FAIL
FAST
SUCCEED
FASTER

Praise for *Fail Fast. Succeed Faster.*

If someone, looking to start a business, does not have a plan and does not seek out the advice of those who have a lot more experience, that business is almost certainly dead even before it starts. The stories of business challenges and failures illustrated in Sunil's book, *Fail Fast. Succeed Faster.* should provide entrepreneurs the impetus to seek out this advice as soon as they can.

– Joe Atkins, Chairman & CEO – Bowers & Wilkins

Most entrepreneurs don't have the accumulated wisdom from their own past experiences. *Fail Fast. Succeed Faster.* allows entrepreneurs to learn from others, accelerate their own learning and is a great tool for anticipating potential obstacles and quickly recovering from the bumps in the road that do happen.

– Tim Fowler, Former Sales Vice-President,
Tropicana Beverages at Pepsi Beverages Company

The purpose of Sunil's book – learning lessons from the failures of others – is extremely valuable for current and future entrepreneurs. My belief is that success happens through a series of failures that are recognized and acted upon. It's that simple. If you've had no failure, in my opinion, you probably are actually not succeeding properly. Reading *Fail Fast. Succeed Faster.* will help you recognize potential failures sooner so you can act accordingly to avoid them. Let Sunil's book help you to succeed faster.

– Kelsey Ramsden, Founder – kelseyramsden.ca
and Sparkplay, 2012 PROFIT/Chatelaine magazine's top
Canadian Female Entrepreneur of the Year

FAIL FAST SUCCEED FASTER

Lessons on how to avoid business failure

Inspired by real life stories of failures and challenges

Sunil Godse

Radical Solutions Group Inc.

To entrepreneurs, current and future.

CONTENTS

Acknowledgements

This book would not have been possible without the valuable amount of time that all my interviewees have given me for both the interview and the updates and clarifications they provided. Each one of them truly believed that it was extremely important to share these stories of business challenges and failures so that others could learn from them.

I would like to thank the various alumni from the Richard Ivey School of Business, located in London, Ontario, Canada, many of whom were interviewees and some who gave me their advice and words of encouragement in taking this project forward as they all believed in the tremendous value that this book will bring to entrepreneurship in general.

The next vote of thanks goes to my family members. In particular, my parents have given me incredible encouragement throughout this long journey. A big hug goes to my wife, who I continually lean on for her thoughts and advice. She took on more of the family responsibilities so that I was able to tuck myself away in my home office to work on the manuscript. To keep my sanity, my two daughters would sneak into my home office from time to time to give me a well-deserved break.

I would also like to thank my many friends and colleagues, too many to name, who provided incredible support in my journey and who also gave me their opinions on book cover designs, the book sections, the stories, and other general comments.

The next set of thanks goes to those who worked behind the scenes to make this book possible:

- The concept and branding from Mark Brown and staff at adHOME Creative

- Video production for my website and conference from Adam Caplan of web.isod.es

- Ryan Ford, my editor who kept me on track and ensured that I was coherent, and was lightning fast in sending me his edits

- Daniel Crack from Kinetics Design, who takes my manuscript and makes it readable with a professional book layout

The final vote of thanks goes to you in picking up my book and giving it a chance to have a permanent place in your library collection. I certainly hope you enjoy the stories and hope you are able to encourage others to purchase a book for their collection. Thanks once again.

Sunil Godse

Introduction

The most successful people are the ones who learn from their mistakes and turn their failures into opportunities.

– Zig Ziglar

Business success is a direct result of learning from failures. Reading the title of this book, you may think that it is about business failure. Certainly, all the stories showcased in this book are about business challenges and failures that others have experienced. But the premise of the book is simple.

Learning from the business challenges and failures of others should prepare you to tackle similar challenges and failures, and being better prepared will save you time, money, and resources, and help you succeed faster.

The reality is that most businesses will fail even before they get started. Someone has an idea that seems to gather momentum and excitement, and in this euphoria, an entrepreneur moves quickly to grab that seemingly small window of opportunity to start a business, neglecting to get proper advice on all the aspects of running a business.

Soon after, both the entrepreneur and the business are taken on an incredible roller coaster ride with endless unexpected dips, twists, and turns. If the entrepreneur is not prepared for this ride right at the outset by understanding where the business hurdles may lie, the business may leave the tracks and fail.

What do the statistics say?

According to Industry Canada[1], as of December, 2012, small

---

1 http://www.ic.gc.ca/eic/site/061.nsf/eng/02804.html

businesses – those with less than 100 employees – represented over 98% of the total number of employer businesses.

What should be a glaring concern is that the majority of these businesses will fail.

A publication by Industry Canada[2] has shown that between 2002 and 2008, 99,000 businesses were created, and within that same time frame, only 8,800 survived, representing a **91.1% failure rate!** Fewer than 1 in 10 businesses actually survived!

A publication by Statistics Canada[3] that tracked new firms entering the market between 1984 and 1994 showed that a firm has a 50% chance of surviving after three years. Of course, this data does not include firms hit by the dot-com crash or the current recession, which certainly would have pushed this percentage much higher.

A 2005 study[4] by the US Department of Labor's Bureau of Labor Statistics showed that "66 percent of new establishments were still in existence two years after their birth, and 44 percent were still in existence four years after. It is not surprising that most of the new establishments disappeared within the first two years after their birth, and then only a smaller percentage disappeared in the subsequent two years. These survival rates do not vary much by industry."

Some may argue over what the actual failure rate is, citing other research publications. Interestingly, a January 2011 Dun & Bradstreet report[5] showed that there were 41% more business failures than official bankruptcies reported by the US government, suggesting that the data being captured by some of these studies may not truly be representative of failed businesses.

For example, research on business failures may use data that tracks companies that have filed for bankruptcy, but a business could have failed in the first year or two and have no revenues whatsoever, yet still maintain a business number. These businesses would not be included in the dataset, although they have failed.

Furthermore, a research project might use a dataset gathered from companies that stopped submitting payroll information to the government as a proxy for failed businesses. If businesses did not have any

2 Key Small Business Statistics, July 2012, Cat. No. Iu186-1/2012-1E-PDF, www.ic.gc.ca/sbstatistics
3 Failure Rates for New Canadian Firms: New Perspectives On Entry And Exit, No. 61-526-XIE
4 http://www.bls.gov/opub/mlr/2005/05/ressum.pdf
5 U.S. Business Trends Report, www.dnb.com/government/lc/economic-report-us-business-trends-quarterly-report-january-2011.html

employees, such as many single-person run businesses, and failed, these businesses would also be missed.

The definition of business success varies from one entrepreneur to another. Success to some could mean owning a business that generates enough money to pay the day-to-day bills and earn a decent living, or a lifestyle business. To others, success may be growing the business exponentially as fast as possible to become a very large company.

When thinking of business failure, one may immediately think about the financial collapse of a business. However, the definition of failure could also include a failure in the characteristics required of an entrepreneur, a failure to bring in the right team, a failure in a process, and so on.

These broad definitions, particularly those of business failure, were the parameters given to the interviewees, and it was up to them to recollect a particular failure or challenge that they felt was important enough to provide an insightful lesson for others.

The book is divided into a number of sections that, in my opinion and experience, cascade in importance when determining whether the business has a high probability of success.

The sections are as follows:

- Section 1 –Are You An Entrepreneur?

- Section 2 – Do You Have A **BUSINESS** Plan?

- Section 3 – Do You Have the Right Team?

- Section 4 – Can You Run A Business?

- Section 5 – Can You Move the Business Forward?

Others may argue that the sequence of importance of the sections when determining business failure should be different. However, when looking at the sections in totality, the ingredients for running a successful business include competencies in each of the sections above.

Each section is further divided into individual chapters with related stories of business challenges or failures shared by one or more interviewees. To maintain the integrity and accuracy of each story, every interview was transcribed and sent back to the interviewee for review to be approved, with appropriate updates incorporated into the story.

While reading the various stories, one may argue that the reasons for the business challenge or failure could have been due to some other factor, different from what was mentioned.

My responsibility as an interviewer was mainly to listen to the story and to clarify any subtle definitions or aspects of the story where more detail was necessary. I was not to make any judgements, interpretations, or suggestions; it was very important to ensure that the reason for the business challenge or failure was defined by the interviewee. If an interviewee stated that the reason for the failure was 'X', then this was the reason that caused the business to incur its hurdles.

Some interviewees requested alterations to their names and/or the names of their businesses to protect the identities of their associates and families, as well as themselves. Nevertheless, every story contained in this book was based upon a true story, related by an entrepreneur during an interview.

In some cases, a number of factors might contribute to a particular story of business challenge or failure. This goes to show that there may not be one single factor, but a combination of them that work in concert to take entrepreneurs and their businesses through some difficult situations.

In the end, the book is about learning from the challenges and failures of others. It is hoped that after reading these incredible stories of business challenges and failures, it not only gives an appreciation for the sheer complexities involved in running a business, but it should give one pause to ask some tough questions before considering going into business.

What is crucial is that these questions are answered with complete honesty. Not doing so could result in the business experiencing the same hurdles that the interviewees in this book have experienced.

Enjoy the book, and, if you are a current or future entrepreneur, I hope you are able to learn many lessons from the incredible collection of interviews from the many interviewees who have given me, and you, their precious time to share their stories.

Read on.

Fail Fast. Succeed Faster.

FAIL FAST

FAST

SUCCEED

FASTER

PART 1

Are You an Entrepreneur?

*Failure is just a resting place.
It is an opportunity to begin again
more intelligently.*

– Henry Ford

What does it mean to be an entrepreneur?

The Oxford English Dictionary defines an entrepreneur[6] as a person who sets up a business or businesses, taking on financial risks in the hope of profit.

Others define it as follows:

- Joseph Schumpeter – "Entrepreneurs are innovators who use a process of shattering the status quo of the existing products and services, to set up new products, new services."

- Peter Drucker – "An entrepreneur searches for change, responds to it and exploits opportunities. Innovation is a specific tool of an entrepreneur hence an effective entrepreneur converts a source into a resource."

- Richard Branson – "Being an entrepreneur simply means being someone who wants to make a difference to other people's lives."

The definition I like to use is that an entrepreneur is someone who has the skills, abilities, and attitude to successfully develop a product or service, using whatever resources necessary and available, that addresses a real opportunity that exists or fills an important void in the marketplace.

As the old adage goes, success in business is really 90% execution and 10% strategy, and execution requires the entrepreneur to possess a certain set of skills and abilities. If some of these skills and abilities are lacking, the entrepreneur needs to have the wherewithal to properly learn them, or bring in others who may be strong in those areas.

When looking at an entrepreneurial opportunity, the intertwining skills, abilities, and attitude of the entrepreneur often act as starting

---

6 http://oxforddictionaries.com/definition/english/entrepreneur?q=entrepreneur

reference point for those evaluating whether the business opportunity will be successful or not.

The stories in this section are told by interviewees who touch upon a certain skill, ability, or attitude that an entrepreneur should have. It does not mean that they believe that only one particular skill, for example, is required to be a successful entrepreneur, but rather an important one, and they illustrate this through a business challenge.

The skills showcased do not represent an exhaustive list by any means; there are many more skills required than those illustrated here. The take away from reading this section should be that success as an entrepreneur requires a complex set of skills, abilities, and attitudes that work together to take an idea forward and create a successful business.

Being Passionate

The success of investments that my team and I make depends heavily on the characteristics of the entrepreneur and the management team. If you lack passion, have a defeatist attitude or focus solely on the money, we will simply walk away from the table.

– John Ruffolo, CEO – OMERS Ventures

Passion drives entrepreneurs to ensure that the products or services they have developed will make it to market, no matter what obstacle comes along. Given that the product or service is unique and serves a need, passion will help drive the entrepreneur forward, and success, personally, professionally, and financially, will follow.

While passion is desirable, an entrepreneur needs to take care that the passion does not cause business blindness. Sure, passion will help entrepreneurs push through the many business hurdles that will be experienced, but simply having passion to push through a terrible idea will most certainly result in the business failing at some point.

That said, when looking at a business opportunity, either to evaluate or to invest in, the characteristics of the entrepreneur are often used as a starting point. This is the same starting point used by John Ruffolo for the ventures in which he invests. In particular, John wants to see passion in the eyes of the entrepreneur and the management team. He knows this passion extremely well; he followed his passion to become CEO of OMERS Ventures, making him successful today.

OMERS Ventures invests in companies in the technology, media, and telecommunications sectors. When John evaluates an investment or an opportunity, he does not look at failure as a failure, but as a learning opportunity. When one is successful at something, one does not stop to think about what made one successful. But when one has failed at something, one generally agonizes over finding out what caused the perceived failure.

"My company believes that, as an investing organization, it is the failures that make you learn, not the successes," he says. "When you translate that in terms of looking at investing in the business, the number one criteria is the management team. I have to have the confidence that an entrepreneur is able to identify an obstacle and move around it."

John and his team look for entrepreneurs that have a passion for solving problems and are not focused solely on money. He notes that Facebook arose out of Mark Zuckerberg's passion for finding a way to connect with women, which morphed into finding a way to connect the world. John attributes Facebook's success to Mark's passion in the face of others pushing him to monetize the idea early. Bill Gates had the same passion, wanting a PC on every desktop, and Steve Jobs had a passion for marketing and ensuring that Apple put a premium product in the hands of consumers. This passion drives entrepreneurs through failure after failure. Despite financial failures, those with passion will find a way to persevere.

For those who have had the unique opportunity to come to John seeking investment, John walks away from the table if he senses that the core management team before him lacks the passion to solve a particular problem. He avoids management teams with defeatist attitudes, those who, when faced with possible impediments, provide excuses such as a lack of capital or a technical feature not being set, compared to having a vision of changing the world. John also stays away from those focused solely on money. If an entrepreneur is passionate about what he or she is doing, success and money will eventually follow. A perfect example of this passion is near and dear to John; his passion led him to become CEO of OMERS Ventures.

In 2010, John was a partner at Deloitte, leading the technology industry practice. At that time, he received a call to meet with a good friend, Michael Nobrega, President and CEO of the large pension fund company, OMERS. Michael and John had known each other for over 20 years, first meeting while both Michael and John worked at Arthur Andersen, Michael as a senior partner and John as a first-year associate.

John was approached by Michael to talk about launching a company, OMERS Ventures, which would invest in the innovation space. John was excited about this announcement, yet surprised, because, at that time, pension funds generally avoided investing in innovative companies due to an increased level of risk.

When asked as to the reason why the pension funds were shy about investing in start-ups, John says that the aversion was actually due to the history of bad investments.

"It's even more blatant than that," says John. "There was a long history of very poor financial returns for that asset class. When you look back, when did they make their biggest investments? Around 2000. Guess what happened shortly thereafter – the whole dot-com bust. So they all got burned."

After this financial lesson, the pension funds shied away from investing in innovative companies, for which John had criticized them.

"I was poking fun at all the pension funds in not supporting the future of our country, the future of our kids, and all that sort of stuff," he recalls.

Michael was essentially asking John to put his money where his mouth was.

"What turned out to be a discussion to get my thoughts, ended up with me being the guy to actually build the venture program in OMERS and lead it, starting in 2011," he says.

Despite some bad financial experiences, OMERS never wanted to abandon investing in innovative companies; OMERS was frustrated in investing in the sector indirectly through venture capital firms. Michael was simply looking at an innovative way of how OMERS could invest directly in the innovative companies themselves.

John states that "Michael is not only the only guy in Canada, but, in the world, who came to that conclusion. When he told me his conclusion on that, I just thought, 'Wow, I know that I want to be the guy to execute that vision.' I found this vision of OMERS unique – not only unique in Canada, but I was not aware of any pension fund in the world thinking of doing the same thing."

John's passion for this investment area lit up and he had serious thoughts of joining Michael. This would also allow him to address his big frustration with the lack of investment capital in Canada for innovative companies. In his heart, he knew that it was his life's mission to solve this problem.

"I felt that I had a duty to my kids, and I had a duty to this country to actually do that and follow the passion," he explains. "I had been fighting this passion for years, but really in the mid-2000s, around 2005, I really spent a lot of time with various levels of government and politicians trying to solve the problem."

However, the decision to move away from Deloitte was not easy. John agonized over this decision for months. It was much easier for John to stay at an organization that treated him well. He was a star at Deloitte and was extremely comfortable where he was financially. He would be leaving a great organization with lots of great people that he worked with. In particular, he was on the board of Deloitte, which made it even more difficult.

But, after thinking about his criticisms of the lack of capital in the innovation space, and being presented with an opportunity to be an integral part of solving the problem he knew existed, "It felt more like not only was it a passion, but it also felt like a sense of duty," he says. "I felt like I had to do it. I didn't have a choice. It ended up being a fantastic decision. To the shock of my partners and to the shock of my clients, I told everyone that I basically have to follow my heart. I did that with massive trepidation."

Ultimately, the passion gnawing inside John vaulted him over the anxiety hurdle.

In January, 2011, John joined OMERS Ventures as Employee Number One with literally nothing but a computer, a desk, a chair, and a phone. He had to build everything right from the ground up. He came into the position as a complete start-up, albeit with some resources from the parent company, OMERS, such as finances, information technology, and human resources, which he could tap into to accelerate growth. But starting this venture was not a problem for John because he had already started a number of "ventures" within Deloitte.

"I would like to think of myself as an 'intrapreneur' at Deloitte," he says. "I've built many practices and businesses inside of Deloitte. In many respects, it was building the same thing inside an organization, so I've done it for many, many years. I knew exactly what the steps would be in building the business from a people, infrastructure, and strategy perspective. But at the end of the day, I knew who the people would be to build the team. If you have a good sense of who the people might be that you would hire, that is really the hardest part."

It was easy for John to find companies to invest in. He knew many of the players in the industry and had already served as an advisor to the companies that he would eventually invest in. He just had to make the leap from being an advisor to being an investor. This gave him the ability to accelerate the business at a rapid clip.

Ten months later, in October of 2011, OMERS Ventures was open to the public.

By following his passion, not only has John satisfied his life's work and ambition, but he is elated to come into work every single day. Clearly, he was good at what he did and he did whatever it took to win. Under his direction, the pension fund made incredibly successful investments, and with the pension fund being successful financially, so were John and his team.

"When I came here, I very quickly realized that not only is this satisfying my life's work and my life ambition, I'm so pumped to come into work every day," he says. "When you focus on the passion, and you are really good at it, no matter what, you're really going to win. We started making incredibly successful investments because we are so passionate about it."

John's track record to date for investing in deals has been consistent at approximately one deal per month, with an average deal size of $8 million.

When suggesting that it was really the passion that allowed John to accelerate the growth so fast, he quickly replies, "That's absolutely right. You really feel it. It's that mission. It's that purpose, that greater purpose of trying to solve a problem, a multi-generational problem. That's the driver. And all the other stuff, the experience and knowing the ecosystem, that's more risk mitigation so you can actually execute."

John was flabbergasted at the fact that he was doing the one thing that he wanted to do in his life and was rewarded for it at both the personal and professional level. Perhaps taking that call from his colleague, Michael, represented an unforeseeable opportunity that his passion prepared him for.

Sitting across the table from a group of young entrepreneurs and innovators looking for funding, John has to assess their potential as investments, and he ranks passion high on his list of priorities. He understands better than most where their passion will take them. His own passion has taken him from a cozy position at Deloitte to the head of the table at OMERS Ventures. Although he may not be sitting across from the next Mark Zuckerberg or Bill Gates, he knows that investing in passion tends to pay healthy dividends for everyone. Every meeting could be as fateful for a young entrepreneur as his own meeting with Michael.

While entrepreneurial passion helps to move a legitimate business opportunity forward, one must be careful that blind passion does not lead the entrepreneur to chase an idea that is not a good BUSINESS idea, a topic discussed in Section 2.

Personal, professional, and financial sacrifices will be required to make a business successful. In some cases, entrepreneurs might make a hasty move to get the business going, without taking a step back to honestly question why they are opening a business. This was vitally important for Jean-Pierre Taillon as he describes the moment when he found answers to that question; it started with a call at 4:00am telling him that three of his employees had been shot and killed.

Define Why You Are in Business

I got a call at 4 AM, Friday, June 15, 2012, from my Vice-President of Security telling me that four of my Cash in Transit security guards were shot, three of them were killed, one of them seriously wounded, and one missing. This incident really defined why I was here, running this company. Entrepreneurs should all ask themselves, honestly, why are you looking to run a business, and when everything is on the line, what kind of decisions are you willing to make?

– Jean-Pierre Taillon, President & CEO – G4S Solutions Canada Ltd.

Starting a business is extremely exciting, and after talking about how an idea can transform itself into a business, entrepreneurs often run to start the business, fearing the window of opportunity might be missed. However, what does get missed is the entrepreneur sitting back and thinking about why he or she wants to start a business without weighing the appropriate risks, or preparing for the business challenges that lay ahead.

If the entrepreneur does not sit back and define why he or she is starting a business, then whatever risks that come when encountering business challenges could crumble the entrepreneur both emotionally and financially. At these moments, the true reason why the entrepreneur started the business comes to the forefront. This definition was incredibly important for Jean-Pierre Taillon starting when he answered his phone at 4:00am.

In the early morning hours of Friday, June 15, 2012, five armed security guards working for G4S Security Canada (G4S) drove their truck onto the University of Alberta campus, located in Edmonton, Canada. Four of them walked into HUB Mall, a combined shopping mall and student residence, while a driver stayed with the truck. HUB Mall had a number of restaurants and a few ATM bank machines.

The security guards approached a door that would take them behind the ATM to transfer cash from the various ATMs in the city as a part of the contract G4S had with one of the banks. After three of the four guards went in, the last one took a look to see if there was any suspicious activity outside the ATM, and finding none, locked all four inside the room to do their routine duties.

BANG........BANG.........BANG

Just like that, three of the security guards were shot at point blank range in the head, killing two of them instantly and critically injuring the third. The fourth, Travis Brandon Baumgartner, walked back to the security truck, and, **BANG, BANG, BANG**, shot the driver three times, killing him.

Travis drove the truck back to the office, took over $300,000 from the truck and put it in his personal truck, drove to his residence, dropped some money on the table for his mother, took her license plates and attached them to his truck, and then proceeded to the US border in British Columbia with the rest of the money. With no passport in hand, he was arrested 40 hours later at the Canada-US border without incident. He displayed no remorse whatsoever for his actions.

The president and CEO of G4S Security Canada, Jean-Pierre Taillon, received a call that Friday morning at 4:00am telling him that four of his employees were shot, three of them were killed, the fourth was in critical condition, and the fifth was missing.

"The first thing I thought about was that there were some bad guys held up, robbed and stole the cash in transit, and kidnapped one of my guards," he recalls. "I was shocked, and just never expected this to happen."

After the call, terrible thoughts raced through Jean-Pierre's mind. Most terrible of all, Jean-Pierre found out soon after that one his own guards shot the others.

"I never suspected that it was one of our own," he says. "You think about your company, you think about what was done, the training that everybody goes through, the screening processes, and of course at the end of the day, you wonder what failed in the organization to allow this to happen."

At that moment, Jean-Pierre reminisced about why he was there, why he was running the company, and what his personal and professional values really stood for. His mind swirled with all of these thoughts and definitions, and he went through a tremendous range of emotions. But, despite any doubts, he knew what he stood for, and why he was doing what he was doing.

Jean-Pierre came from a technical background, previously working in the telecommunications area. He joined G4S on December 16, 2008 after the former president retired. He had to pivot his skill sets from a logical, engineering and technical background to one of policing, criminology, and security, much different from his previous career. However, because of his previous career, he was treated like an outsider.

"My peers used to chide me publicly, saying, what does he know about security? He came from an environment where you get terrible customer service. So, that is what you are going to get from this security company," he recalls.

The company, at the time, was pursuing deals where the profits on each deal were smaller, the company did not have a structured story as it wanted to supply security for everyone, and it did not have an elevator pitch[7]. He found better value in focusing on the high risk-high value security market.

He brought in some familiar individuals from his previous career and hired salespeople to execute on his focus, going through a number of salespeople in rapid fashion to ensure that he found the right ones to move his vision and his strategy forward.

With the right team in place, Jean-Pierre grew the company organically from $165 million to $520 million, effectively quadrupling the organization. He had success growing the company because he understood the market and helped realign the company with the direction of the market. He refocused the company from supplying security to

---

[7] A short narrative that usually defines the products and services a company offers, including what value the company offers to customers and the marketplace. A verbal elevator pitch is usually 60 seconds or 90 seconds in length, the estimated time of a ride in an elevator.

anyone looking, to a different market, one that was more lucrative, such as security for the banking industry; G4S won enough business from the banks to represent approximately 70% of revenues.

This helped Jean-Pierre build the corporate brand and reputation across the country. He has security guards, undercover and uniformed, working at retail outlets. In addition to moving money around, G4S transports gold and prescription narcotics from one place to another.

Despite providing security to some of the world's least secure locations, such as Afghanistan and North Africa, and involving high risk activities such as clearing mines and providing safe houses, Jean-Pierre had never faced a situation like the tragedy in Edmonton. To find the direction to take the next step, he looked inward to his personal sense of purpose for running G4S and his core values.

"The natural instinct is to ask yourself, well, what you do next?" he says. "The first thing we did was call all the families, put together some money in a trust fund, fly them down, make sure they had food, make sure they had a hotel, and make sure they were taken care of. It was more important to take care of this and the whole healing process. Taking care of the company came second."

For Jean-Pierre, this incident was more about defining why you run a business and what is the most important priority for him.

"The lesson is that in business and leadership, you have to dig inside and wonder, 'What's the most important priority,' and it's family," he says.

Certainly, he had a few options on the table, but none even remotely resonated with what Jean-Pierre thought was the right thing to do.

"Here's the bad way of doing it. I could have stood up there for an hour denying everything, saying nope, G4S is the best," he says. "We screen everybody. This was a freak accident. The incident should have never happened. Our process and procedures are great......No.......No. This guy slipped through somehow, and there's things to be looked at. So when the press was asking, 'What is your biggest priority now,' I said 'Look, this happened yesterday. Take care of the families and the victims, fly them in, make sure they're supported, make sure they've got money, make sure we still pay them, and then we'll worry about the rest after it.' I thought that was the right thing to do. The corporation was saying no – protect the brand, protect the brand. And I said no. We have the best practices and procedures in the world, but at the end of the day, something did not work."

This incident touched off a long conversation between Jean-Pierre and the regional Vice-President, Rob Murray, about personal values. Despite opposing views from his legal team, Jean-Pierre told his lawyers that they would have press conferences, answer questions, and try to explain what was going on, in the context of this being an ongoing police investigation, as Jean-Pierre was quick to note that the police were in charge.

Jean-Pierre immediately began an internal investigation to provide a more detailed examination of the screening process, and any other processes and business areas that might point to what could have been done differently.

Jean-Pierre's company had already instituted a number of regular checks and balances to prevent tragic incidents from happening. In fact, a process called "walk the talk" is carried out at the start of every employee's shift. Every employee's supervisor or manager checks whether that employee is sober, had a bad night, or for other warning signs – essentially, a final check to ensure that all employees could perform their job to the best of their ability on that particular shift.

Clearly, Travis Baumgartner showed that he was competent to work that night, and no negative warning signs were reported in Travis's behaviour during that shift. Yet, in a sudden fit, Travis shot and killed his colleagues at point-blank range.

Everyone reviewing the processes, including the police investigators, realized that the company did everything that it could. But Jean-Pierre still agonized over why this had happened.

"The checks and balances we put in place went above and beyond any measures that were required by law," he says, "and we even went beyond that. There was so much trust in the workplace that I had honestly thought that someone had kidnapped Travis."

Given that Travis had passed the proper medical tests and checks and had received the proper training, it was virtually impossible to predict his betrayal. Arguments could be made for more testing, or more checks and balances, however, this is exorbitantly expensive and targeted to prevent the failure of .001% of an incident. Providing this level of security would bankrupt any company.

No company or individual can evaluate an employee's ability to work based on a stressful situation in the past. For example, if an employee had a fight with their spouse, it would not necessarily mean that they would not be able to work the next day, and many individuals would never show signs of stress in these situations. To take this even further, if someone made a social media post that was negative in nature, firstly, it would be extremely hard to monitor on a constant basis from both a resource and financial perspective, and secondly, this in itself does not mean that one could not work competently the next day.

Right away, the media jumped on Travis Baumgartner's social media footprint to see if there were any signs of mental instability. Apart from a skull and crossbones taken from a game that was displayed on a website, which may not seem odd for a 20-year-old, interviews with coworkers and friends, and extensive reviews of Travis's social media accounts, did not indicate any harmful text, pictures, opinions, etc. that would remotely suggest he had problems.

"Trying to find that golden answer that would have prevented this situation was next to impossible," says Jean-Pierre. "The other question to ask is that if only .0005% of all employees over time may potentially be a bad employee, how much screening do you put the other 99.9995% of the employees through to catch that one, especially in a very trusted environment?"

Despite doing everything the company could, Jean-Pierre further increased his screening processes, but did so with caution; too many screening processes would turn people away from working for G4S due to the lengthy process in just getting the job.

Internally, employees who became desensitized after performing their jobs time after time became re-sensitized to the nature of their employment. These employees would be carrying $1 million, have a gun and have body armor, but did not think about whether they would get shot that day. The shooting in Edmonton brought the nature of the job back to reality: this was a dangerous job. One employee resigned after having a long chat with his spouse. Luckily, Jean-Pierre had a number of employees across Canada ready to jump at the opportunity to work in that role, despite the risk of danger.

After searching for preventative measures, Jean-Pierre had to rebuild confidence in his brand. Fortunately, many recognized not much could have been done because the incident happened internally, which was abnormal. The brand would have been hurt more had their guards been held up by others. Employees go through an extensive amount of on-going training to provide a resolution to such a situation.

Because Jean-Pierre focused on the right things, and did not initially worry about how the brand image projected to the public, to his surprise, the community supported him and his company's efforts.

"The banks were great, and the clients understood," he says. "In fact, the industry worked together. The next day, some of the other companies helped us out as we still had packages to deliver and orders to fill. We all got together and agreed that small decisions are important, but when something like this happens, we need to work together. The next day, all the presidents of G4S called me up to give their support, and I got some beautiful letters from a lot of the banks. And I thought that was nice."

The people of Edmonton, a city of over one million, also rallied around and supported each other during the tragedy. Everybody from the emergency medical services team, the police, and corporations in general all rallied to help the situation in whatever way they could. A fund for the fallen employees' families was opened three days after the incident, and the media assured that the word about the fund got out.

Jean-Pierre avoided a failure – which would have been a big one if he had protected the brand. The media could have had a field day with him, accusing the company of not being sensitive to the loss of human life, criticizing it for protecting their investment in the Canadian market, and faulting it for not recognizing the signs such as skull and crossbones on a website, among other things.

Instead, the media joined Jean-Pierre's efforts. His peers and everybody that worked for him began treating him like a peer rather than an outsider. The other presidents that ran G4S globally realized, after this incident, that Jean-Pierre was not this person who only understood technology; he understood the security business and knew how to drive it forward.

At a subsequent conference, where Jean-Pierre was a panel member, his competitors congratulated him on a job well done, and the comments about Jean-Pierre not knowing anything about the security industry stopped. This became a personal branding issue for Jean-Pierre where he was now treated with more respect, something that he cherished.

Because Jean-Pierre knew who he was and what his company stood for, he has always operated with honesty, integrity, and openness. When asked about sharing his values with his employees, he is quick to point out that he communicates his values as much as he can. Having openness, honesty, transparency, and constant communication is the way Jean-Pierre has operated with his clients. These same qualities also helped him win a major security contract.

When bidding on a contract for one of the major Canadian banks, the decision-makers had told Jean-Pierre that his firm was one of two finalists, and had to go through a further bidding process before a final decision was made.

Jean-Pierre saw what the other company had been doing, but more importantly, he impressed the decision-makers with what he and his team did differently.

"The other company came in and essentially did a presentation, making a bold assumption that that would be enough to win the bid, and also made the false assumption that because of my background, I would not have a clear understanding of what security requirements would be needed," he recalls. "But we maintained a constant pipeline of communication during the bidding process to ensure that we were able to deliver on what the bank required. In the end, the banks saw facts and data from me and my team, and nothing from the competitor, and gave us all the business."

G4S went on to win other contracts with other banks as either sole providers or as partners in providing security, slowly gaining incremental market share over its competitors. This would not happen if G4S did not have a solid reputation of delivering value to its customers.

"When you buy from somebody, you are placing a bet," says Jean-Pierre. "If they fail, you fail. That was your reputation that has been reflected. And you think about that all the time. At the end of the day if I buy something from you, and you are messing it up, it'll be my boss that will be all over me. This follows the philosophy I have. If something goes good or bad, doesn't matter, tell them right away."

Jean-Pierre's guiding principles came to light with the shootings in Edmonton, when he had to strip away the layers of ego and noise, and get down to the basic question of why he wanted to run a business.

"Why are you running a business? It gets back to heart versus mind," he says. "You know, your mind might be telling you one thing, but you need to ask yourself, 'What's the right thing to do?' You know, corporations are human entities. Corporations are made with people. People run corporations. You need to strip off everything and say, 'What do people need?' After the fact, it sounds simple. But believe me, at 10:00am on the Friday when we found out that it was our guy, and lawyers are saying 'Deny, don't say anything, don't call anybody,' it is not so simple. For me, it was about calling the families and saying we are supporting you. When I was calling the families of one of my guys, his wife had just given birth to a baby, and I basically had to tell the mother of his child that her husband was just killed. Right? So you have to do the right thing."

In September of 2013, Travis Baumgartner pleaded guilty to two counts of second degree murder, one count of first degree murder, and one count of attempted murder in the HUB Mall shootings. The 15-page statement of facts read in court revealed Travis was heavily in debt, owing $58,000 with just 26 cents in his bank account. The statement of facts also reported him as telling police he was "just mad at the world". In a precedent-setting judgement, Travis was sentenced to life in prison with no chance of parole for 40 years, the harshest sentence in Canada since 1962. The judge overseeing the case, Associate Chief Justice John Rooke, described the crimes as "some of the most horrendous crimes [he had] ever seen," and said that he "couldn't believe these assassinations and executions were carried out by a cold-blooded killer all for the simple motive of robbery."

Jean-Pierre's ability to "do the right thing" sends clear messages to both the outside world as well as his employees that upholding strong values has its rewards. And rewards have definitely been delivered to him. The Cash Solutions part of the business was taken over by Jean-Pierre in March of 2012 as a part of a strategy to manage business units by country rather than separate lines of business. Initially operating at a PBITA[8] of less than 0.8%, Jean-Pierre and his management team turned the Cash Solutions business around, growing brand awareness, gaining

---

8 PBITA = Profit Before Interest, Taxes and Amortization; expressed as an actual number, or a percentage of revenues

market share, and driving PBITA growth to over 4.6% while in a recessionary market. This company became an acquisition target and was sold for $110 million, an astonishing 14 times PBITA, a true success story.

Although the events that Jean-Pierre went through were extreme and tragic, they gave Pierre pause to deeply contemplate why he was running G4S. An entrepreneur looking to open a business and create value for customers should also do the same type of reflective thinking before jumping into unknown territory, really defining why he or she is looking to run a business. Not doing so simply means that you may be a statistic: one of the businesses that does not make it. But it does not have to be that way. Answer the question of why you want to run the business **honestly**. Not doing so will lead you down a path that may be ripe for failure.

Once this important question is asked, an entrepreneur should be able to get the business moving ahead. In the process, an inordinate number of business hurdles will be faced. Jumping over these business hurdles will require perseverance, which was what Hank Vander Laan needed to rescue his business from a fire that almost wiped the business out.

Perseverance

Most entrepreneurs will tell you that if they had known of all the problems they were going to have, they would have never dared going into business. It's like getting into marriage. If I would've known all the fights we were going to have, I wouldn't have married you. The beauty is that if you can work through those problems, you build a super marriage and have a great relationship.

**– H. J. (Hank) Vander Laan, Former
Chairman & President – Trojan Technologies Inc.**

Unfortunately, entrepreneurs can count on one thing from business: there will always be a business challenge and there will always be some kind of failure that they experience. If you cannot handle making risky decisions and having your emotions played with, with the possibility of the business shutting down for good just around the corner, then running the business may not be for you.

For those who choose to make a go of it, the "ups" are obviously enjoyable, but pushing through the "downs" to move the business forward may be the deciding factor. Persevering through the "downs" and making difficult decisions despite the situation around you is essential. Such was the case for Hank Vander Laan.

Hank Vander Laan is former Chairman & President of Trojan Technologies Inc., a leader in the development of water treatment solutions using environmentally friendly ultraviolet light (UV), with the largest installed base of UV systems in operation in the world.

Hank started as an entrepreneur by buying a metal fabrication business back in 1976. He was not fond of that business because it involved metal bashing and low margins, but he used it as a base to provide a source of income. This company allowed him to develop ultraviolet technology as a disinfectant for water, which Hank had a hunch would be a global business. He was excited about the global application of this ultraviolet technology and at this stage never focused on anything else, such as compensation, always believing that, "if we strove for excellence in water process technology development, all the other pieces would at some point fall into place."

Hank faced an incredible number of business challenges, but it was his and his associates' perseverance to get through them at a time when he was down and out that made him and the business successful today. To make it through the tough times, he had to make key business decisions, which had the potential to be unpopular at times, but were necessary to move the business forward.

Hank encountered one of his fiercest challenges when he got a call from the fire department at 4:00am telling him that the plant was on fire. He rushed to the plant, only to find a firefighter standing on the roof with flames shooting high into the sky. The plant's sprinkler system activated immediately, saving the building from becoming totally unusable. However, the plant suffered a tremendous amount of water damage.

Hank sat at his desk, knee-deep in water, wondering what to do next. Not only did he have to think about how to get the plant back up and running, but he also needed to find a way to make payroll at the same time, as the bank account was low.

At about 11:00am, the bank manager called.

Bank Manager: "How's the day?"

Hank: "It's a busy day. Pumping water like crazy. "

Bank Manager: "That's good Hank, but I have a cheque here that you have written, but you don't have any money in the bank."

Hank: "Well, that is what I have a banker for. What do I need a banker for if I don't need any money?"

Bank Manager: "Hank, you have a cash flow problem, and as a start-up company that's very difficult. I will let it go this time, but next time, please call me first."

Hank agreed, and put the phone down.

The next morning, there was a picture in the paper of Trojan Technologies, much like the first view of his plant when Hank arrived. The picture showed a person standing on the roof with flames coming out from the roof with the caption, "Trojan Technologies on fire!"

The same banker called him the next day.

Bank Manager: "You were lying to me!"

Hank: "I wasn't lying! You asked me how are things and I told you we are all busy trying to get product out and we're pumping water out like crazy!"

Surprisingly, the plant was fully operational by Monday morning despite the fire on Friday morning, with the insurance company covering the damages. However, the company was at a tender stage financially. Despite the fire and the financial "treading of water", Hank was a master at managing cash flow and proudly survived this as just another glitch.

Hank encountered another stressful situation in 1999. At that time, Trojan Technologies was one of the first companies to take on an enterprise accounting system from a particular vendor. Because of the complexity of the accounting system, data was being entered into the system incorrectly.

As a result, the accounting system reported erroneous figures. What was supposed to be reported as Cost of Goods Sold[9] on the Income Statement was reported as inventory on the Balance Sheet; this resulted in the accounting system showing an extra $10 million of inventory in the plant when in fact this inventory did not physically exist. And on paper, profits increased by $10 million; these profits also did not exist.

On a Friday night just before a long weekend, accounting staff had approached Hank with the discrepancy of $10 million in inventory. Hank, being close to all aspects of the business, reviewed all the reports from the accounting system and immediately questioned them. What the accounting system reported just did not make sense.

Hank knew that the people on his team were extremely trustworthy, and $10 million in inventory just did not walk out the door. So if the

---

9 Cost of Goods Sold – A figure, seen on an income statement, that represents the actual cost of items incurred by a company when selling them to a customer

people were not the problem, it had to be the software. To answer questions surrounding how this had happened, Hank and his staff resorted to a manual count of the inventory and the processes. In the end, because of the sudden shift in profitability, Hank had no choice but to let people go, an unpopular and difficult decision.

Hank immediately contacted an external independent auditor to work together with his team to ensure that the process was corrected with proper testing being performed. Once that was complete, Hank's faith in the accounting system was restored, and they continued to use it for some time.

The software malfunctions were complex to deal with, but in the end, Hank learned that software providers, both externally and internally, had to be taught that they are there to serve the organization and not the other way around.

"Quite often, the 'techies' in the software business have a tendency to hold captive their audiences with their wizardry and forget who is paying the bills. This still happens to this day where software products are not user friendly, and this could be construed as a function of control and security for the software provider."

When Hank was asked whether the ups and downs were worth it, he wrote in an email:

"Trojan as you know was acquired by the Danaher Corporation in the fall of 2004 for the sum of $248 million. Since that time, the original team we built Trojan with have, over the years, added additional talented people, which more than doubled our staff and tripled our revenues. The merger with an excellent corporate partner like Danaher gave us access to capital and superior operational business systems allowing us to make a number of key strategic acquisitions, expanded R&D – a combination which then positioned us to serve broader markets globally."

"To answer your question "was it worth it". Obviously we have built a company that thrives in its place of origin, that is London, Ontario; but not only that, it now delivers product and services in over 100 countries. I could not think of a more rewarding result where everyone wins, shareholders, business associates, suppliers, customers, the environment, our local communities and the countries we operate in. Dreams are made of these!"

Over the years, Hank faced major incidents involving emotional decisions, complex thought processes, and weighing of options. Often there is no black or white solution and entrepreneurs like Hank have to determine what is best for the situation given their experience and gut feeling. It is easier to hoist the white flag and surrender, and life goes on.

The more difficult path is the one where perseverance picks you up from these situations and pushes you to work through the difficulties, no matter what. It takes a lot of internal strength, support from family and friends, and willpower, but if you have the perseverance, you will find the solution. And, as Hank aptly put it, in the end, everyone wins!

When facing seemingly insurmountable challenges, entrepreneurs need to tap into perseverance to overcome the business challenges that will test their resolve. Some will fall, some will hesitate, and others will push on ahead.

Yet another quality that helps tackle business challenges is tenacity, defined as maintaining, adhering to, or seeking something valued or desired[10]. Given some of the challenges that could be faced in business, emotional and physical ups and downs will begin to eat away at an entrepreneur. Tenacity is needed to keep everything together during such difficult times. Tenacity helped Jonathan Ehrlich, Jean-François Tremblay and Clare McEwan learn some lessons from their business challenges.

---

10 http://www.merriam-webster.com/dictionary/tenacious

Being Tenacious

Having a vision and a focus going after a big market is essential. But if you cannot combine those with tenacity, then there's a good chance that you will not be able to tackle the business hurdles that will be thrown your way.

– Jonathan Ehrlich, Co-Founder – Utah Street Labs and Copius Inc., Former Marketing Director – Facebook

Where I was not tenacious enough, was pushing back on my partner sufficiently to say: 'Okay. Stop it already.' I tried and tried, but when you're a 50-50 partnership, there is only so much you can do until it breaks.

– Jean-François Tremblay, President – JFT Consulting

I faced a number of situations where I could have justified shutting the business down, but I was tenacious and had a passion for what I was doing so I chose to push forward and to keep going.

– Clare McEwan, Founder – Air Safaris International Inc.

One of the essential qualities an entrepreneur must have is to be tenacious and continue forward despite the business hurdles that get in the way. Whether it is through competition, internal challenges, or some other factor, the business will continually face challenges right from inception. Hence, entrepreneurs must have some element of risk appetite.

A tenacious attitude will give entrepreneurs the ability to leap over hurdles and continue in business – provided the business makes sense, the vision is solid, and the entrepreneur is able to execute. Of course, some unavoidable situations may require the entrepreneur to step back and possibly discontinue the business, but it is hoped that these situations are rare.

If an entrepreneur becomes overwhelmed after facing constant challenges, not being tenacious may result in folding the business. For Jonathan Ehrlich, his experience as an investor and a serial entrepreneur gives him an excellent opportunity to see companies with business owners that have, and do not have, tenacity.

Jonathan Ehrlich, former Director of Marketing for Facebook and current Co-Founder of Utah Street Labs and Copious Inc., is a serial entrepreneur and investor. He previously co-founded a company called Mob Shop, which used the Groupon concept 10 years earlier. The difference with this particular concept as compared to Groupon, which made things difficult, was that Mob Shop operated in an environment without email or an email structure, and a limited focus on small business. Unfortunately, the team simply ran out of gas despite having some money in the bank and, after four years, called it quits. Had the company reduced its staff and hung on for a few more years, it likely would have been one of the most successful IPOs to hit the market.

When it comes to tenacity, Jonathan points to a couple of companies tenacious enough to stay with their original game plan.

"If you look at the Netflix stock chart, it went from about $30 a share to about $4 within three months while Blockbuster had about $6 billion in revenue and $3 billion in profit," he says. "And then Walmart entered the market. The only way to survive somehow is in having focus on building a great culture and being tenacious enough to not be distracted by whatever the competitors are doing. Also, within the last year, Netflix stock dropped from $300 a share to $60 a share and is now back up to $200. The only way Netflix can survive this kind of a situation is to not be focused on anything other than building a great service. The tenacious can survive when people get their knives out."

To support tenacity, an entrepreneur needs to believe so strongly in what they are doing that nothing would stop them, pushing through emotional ups and downs from uncertain business hurdles. It is during these uncertain times that entrepreneurs must have a high level of motivation and comfort as both of these will support the entrepreneur's tenacity. So when one encounters a business hurdle, such as a product that has no customer appeal, the entrepreneur needs to take a step back and pause to think about the best way to overcome the hurdle.

"Entrepreneurs still need to know what mountain top they are going towards, but the route that they may take may change," says Jonathan. "You build a product, you ship it, and nobody likes it. The vision may still be correct, but the product and the execution associated with the vision may be wrong. The key gene for founders is to know whether the vision is wrong, and that is harder, or whether the vision is right and the execution is wrong."

In some cases, tenacity may be a quality that first-time entrepreneurs have because they simply keep trying to find solutions to problems, as they do not know any better. In Jonathan's experience, and given his vast network of entrepreneurial contacts, many of the successes he has seen are from first-time entrepreneurs. He notes that most of the great consumer Internet companies were founded by first-time entrepreneurs, citing examples such as eBay, Facebook and Google.

"The fact that someone has experience in solving a problem may or may not have an advantage. The first go around, you just don't know how hard it is," says Jonathan. "And you really don't know anything else. You just know that it is really hard. You are also really bold because you really don't understand the consequences of your actions. You think it's supposed to be this way, and you just keep on going."

To provide an example, Jonathan cites Netflix's management team's continued focus on their core vision, and the execution of that vision. They were tenacious and ignored both the competition and concerned shareholders who saw a slumping share price. The company knew what it stood for, what it was delivering, and knew that there was tremendous value to its customers. In the end, Blockbuster filed for bankruptcy, due at least in part to competition from Netflix.

Netflix's management team stayed the course and succeeded, but what if there are differing opinions on the management team as to where the company should go? Key members of the management team may be affected by issues such as the competition or market trends, and may lose focus, resulting in the company constantly changing directions. It is up to management to reach a consensus, and as a unit, be tenacious enough to not let these influences affect the company's direction. Such was the case for Jean-François Tremblay.

Jean-François Tremblay is currently President of JFT Consulting, a firm providing advice in digital media marketing. Jean-François has had a long career in marketing, and has previously been involved in a number of start-ups in various management roles, co-founding the last one.

After this last company opened its doors providing high level digital media strategy, Jean-Francois and his partner used their expertise and contacts to secure some large customers. Soon after starting, Jean-François's business partner began discussing changes to the company's strategy. Swayed by the latest and greatest buzz in the digital media market, he strongly felt that the company should rally its resources behind this bus to gain experience. The problem was that there was constant change, as his partner rarely stuck to an agreed-upon strategy.

"Every 6-12 months, he would come out with an idea for what the agency should stand for based on what he would like to do or veer towards," says Jean-Francois. "2000-2001 was the year of e-business for the company, 2001-2005 we were doing websites, 2005-2007 we wanted to do marketing campaigns, 2007-2008 we were a no-nonsense agency, 2008-2009 we were about branded utility, 2009-2011 we advertised that we were going into digital branding, 2011-2012 we were storytelling. And while we were changing what our strategy was, we also changed the type of client we wanted to go after and also the geographies we would work in."

Although Jean-François intuitively knew that the company had to pick a direction and stick with it, he ignored his intuition as the reasons for making each change somehow seemed reasonable. Each time a change in direction was proposed, the management team agreed to move the company forward in the new direction. And to justify the move, the team would backfill the reasons for the change with convincing financial models.

"In our day, you can model everything. You can come up with any business, financial, or whatever model to post-rationalize anything," says Jean-Francois. "And after it fails, we post-rationalize the situation because we had the model that told us that it would work. We would then realize that we made the numbers go where we wanted them to go. Once we made the change every 18 to 24 months, we would try and justify it by saying, 'Yeah but okay, here are our types of clients, here's what we do, and here's where the market is going.' Imagine restarting that wheel every 18 to 24 months!"

With so many changes, the company could not gain enough experience, wasting time, energy, and talented resources in the process. This began affecting the company both internally and externally. Internally, the employees stopped believing in the management team and became frustrated with the constant changes. The employees were not putting their heart and soul into their projects because they knew the strategic direction would change and they would have to work on a different project. Externally, clients became confused with what the company was trying to do. As the company hopped from one strategy to another, clients received mixed messages from the management team, and a few finally left.

Jean-Francois had a chance to reflect on the problems the company had.

"One could blame the market changing, being in marketing, being in advertising, being in digital, but at one point you got to have that vision that you keep in sight of for the next 10 years," he says. "You can't change it every 18 months. That causes people to stop either believing or taking you seriously as they will ask, 'Well, we're changing again. Why are we doing that?'"

Jean-François's partner became so enamoured with the trends in digital marketing that he began to make decisions fueled by emotion. The rest of the management team members blindly supported the change, saying yes to every decision. The role of management should have been questioning the changing strategy and looking at the effect of the change on areas such as internal resources, capabilities, and customer perception, among others. But there was no debate.

Although the management team took the partner's advice and supported him with data after the decision, Jean-François should have been much harder on his partner. He takes full blame for the company suffering. He realizes that his lack of tenacity resulted in the swaying strategy.

"Where I was not tenacious enough was pushing back sufficiently to say, 'Okay, stop it already. Enough of the flavour of the month. We need to stick to our guns and keep that going to create sufficient momentum,'" he says. "I tried and tried, but when you're a 50-50 partnership, there is only so much you can do until it breaks."

In 2012, Jean-François had had enough and walked into his partner's office and told him that he wanted to sell his shares. With a cheque in hand a few months later, Jean-François went out on his own to start his own consulting company in the digital media area.

As far as he knows, the previous business is still operational with the original partner as sole owner, but with a small number of employees and a small customer base. Jean-François is not sure what the strategic direction is, and wishes his former partner well, but he cannot stop thinking about the company's strategic direction changing when he reads about new fads in the digital media space.

In some cases, business hurdles are so great that they test the will of the entrepreneur to go ahead. These challenges may bring the business to the brink of failing, and the entrepreneur may need to make a serious decision to either move ahead or call it quits. Closing the business may be a smart option as there tend to be a multitude of issues at play. Making the decision to move on requires guts, and the entrepreneur takes a calculated risk in doing so. This is where tenacity is needed. Just ask Clare McEwan.

Clare McEwan left a long and successful career in the sales and marketing area to open Air Safaris International Inc., a firm that provides customized flying vacations for clients who are looking for a different type of vacation experience. Clare opened the company because it combined his love of travel and aviation, and he believed that people wanted a travel experience that was different from visiting the usual tourist spots. Because the vacations were designed to offer a premium travel experience for a small group, the pricing would be in the order of $12,000 to $15,000 per person for a two-to-three week vacation.

The Air Safaris package appeals particularly to pilots because, as part of the package, Clare rents aircraft for them so they are able to fly themselves. At the same time, Clare and a local commercial pilot lead the group and take care of all the logistics. For the non-pilots in the group, Clare arranges for a pilot to fly a plane for them. Because the aircraft flown are small single-engine planes, the group gets a unique perspective as they fly low and slow over the landscape. The use of small aircraft also makes it possible for the itinerary to include stops at remote locations that would otherwise be inaccessible.

The concept was well received, and Clare secured a number of initial clients by attending aviation shows and advertising in aviation publications. However, shortly after launching the business, Clare faced a number of challenges.

The first challenge Clare met involved starting a business based on flying at a time when aviation was in a decline following the 9/11 attacks in the US.

"It was ironic that I was sitting in a government office on University Street registering my company in 2002. There was one minute of silence as it was the anniversary of the September 11, 2001 attacks," he says. "I had to ask myself if this was the worst possible timing or whether it would end up being wonderful timing. It certainly would make a great anecdote."

Despite his concerns, he moved ahead and, with a sigh of relief, successfully registered the company.

Clare chose to focus his tour offerings in Australia because of his extensive travel experience there and because the weather was conducive to flying most of the year. The next step in the process was to recruit an Australian lead pilot and to find an aviation base from which to operate. Once that was in place Clare would be ready to entice interested travelers in his vacation excursions, bringing much-needed revenues to the business. But once again, Clare faced a delay due to changes in the Australian rules for pilots.

"The problem was that every pilot in Australia had to go through an additional security screening as a result of the World Trade Center attacks," he says. "The new Australian regulations required every pilot to have a federal police security check. This created a huge backlog and it was impossible to get clearances for foreign visiting pilots. The process was also time consuming and somewhat unpredictable. This is one point where I thought that I may have to close the business."

This waiting period almost killed Clare's business, but he did not give up and continued to push forward in spite of the financial pain on the belief that the challenges with security checks would be resolved.

In order to survive this difficult period Clare needed to keep his expenses at a minimum. In time, he overcame the security clearance issues and began running tours again, thereby generating needed cash.

Things were going well for Clare, with a healthy number of clients using his services – and then the economic downturn of 2007 and 2008 hit. Because of the negative financial consequences for most of Clare's customers, many of them chose to delay their tours for one or two years.

"Because of the depth of the downturn and because it was something that was beyond my control, I wondered if it was realistic to carry on as it appeared it would take some years for the market to come back," he says.

Adding to Clare's challenges at the time, the Australian dollar was strengthening so his clients faced significant increases in the cost of their trips. With drastically reduced potential sales, Clare once again wondered if it made sense to continue.

"I had a few sleepless nights and I joined the ranks of those entrepreneurs who have said that if they had known how difficult it was going to be, they probably would not have started it," he says. "I had to ask myself, 'Where do you see this going? What else might I to do?'"

Clare had to look deep inside himself.

"I had to ask myself, 'If I had unlimited resources and did not have to work, what would I want to do?'" he recalls. "And the answer was I wanted to travel and I would fly. In other words I would do what I am trying to do with this business. So while I may not be making a lot of money, I am happy to be doing what I am doing. I am meeting great people and I get a lot of satisfaction when I see them have a wonderful trip experience. My family is very supportive of what I do and I feel I have a good balance in my life. For me that is success."

Clare persevered and his efforts began to pay dividends. His creative thinking drove him to establish solid partnerships with travel agencies, aviation clubs, travel associations, and airplane owners. He has been able to begin filling his sales pipeline again.

Today, Clare has a robust set of clients and operates a healthy business with a steady stream of clients and a continued happy personal and professional life. One cannot sum up Clare's love for his business and his customers any better than he does himself on a video that is posted on his company's website.

"I get a lot of satisfaction seeing the smiles, seeing the friendships develop on these tours, friendships that last a lifetime," he says in the video. "My goal is for everybody to have the best vacation ever."

In two of these cases, the tenacity by Clare McEwan and Netflix got them through incredibly difficult times where the survival of the company was at stake. In the third case, with Jean-Francois, a lack of tenacity resulted in the partnership breaking, in addition to confusing both customers and employees. Of course, tenacity is usually combined with other business elements and attitudes, as Jonathan Ehrlich points out when he combines tenacity with focus and attention on a big market. Nevertheless, a tenacious attitude helps a business push through the hurdles it faces.

If an entrepreneur has both tenacity and perseverance, there could be a tendency for the entrepreneur to become aggressive when trying to achieve that end goal of business success. That aggressiveness could put the business in risky situations, as John Adamson experienced.

Being Aggressive

*Being overly aggressive got me into a situation where
I was close to depleting what little savings I had.*

– John Adamson, Serial Entrepreneur

For the entrepreneur, talking about the product or service to be launched and having people agree that the venture will most certainly be successful instills confidence in the entrepreneur that his or her venture will, in fact, be successful.

If the launch of the venture succeeds in attracting customers, while being aggressive may potentially be a good sign to help move the business forward, entrepreneurs may become too aggressive, getting into businesses or projects that may be a bit too risky, not taking the proper time to fully understand what they are getting into.

This happened to John Adamson when he took on a number of business opportunities prematurely, hurting him financially.

John Adamson ran a firm called Optical Recording Corporation (ORC) that, in 1985, purchased a number of patents from a bankruptcy asset sale related to the laser recording of an audio or video signal onto portable media. John, through ORC, began a project to develop an electronic data storage device to write CD-like data density and capacity onto a credit-card sized health record. However, with the assistance of the inventor and patent professionals, John learned that the Compact Disc or CD, and then DVD, only worked by using the ORC patents.

The CD technology was just then, in 1987, being introduced by a partnership of Sony of Japan and Phillips of the Netherlands. After years of fruitless meetings about a license agreement with Sony Corporation, John had ORC bring patent infringement cases against several large manufacturers such as Time-Warner. In the summer of 1992, ORC received a jury judgment of infringement and a significant damages award against Time-Warner in an American court. This judgment and damages award was, for John, the culmination of a series of entrepreneurial efforts and learning experiences.

"In my first entrepreneurial venture, started in 1974," he says, "one challenge that I faced was being overly confident and aggressive, which resulted in me not fully understanding the capital requirements of the project."

He had started a general contracting business with a pre-engineered steel building dealership from an American firm called Behlen-Wickes, which custom-designed and manufactured large span building systems.

These buildings were unique because they protected against harsh winters and were ideal for providing a roof over large open areas, with no interior posts, such as warehouses or hockey rinks. As project manager for an airline, John had constructed this type of building in Iqaalik, Nunavut (then Frobisher Bay, NWT). With his Frobisher Bay experience, John decided to offer this type of building construction to Southern Ontario. Early in this venture, John bid on a hockey rink project in Beaverton, Ontario and would have won had he not withdrawn his bid.

"I had gone through the capital requirements of my bid before but on review I feared that any delay in construction could turn into a complete debacle," he says. "With my young family, I could not risk what I had left of my small savings and I found employment as an administrative manager for a performing arts company in financial trouble."

Two years later, in 1977, he became Controller for MCM Computers, a Canadian computer manufacturing start-up who introduced their desktop microcomputer five years before IBM launched their PC in 1981. As a pioneer, MCM had continuing sales trouble and, after 18 months of constant scrambles to meet payroll, John decided to open his own dealership for the MCM product, targeting the Toronto financial community. John did well and had three profitable years. Then the IBM PC was introduced, and MCM collapsed just over a year later. With no

MCM product, John lost all of his investment in software developed for the MCM product and, at that time, could not get wholesale access to the IBM PC.

So John took on a PC dealership with Olivetti of Italy, a noted office products manufacturer. The Olivetti Company had promised their new PC dealers all the software necessary to make their PC product useful to many markets, but no software came. One year later, once again John lost a large sum of money.

To recoup, John went on a one-year consultant contract with DMR & Associates, a systems consulting firm keen to expand their footprint in the Toronto financial community. At the end of that year, John decided to pursue another venture and, through an MBA classmate, found the project opportunity that he subsequently named ORC.

"I remain committed to the view that there is no wasted time and experience in a career," he says. "The skill set and awareness gained from some tedious, seemingly irrelevant task that you hated to do years before, will place you at the head of the line in some new business opportunity."

With his experience at MCM, John learned of the importance of data storage capacity as a design element in computer systems. This element determined the limits of a computer's functionality and thus the size of the accessible market. ORC was all about data storage capacity in that only with the inventions of James Russell – whose patents ORC had purchased in 1985 – was there sufficient digital data storage capacity in a portable format to allow the development of the CD and DVD. His patent licensing success rode the wave of these products in the marketplace, getting in this business on the basis of his earlier experience developing and implementing business systems with the MCM computer.

Olivetti was an equally useful experience, but in a different way. Whereas John had worked hard and made his first small fortune of $300,000 in two years with his MCM system integration business, he lost money, $125,000 to be exact, in the year that he was committed to introducing the Olivetti PC to the downtown Toronto business community.

"What went wrong? In retrospect, I remember being desperate about being shut out of the marketing of the IBM PC," says John. "IBM had designated only two market channels for this product: Computerland, and their own sales force. As it was, in the first year, IBM could not meet the demand for their PC. So, Olivetti came out with basically a knock-off of the IBM PC. Buoyed by the hubris of my earlier MCM success and my desperation to be in the PC market, I leapt before I looked. I committed to a dealership for the Olivetti PC on the strength of their "commitment" to deliver software for system compatibility with existing mainframes. At that time, CIOs were demanding that the PCs be able to share data with their in-house mainframes. Olivetti never delivered and I was left high and dry, basically no sales for a year, 12 units at about $1,500 a piece, and I threw in the towel. This is probably one of the few times that I cut my losses when I should have and this, only because I got tired of looking at my two salesmen, on full draw, working the phones hard but with long faces at the end of each day."

John also believes that timing and the right people are key. The entrepreneur is the driving force who stays awake at night testing, planning, and plotting their next move, but without the right people for the execution of that next move, the result will be similar to "one hand clapping" but considerably more painful.

Young entrepreneurs, as a group, tend to be overly confident and overly aggressive, which makes them prone to committing to a venture long before they fully understand the economics of the project or all of the skill sets required for success. This fast action can be a strength because many opportunities have short fuses and evaporate if not acted on with dispatch. However, while sheer effort may force the ill-planned venture to succeed, in many cases the deck is stacked toward failure. Too often, the entrepreneur's hubris also puts his or her personal commitments at a greater and unnecessary risk.

This hubris is dangerous as it will result in a loss of objectivity, and a loss of objectivity may spell disaster for the business, as witnessed by Mitch Baran.

Being Objective

*Look objectively at all aspects of the innovation,
including potential marketing barriers. Do not get hung up on
your perceived genius. Otherwise, you risk business failure.*

– Mitch Baran, CEO – Trudell Medical Ltd.

It is impossible for an entrepreneur to not become emotional when getting into a business venture. This emotional drive combined with passion, excitement, and tenacity, are needed to move the business forward. But this emotion can also drive an entrepreneur to lose objectivity and make irrational decisions.

It is hoped that the entrepreneur will seek proper advice to ensure that any irrational decisions are identified and corrected. But over-whelming emotion may cause the entrepreneur to disregard advice or worse yet, move forward without advice, losing objectivity, and possibly resulting in the business being negatively affected right from the start.

Mitch Baran has seen a loss of objectivity from entrepreneurs trying to move a business forward all too often.

Mitch Baran is CEO of Trudell Medical Ltd., a leading global medical device company. His experience has led him to not only push through challenges in his industry, but also recognize challenges that others will face.

One challenge Mitch often sees is the need for business owners to be objective. Typically, at the university or college level, there are people wrapped up in a particular idea itself, and they lose sight of developing the business plan and processes needed to successfully commercialize the idea. Someone with an idea must understand that getting market share is difficult. Issues such as product pricing or market readiness are often sidestepped, creating difficulties that will guarantee that a company will have an extremely hard time getting to market.

"To ensure that this does not happen, a business owner needs to keep a passionate focus on the market and remain objective of how the market will accept a product," Mitch says. "Take advice from advisors, initiate focus groups, and look for signals that give hints about market readiness. Too often, the advice or signals are dismissed and are treated as being offhand in nature. Of course, nobody has the ultimate answer regarding the marketplace, but risks must be managed by an appropriate planning process."

One company that had not properly assessed the process of getting its product to market approached Mitch with a new way to process pharmaceutical products. The idea was excellent, and Mitch leaned on his network of contacts to find out if this idea had a reasonable chance of success. The feedback Mitch received was that a company that adopted the new pharmaceutical process would have to go through the entire regulatory approval process, costing time, money, and exposure to significant regulatory risks. Thus, the savings gained by process adoption could be effectively wiped out. The company was not convinced that this was an issue and eventually got funding, but folded soon after.

"Unfortunately, the company was biased to the extent that their equipment was superior, but there was no market because the pharmaceutical companies were not prepared to purchase a piece of equipment which would disrupt their already approved FDA process inasmuch as it meant new clinical trials and waiting time for approval – all at a very significant cost," says Mitch.

In the end, failure should not be seen as a bad thing. Mitch mentions a parable: if failure does not kill you, it makes you stronger. Failures will push your emotions through a roller coaster ride, but you eventually harden, and you are more apt to learn from them. Every entrepreneur has a sense of not wanting to fail, which is a tremendous driving force. But, one has to be a smart driver, and not one that is rash.

The loss of objectivity, in the case described above, resulted in the business folding. If business decisions are continually fueled by emotions, there is a good chance that the business will find itself continually fighting to survive, losing out on potential revenues that could be gained because the business model was actually quite good.

Putting emotion aside and making decisions with objectivity is part of being a good leader. But that is only one aspect; there are many other characteristics required to be an effective leader. Most will assume that they can lead, and continue running the business ineffectively. Realizing that one is not a leader is important as business needs excellent leadership to move forward. George de Vlugt found this out early.

Can You Lead?

I failed to realize that I was not a CEO that could lead with a vision. If I can be led, I can take a vision and make it happen very successfully.

– George de Vlugt, Former Pastor

Being able to lead is an extremely important trait for entrepreneurs as they need others joining the company to buy into the strategic vision and to get the business's products or services into the hands of potential customers. Without this leadership quality, it becomes hard to articulate what the business is to both the team and the customer. Of course, a partner can help do this, but for George de Vlugt, there was no such partner and he had to come to terms with the fact that he could not lead the vision.

"I grew up in a very conservative religious denomination," George says. "This denomination had a strict set of rules set out by the church founder, which we needed to follow in order to please God. The congregation followed these rules very tightly, rarely accepting the practices of others."

Because of the unique nature of the philosophy – one not shared by any other church – George's church became a geographic one, pulling people from the surrounding areas. With churches in London, Windsor, and Sarnia, people would come from areas surrounding these cities, with some even driving long distances, coming across the US border to attend.

At one point, George had an opportunity to pastor all three of the churches.

"I was okay financially because I was able to draw a salary from the congregation's head office, which collected donations from the congregation members," he says. "One of the strange rules was that each member was required to submit 10% of their earnings to the church on a regular basis, and this would help pay for all of the costs in running all the churches. Even when I was a young kid, I got paid 25 cents a bucket to pick strawberries. I had to donate some of that money to the church!"

When the church leader passed away, "all of a sudden the congregation members did not have a leader to dictate the rules," George recalls. "Our members went from being almost child-like in following rules, to becoming adults, trying to figure out what the best rules were for everybody."

The next leader began discussing re-evaluating the values, and the congregation members began re-evaluating the way they thought as well. The members of the congregation felt that they did not need a lot of rules to please God and decided to be more accepting of other people. After finally being able to think for themselves, a number of the church members became disillusioned with the original values the church held.

The reaction to the old values was quite stark. Some members of the congregation felt controlled, cheated, and lied to by the former church leader, whereas others were relieved that they did not have to drive so far to attend a church that was similar to one in their own community.

Because members of the congregation were more upset at the late head of the congregation, George still had a good relationship with them. He tried desperately to keep the congregation together by trying to be collaborative. However, once a number of members left the congregation, their friends started thinking the same, and eventually they left, which triggered more people thinking about leaving as well. Soon, the congregation numbers started falling quite rapidly.

George was excited about these changes, and thought that he could start a new church based on these new guiding principles. He thought that while he was pastoring these three churches on the Saturday, he could start a new church on a Sunday and did so, starting a new church in nearby Strathroy.

Within a short period of time, George drew a number of families in the area to the church. The challenge was now to get the church self-sufficient through donations. George no longer had the luxury of a flow of cash from the old church's head office to cover both his salary and any operational expenses for the church. However, given his past experience in connecting with the congregation members from the old church, he thought that he would be able to convince the new church members to donate to the cause.

Initially, George was able to convince the old church's head office to help him financially with a small salary. But this stipend was not enough, and George put in his own funds and worked extremely hard to make ends meet.

"There was interest from a good number of families," he says. "The challenge was that I could not get these families to believe in the values strong enough to donate to the cause. I had to work seven days a week just to make things work financially, and I was really getting burned out."

Both personally and financially, George was at the end of his rope.

"I saw the writing on the wall," he says. "The original congregation numbers were slipping and that meant that my salary from the head office was shrinking because they were cutting salaries across the board. This model could not continue for me and I had to start thinking about me."

George finally left both churches and got into sales, selling furniture part-time. Much to his surprise, he did extremely well. He was able to leverage the relationships he had established in the town he was living in, and these people supported him by buying furniture from him.

When George thought about the success he had in sales, he found that he did not know himself very well. He now knew that he was not good as a CEO but was good at being second-in-command. He could not lead a team of people, but he was capable under the direction of somebody else. Give him a vision and he could execute that vision, as long as someone else comes up with the vision.

However, when starting a new church, George had to create the vision and execute it. Once that was done, he knew the donations should come in if people connected with the church's vision. George was never able to create that vision, and hence, he was not able to get any donations. He had no choice but to step away and take care of his own needs.

"It has been eight years for me now, and it is water under the bridge," he says. "In the end, this was awfully good for me. Had I not gone through that crisis, I would be stuck in a situation, and I would not be able to talk to people like you."

George likens the experience to coffee pod or disc machines.

"There are a lot of free samples, and a lot of people will use the free samples, but very few will actually buy the coffee machine," he says. "One has to think about the cash coming in from those buying the coffee machines that would need to pay for the free samples." For George, the new church gave initial members a "free trial" with some values that they could connect with, but once the "free trial" was over, not too many people wanted to pay for the overall product.

George's story has incredible implications for those looking to start a business because many feel that they have "the right stuff" when looking to lead others, when in fact they simply do not. In George's case, he realized early on that he was not a leader, and made the decision to move on.

However, others are not so lucky. Some entrepreneurs simply do not have leadership qualities and are hard-pressed to bring other resources on board. If the business requires strong leadership from the beginning, then the business whipsaws along with little to no revenue. It is only a matter of time before the entrepreneur realizes that a leader is needed or, with little to no revenues, it just does not make sense to continue the business.

There are a tremendous number of aspects to leadership, and picking up a book or taking a weekend course will not make an entrepreneur an effective leader. The best advice would be to bring on another resource or get some guidance from a qualified mentor.

If successful at being a leader, an entrepreneur needs to have a good balance in being proactive and reactive in different situations. If an entrepreneur is too proactive, this could lead to an overconfident attitude. This could spell trouble for the entrepreneur, as it did for James Robertson.

Taming Overconfidence

I had a chip on my shoulder and a sense of entitlement, but as the owner, I needed to mature and be accountable to a higher degree.

– James Robertson, Vice-President – Robertson Hall Insurance Inc.

For entrepreneurs with a track record of success, starting a viable business the second or third time around should be much easier. But past results, despite being positive, may not necessarily result in a new venture also experiencing success. Each venture must be treated as a separate entity. Of course, one needs to leverage what worked before to this new venture, as long as it is relevant. But the entrepreneur should not make an assumption that success will just happen. This leads to overconfidence, which could stall the eventual growth of the business.

Those following in the footsteps of their parents and getting a chance to run the family business could believe that running the entire business is not hard. Ideally, the family business would hire the children in hopes that they take over the business at some point, but just because the children get some experience in the business does not necessarily guarantee that the children can manage the business.

From the children's perspective, knowing that eventually one of them may run the business can foster a sense of overconfidence without gaining the proper experience. This plays out in different ways. For example, it could lead to an inability to make some key decisions or possibly impact the overall culture of an organization.

For James Robertson, overconfidence and a sense of entitlement did not bode well.

James Robertson is Vice-President of Robertson Hall Insurance Inc., a full service insurance brokerage dealing in personal and commercial lines insurance, located in London, Ontario. His father originally owned the business and after some time, was looking to James to take over the company. Of course, he needed training to learn the business before getting a chance to run it.

James completed a one-year MBA program in risk management initiatives in the United States. Upon completion, James's father sent him to Australia to work for a large international insurance company. Given his seeming enthusiasm, he thought he could go from 0 to 100% in understanding the sales role within a short period of time, but he soon found out otherwise.

Although James returned to London without a full understanding of the sales role, he was not affected by this lack of experience; he knew he had a job waiting for him because, after all, he was the owner's son.

"Because I was the owner's son, I was overconfident and had a sense of entitlement, thinking that I could make an immediate impact upon my return," he says. "But this was not the case."

He had a chance to shine in the sales role, but much to his astonishment, his sales numbers were weak. He simply did not have the proper training in the sales area, a set of skills he should have gained in Australia. James knew that, being the owner's son, he needed to be accountable at a higher standard than others. He recognized that he had to mature fast.

To be successful in the sales area of an insurance brokerage firm, one needs to understand the behaviour, attitude, and activities that work together in helping close business. One also needs to have patience. With proper sales training, which incorporates all of these elements, a salesperson should be able to maintain a consistent and healthy level of sales and prospecting activity.

To increase his sales skills, James began weekly counselling with a sales coach and completed an online sales training program. This combination worked well for him, and the results spoke for themselves – his sales income was consistently higher than that of the other insurance brokers. Robertson Hall Insurance even adopted the online sales training as a standard requirement for any new sales hires.

Having the self-awareness to recognize his overconfidence, James leveraged that experience to save his company from establishing a potentially bad partnership. James looked at partnering with a firm that promoted a line of insurance products different from Robertson Insurance. The owner of the other firm had aggressive growth projections and wanted to locate downtown to help drive revenues. However, James noticed that the owner was quite naïve and impatient, signs of the overconfidence that James once had. The warning signs made James back away from the partnership. A short time later, the other company imploded and, thankfully, James saved a lot of time, money, and effort.

Overconfidence may lead you to believe you are right, when in fact you may be wrong. According to a Forbes magazine article[11], a study by University of Oregon psychologist Lewis Goldberg found that in nearly 15,000 judgements, when participants believed they were correct 98% of the time, they were wrong over 30% of the time. The same article goes on to mention that these inaccuracies could lead to tragic circumstances, such as the Chernobyl disaster and the NASA Challenger explosion, where overconfidence was linked as a contributing factor.

For an entrepreneur, not being able to tame overconfidence could be the difference between the business moving forward or shutting down.

With a failure in business comes a tremendous mixture of negative emotions. However, these failures must be seen as positive events because, learning through these failures, one becomes successful. Of course, failing is shameful, but it is okay to admit that, as Sean Miller did.

11 http://www.forbes.com/sites/nathanfurr/2012/11/13/why-confident-entrepreneurs-fail-the-overconfidence-death-trap

Ashamed After Failing? It's Okay.

*I think, to fail fast, you need to lose your pride.
Here, in this case, we failed in creating a successful
business, and one of the reasons I didn't talk about it
with you before was because I was ashamed that
I failed on my strength: being a lawyer. To sit back and
say that the business did not succeed because
we didn't create proper employment or supplier
contracts at the beginning, this is shameful.*

– Sean Miller, Former Clothing Store Owner

The hardest part of talking about failure is that someone needs to be honest about what happened. Admitting failure is hard, especially when putting on a good face and telling the world that things are going great, which seems preferable.

For the majority of the over 200 interviewees I have had the pleasure of interviewing on their business failures and challenges, what was more important for them was to be open and honest about their experiences. Accepting failure is okay. It is also okay to say you have lost your pride, and you are ashamed at what happened.

For Sean Miller, opening a retail business was a dream. But for him, to admit that the business did not flourish because he did not create proper employment and supplier contracts early enough, despite being a lawyer, was devastating to him personally. Although tough to swallow, and with the business now sold, he now happily talks about the shame he felt – although he did not talk about it during our first interview, but came to terms with it much later.

After graduating from university with a law degree, Sean joined a local law firm as an articling student. While at the law firm, Sean and his brother took advantage of an opportunity to open up a clothing store, a business that he and his brother were thinking about for quite some time.

Sean and his brother, also a lawyer, joined two friends who had retail experience to help open a retail clothing shop that offered young, fashion-forward clothing at a reasonable price point. Early into venture, the two friends could not commit to helping with the operations as much as originally hoped. Because of this, both brothers had to take on more responsibilities than originally thought. Sean's brother had to manage all of the operations of the business while Sean helped with the marketing and business development roles.

From a marketing perspective, Sean implemented many different marketing campaigns, and in every case, he saw a subsequent lift in sales.

"In the retail industry, when somebody needs your product, you need to be top of mind," Sean says. "I drove the marketing campaign and advertised in several newspapers and had some radio spots going. The business had a very robust following on Facebook, but it was difficult to track which advertising route worked. I would run various advertising and marketing campaigns and see sales go up, and then run another set of advertising and marketing campaigns, and see sales flat-line or slowly decrease."

Sean decided to open his own law practice, limiting his attention for the clothing store. With less time devoted to advertising and marketing of the business, sales started to drift downward.

"This shone a light on a lesson that we learned very early, especially in the retail industry, which is that you need to be there all the time," he says. "And whoever is there has to have skin in the game."

The lessons did not stop there. Sean also learned the hard way that he needed to have a handle on the legal side of the business from the start. Sean's brother was busy running the daily operations, and despite knowing they needed legal contractual agreements with all employees and suppliers, it was not top of mind when considering all the other priorities when opening and running a new business. They simply did not have enough time to dedicate to the legal side of the business.

Not having employment contracts in place resulted in a number of employees asking for a significant amount of overtime pay despite not being approved for working these hours. Although there were verbal agreements in place, both brothers knew that this would not hold up in a court of law, and they had to pay the employees out, cutting into their razor thin profits and low cash flow at the start of the business.

A lack of supplier contracts resulted in not being able to return incorrect inventory for credit. Some of the inventory that had arrived had sizes, styles, and colours that were different from what had been ordered, resulting in a skewed selection of clothing items. More inventory had to be ordered to carry the proper selection of inventory for the customers.

With the original inventory unable to be returned for credit, money was tied up in carrying the excess inventory. This was cash that could have been used elsewhere.

Although both brothers were lawyers, they failed to have the proper contracts put in place at the beginning, resulting in hardship for the business.

"The problem that I have, which I admit is my embarrassment, was that a failure came on a legal matter, which is what my expertise is," Sean says. "We knew we needed it, but it took a second priority."

"I take the blame for that," Sean says. "I did not turn to my brother and say 'If this isn't getting done, we're getting someone else to do it'. If I had asked him earlier, the agreements would have been signed three months earlier, and four months later we could have saved $15,000. With an extra $15,000, it would have changed the loan situation, and our advertising strategy, our inventory blunder, and this and that. It would have changed everything."

To complicate the issue of cost, Sean brought in a trusted retail manager to manage the business, but the new manager's vision of what type of inventory should be carried was much different than what Sean and his brother were looking to offer. He came from a renowned retail chain in New York, and stocked the store with the best of everything. Because of the more modest pricing of the majority of the clothing being sold, the high cost of what the new manager ordered left little profit margin on this particular line of clothing.

The store was opened, and although the initial sales were robust, the hiccups that were experienced resulted in expected profits that were very low due to higher-than-expected costs. But this was not realized until much later because there was no financial reporting process in place to validate the costs. So, Sean and his brother were running a retail business with an inexact set of financials, running financially blind.

Luckily, the brothers had initially put in some start-up capital that provided much-needed financial relief. Sean split the funds, allocating 50% of the investment at the start, and withholding the other 50%. When looking back, Sean realizes that he should not have withheld any money, but should have made the full investment available right from the start.

"This extra money would have gone into crucial areas such as providing signage for the front of the business, upgrading the lighting system, and having the proper trained staff in place," he says. "The business had its largest sales month four months in, and we were not ready for it. With the volume of customers, we had put in a very large order for inventory, so we were okay there despite the problems with our suppliers. But we had another big issue staring right into our faces. The issue was the service – we couldn't manage the volume of customers in the store. If we did, we could have drastically increased our sales levels."

Being short-staffed started a series of cascading problems. When starting out, the staff did not know the products well, so they needed more time with each customer. Customers were also new to the store, so they also needed time to go over the products, talk to the staff, and make a decision. This cascade of problems turned into a number of unpleasant experiences for the customers, with many of them leaving with no sale, not returning, and likely the biggest problem, sharing their negative experience with others.

"I would suspect that these customers did not come back nor talk about it," says Sean. "The problem was that these were the type of customers who came to the store because they read about us in the newspaper or magazines. They were the target market. We had them coming in to buy. It was a new business that they wanted to try, and we never had them coming back or talking about it."

Coupled with Sean and his brother's father passing away, and the success of Sean's law practice, Sean and his brother decided to sell the business rather than try and revive it. Sean's attention shifted from running advertising and marketing campaigns to concentrating more on his law practice in addition to finding a deal that would have someone take over the lease.

Upon reflection, Sean feels he should have been able to fail fast rather than fail slowly. He puts the fault of the business not succeeding squarely on his shoulders, and recognizes that it is okay to be shameful.

"I think, to fail fast, you need to lose your pride. Here, in this case, the reason I didn't talk about it was because I was ashamed that I failed on my strength and this was a main reason we were not succeeding – or said another way, failing. If you're not succeeding, you're failing. This concept has taken me a long to realize."

Sean also accepts the failure to affirmatively ask his brother to properly attend to the legal work that was sorely needed at the start.

"I failed on my strength because I was in a personal relationship with the person that was operating the business and who was drafting the legal work that I was then going to evaluate. So asking your brother for legal contracts that don't come, it's a hard decision to tell him that he is not doing that anymore. I didn't make the right business decision because of my personal relationship and that was another reason why I failed in the business. And ultimately, when you then sit back and take a look at this team with its combined legal experience, and then say that one of the cascading problems for the business failure was because we didn't produce adequate legal contracts, this is shameful."

More upfront investment in the clothing store would have also solved a number of problems. With Sean's brother busy running the store, a few more resources should have been brought on and paid to provide legal help, financial reporting, and marketing and business development. This would have allowed both Sean and his brother a chance to discover and address any issues early. Moreover, Sean admits that both he and his brother should have admitted that they were failing much sooner.

"There are two shame comments in this story," he says. "My brother is a lawyer and he should have been able to do the drafting of all the legal agreements. He did not identify that he was too busy and he was ashamed that he couldn't get it done. He didn't say that I failed, and go find somebody to do it. I, as a lawyer and evaluator of the agreements, was ashamed about telling my story, and admitting that we needed help. We didn't need help in expertise; we needed help with horsepower, which is a huge difference. We yielded to our pride as an expert over the need for horsepower and it has taken me a long time to realize that."

Sean struggled to admit that the business was failing when telling his story, which was apparent when I had interviewed him a few months earlier. During our second interview, he had become comfortable enough to let me know that it truly was a shameful experience. As a lesson, being able to openly admit shortcomings is something Sean says is necessary to share with other entrepreneurs.

"That sequence of events happened two years ago," he says. "It has taken me about a year and a half, or two years, to figure out why I didn't want people knowing about this. And so for the entrepreneurs that have the eternal hope, it's all great, but to fail fast you have to accept that you have failed, and you have to recognize it, you have to understand it, and you have to learn from it, and you to need to move on from it, as soon as you can, before you are going to fail more, and slowly."

For a person to openly admit that he or she failed, and felt shameful about it, is extremely tough. Given the professional success Sean has had, a bright career with a thriving law practice and an excellent network of peers, failure was not a part of his vocabulary. But for someone to go through the process emotionally to admit the truth about what happened, I hold tremendous respect for.

It is stories such as these that will truly inform you, and make you aware of the realities of trying to run a business if not properly prepared. There are plenty of rosy pictures drawn in an entrepreneur's mind at the starting stages of a business, but the picture is not so rosy on the way down. It is okay to lament and feel shameful. But then, in the true spirit of entrepreneurship, you pick yourself up, dust off your shoulders, and begin creating value again. Only this time, you look in the rear view mirror to tell yourself that you will not repeat that same mistake, or the mistakes others have made as narrated in this book, again.

Fail Fast. Succeed Faster.

FAIL FAST SUCCEED FASTER

PART 2

Do You Have a Business Plan?

I have taken more than 9000 shots in my career. I have lost almost 300 games. Twenty-six times I have been trusted to take the game winning shot and missed. I have failed over and over again in my life; and that is why I succeed.

– Michael Jordan

Having an idea and having a *BUSINESS* idea are two separate concepts. There are a million ideas out there that are shared among acquaintances, friends, or family in a number of social settings, such as social gatherings, pubs, and coffee shops. These ideas seem to solve a number of problems, some real and some contrived. Sharing these ideas provides for much interesting discussion in any case.

A BUSINESS idea is one that seems to solve an important problem in the marketplace. The entrepreneur creates a product or service that solves this problem and is able to articulate how he or she can convince customers to part with their money and eliminate their problem.

To ensure that this business idea will survive as a real business, entrepreneurs should create a business plan detailing what the goals of the business are, why these goals are attainable, and how the business will attain them, considering all of the risk factors that may be encountered.

If the business plan is created with realistic details, scenarios, and assumptions, those reviewing the plan should be convinced that the entrepreneur has a successful business in the making, assuming that the plan is adhered to. However, if the plan is prepared with emotion, unrealistic assumptions, and rose-coloured glasses, the entrepreneur may be convinced that he or she has a successful business, but not others. Moving forward with an unrealistic business plan will most likely result in the business either not getting off the ground, or sputtering from the start.

The stories in this section showcase a number of issues that should be taken into consideration when preparing a business plan. By taking note of the experiences the interviewees went through and incorporating the lessons learned in a business plan, the entrepreneur stands an excellent chance of producing a more robust guide for the business and its success.

Are You Unique?

In our industry, nobody knew who we were. We were young, and ambitious, and would do anything, but to really be successful, we needed to figure out why we were different from our competition.

– Martin Perelmuter, Co-Founder – Speakers' Spotlight

When introducing a product or service, to be successful, an entrepreneur needs to define what makes the offering unique. Several questions can help determine the business merit of the product or service being offered:

- Is there a unique patent or trademark that others cannot copy?

- Is there a gap in the industry that needs to be filled?

- Is there a solution to a big problem that customers have today?

- Does the product or service offer something of value with the same quality, but at a drastically reduced and sustainable price?

- Does the product or service offer a significantly enhanced value today for the same price as what is currently available in the market?

- Can a significant market share be gained early and quickly as a first mover into a market before competitors begin entering the market?

By answering one of these questions in the affirmative, an entrepreneur has a good chance of success, providing that the entrepreneur can build a business around their unique product or service.

Many entrepreneurs make the mistake of answering these questions with an opinion. They put blinders on and assume that the product or service does answer one of the questions above. For example, a product can come out that supposedly provides a solution for a problem that customers are facing, but either the market for that solution is extremely small, or the problem does not exist. The entrepreneur then begins to manufacture the product, and lo and behold, there are no customers.

Having a unique product or service should provide the business with an early competitive edge to bring in revenues. For Martin and Farah Perelmuter, they needed a competitive advantage to turn a passion into a business. The formula was simple for them: no competitive advantage = no business.

Martin and Farah Perelmuter started Speakers' Spotlight in the mid-1990s with nothing but interest and curiosity. They both gave up lucrative careers to pursue a business that they had no experience or familiarity with because they both knew they wanted to do something different. Prior to co-founding Speakers' Spotlight, Martin was a corporate lawyer at a prestigious international law firm and Farah started her career in the advertising industry.

"It was scary because we went from two decent incomes to zero overnight," says Martin. "The hard part of it was, all of a sudden we didn't have a paycheque coming in. But on the other hand, there's nothing that motivates you like a sense of urgency that, hey, you know, we don't have any money coming in the door now, so you better get up every morning and do something to figure out what works and what doesn't."

They were able to live on a budget because they were both young and relatively fresh out of school, and remembered what student life was all about. It was not difficult – they had no children, no mortgage, and did not have any responsibilities to anybody other than themselves. They also lived a fairly simple lifestyle.

"The fact is, okay, we can't go out for a nice dinner very often, but that was okay because the other 23 hours of the day we were a lot happier," Martin says. "And we really didn't miss it. But it was tough at times because we had friends, and we told ourselves that we will go out for one nice night a month. That was our thing. Other than that, it was renting a lot of movies and spending time with friends, and you know, there's nothing wrong with that. We didn't feel like we were missing out on anything at all."

Neither Martin nor Farah had been happy in their previous careers, and what ignited them was giving people an opportunity to hear from individuals that had an incredible story to tell. After quitting their jobs, they began researching what it took to be successful in the speaking industry.

"We had done some research and we had a sense of who was out there already doing this kind of thing, but really, it was driven by more of a curiosity and an interest that we had," says Martin. "It wasn't like we had identified a gap in the market and thought that there was an opportunity to go in there. This was something more like, this is something we are interested in and we felt that, regardless of how competitive it is or isn't, we're going to try and figure out how to do things differently and make it work."

Martin and Farah quickly found that the way to be at the top of mind when looking for speakers was to be at the forefront of those hiring the speakers. So, in tandem with trying to establish an initial stable of speakers, they began trying to build relationships with the conference planning organizers who contacted agencies to bring speakers to their events. Without them, there would not be a business.

Martin took on the role of sales, but he had never sold anything in his life. He did not know how to make a cold call, and had to figure out what would work and what would not. Without the benefit of experience, he was not sure what "not doing it correctly" meant.

"There was a constant sort of rejection, and you felt like banging your head against a wall," he says. "On an average day, I was making 75 calls a day, and you get voicemail all the time and people don't call you back. But you learn not to take that personally. I just knew that, hey, this is just what you need to do. It's tough when you're not getting anything to show for your efforts. There were days where I would make 75 calls a day, and not one person would call me back."

To compound the problem of not getting through, neither Martin nor Farah had experience or contacts in the industry, so nobody knew who they were. They needed to build relationships and trust just to get a foot in the door; they needed somebody to give them a chance. It was tough, but Martin felt that the short-term pains would somehow translate into long-term gains, believing that his efforts today were helping plant seeds for the future.

"It's tough. When you are feeling like you are working hard, trying to do the right thing, you know, and you know you have a service that can be helpful, and yet, people tell us 'Sorry, we already have somebody that does this for us', or 'We don't need your service' or they don't even call you back, so you don't even know if you're calling the right people," he says. "But it's all relative. People have much bigger challenges, and if it was that easy, then everybody would be doing it. If you know why you're doing it, then those things are minor setbacks."

Martin quickly learned to have patience as trust took time to build. Both he and his wife were in it for the long haul, and knew that if someone was not willing to give them an opportunity today, they may do so months later, or whenever the next opportunity presented itself.

The immediate challenge for them was that, although Speakers' Spotlight represented a couple of speakers, those speakers were also being represented by other companies. To be unique, they had to secure an exclusive stable of speakers that nobody had, that eventually would be in demand. This, they thought, would be their competitive advantage.

"We looked at who was out there. There were at least a couple of agencies out there who claimed to be the oldest and at least a couple of agencies out there that claimed to be the biggest," Martin says. "So, we said we know what we are not: we're not the oldest and we're not one of the biggest. So, we thought, what are we? We knew that we can turn youth into an advantage, and we felt that we were a little bit more on the cutting-edge. The established agencies had older, more stellar speakers whereas we started looking for people who were more up-and-coming and little bit more cutting-edge."

For example, Speakers' Spotlight established a relationship with Evan Solomon, who, at the time, had just co-founded Shift magazine and hosted a show on CBC called *Futureworld*. Evan was young and had a show on digital technology and culture. As his career started to grow and take off, Martin and Farah worked with him along the way to help him with speaking engagements.

To establish another competitive edge, Martin and Farah used online tools and technology, while their competitors operated in a more traditional way, such as sending information through brochures and paper. Speakers' Spotlight was one of the first in Canada to establish a web presence, taking the business online at a time when the Internet was just starting to become a popular medium. Searching for a website name that would also work seamlessly with the corporate name, Martin and Farah found that, surprisingly, although speakers.com was taken, nobody had claimed speakers.ca.

As Internet usage shot up, the competition began moving to an online presence. But that certainly did not happen overnight.

"[Our competitors] actually had to take the business online. It took some of them a while to realize that this needed to be done, whereas with us, this was an advantage for us as we really never had to make a shift," Martin says. "We just started, and we looked at the Internet and said, this is a great way for us to market our speakers. And for the competitors, they were just looking to move their whole brand onto a website by taking the company name and adding a '.com' to it. So, I think we were a little bit ahead of the curve."

Farah's background in marketing and public relations (PR) helped the company receive some exposure in the Globe and Mail and the National Post, two of the leading Canadian national newspapers at the time. They both joined industry associations to increase networking opportunities, and supplemented these opportunities with creative marketing to spread the word about their business, using online tools. Soon, they had carved a nice competitive edge in an industry dominated by a few stalwarts.

"There was that whole idea that a beginner's mind can somewhat be a little bit of an advantage," Martin says. "We did not have any pre-set ideas on how to run this business or how to grow it as we didn't come from another agency. We really built this on relationships and trust and figured it out as we went."

One of the cornerstones of their success was establishing strong relationships.

"We have no differences in how we charge our fees compared to any of our competitors. In the end it comes down to servicing relationships," Martin says. "The challenges in our businesses are similar to advertising, where you can do a great campaign for a client but you have to keep winning their business all the time. You have a bit of an advantage being the incumbent, but companies tend to change ad agencies all the time. We kind of knew this because we did a great job for clients, but there was no guarantee that they would come back and use us the next time."

Their ambition, passion, and focus on establishing strong relationships landed them one of their first speakers, Jack Donahue, who coached the Canadian Olympic basketball team for a few years.

"Jack Donahue was one of the first people that we reached out to," says Martin. "We met with him – super nice guy – and he said that we seemed bright, young, and ambitious and so he took a little bit of a chance on us. That certainly helped. It gives you a little bit of credibility and also the confidence to know that he is willing to associate himself with us and work with us."

The most memorable speaker that generated a significant amount of business for Speakers' Spotlight was Rubin "Hurricane" Carter. Martin had become interested in Rubin before he was well known. Because Rubin had a compelling story, he had been speaking at various events around Toronto, gaining a small reputation as an engaging speaker. His story intrigued Martin, and so Martin began reaching out to him to see if he would give Speakers' Spotlight a chance to represent him.

"I reached out to him shortly after we started the business as I was familiar with his case from law school," he says. "And, I'm a Bob Dylan fan and I knew the Bob Dylan song about him, and I read his book. So, I knew who he was. I knew that he lived in Toronto, somewhere around here, and I had no idea that there was going to be a movie made. I just thought that this was a really interesting guy and I would love to try and connect with him. It wasn't as easy to track him down, I remember. It took about six or seven calls until someone finally gave me a number of someone who might have known him. That went on until finally I got through to him. We met, and he was like, okay, let's work together. We worked together for a couple of years, and it was okay, but it certainly wasn't easy."

With a couple of speakers available, the constant cold calling and the endless networking began, as Martin and Farah worked tirelessly to establish their brand in the marketplace. One day, their lucky stars lined up. The story of Rubin "Hurricane" Carter turned into a major motion picture, starring Denzel Washington. The film premiered on

September 17, 1999 at the Toronto International Film Festival and opened in Canada and the US, December 29, 1999, winning several awards, including two Golden Globes and an Academy Award.

"You get little bit lucky sometimes. And when the movie came out, the whole thing just sort of blew up, so to speak," Martin says. "All of a sudden, everybody is interested in hearing from him. The very next day, I received 20 to 30 emails from organizations around the world to secure Rubin as a speaker."

With that boost, Speakers' Spotlight was well on its way to becoming successful, growing quickly and carrying a vast array of speakers, both notable and up-and-coming stars. But, despite the seeming success, both Martin and Farah continued to "be hungry" and push forward.

"You just have to continue to be proactive and take that mindset of not resting on your laurels because things have been going pretty well," Martin says. "To continue, you have to push the envelope and get better every day. That's the thing. We are a better company today than we were 6 to 12 months ago, and we want to be a better company 6 to 12 months from now than we are today. That is our goal and that is the challenge. You just keep trying to get better. That's really key."

Martin and Farah want their company to be one that provides a specific speaker for a particular event that must add value, and that is where Martin says the company's success comes from.

"There is certainly an advantage for both the speaker and the conference organizer to work with us," Martin says. "From a speaker's point of view, we are out there proactively looking for opportunities and hopefully generating a lot more opportunities for them than they would have generated on their own. For the conference organizer, it's all about finding the right fit for their event. We don't have any particular agenda to book any one speaker. It is really understanding what their needs are, and providing them with the best possible recommendation. Nowadays, with the web, when someone needs a speaker, they can go on Google and find hundreds, if not thousands of speakers on a given topic, but it doesn't mean that they are any good at being a speaker for the event. Really, the most important service that we provide conference organizers, you know, is that we have seen and been exposed to hundreds and hundreds and hundreds of speakers, and it's a matter of finding out who is the right one for this event based on who is in the audience, what industry it is in, and what the objectives are. It is all these things that matter and THAT is what we do best."

Martin and Farah gained a foothold in the speaking industry because of their relentless focus on establishing trust and relationships, showcasing up-and-coming speakers, and using modern tools and techniques to do so. Certainly, they entered an already-crowded industry, but they created an interesting niche in that industry. Today, they continue to add speakers to their current roster, and continue to push the envelope.

Entrepreneurs simply introducing a product or service because there is some inner feeling that it will be successful set themselves up for failure right away. It is not about what the entrepreneur thinks, but more about what the market thinks and wants. If there is no alignment between both lines of thinking, then, most probably, there is no business opportunity. To ensure that the business is successful, the entrepreneur needs to have some sort of uniqueness in the product or service. If not, then much larger, well-established companies, with much deeper pools of resources, will replicate the product or service, and sweep the entrepreneur under the rug.

Being unique is a quality that a business's products and services must have, but those products and services must have value to potential customers. This value has to be established by the customer, not assumed by the entrepreneur. If the product does not resonate with customers, the result is simple – nobody buys it. This was experienced by both Bill Johnson and Tim Fowler.

Know What Your Customer Wants, and Does Not Want

The success of your product or service is to know both what your customer wants, and does not want. We, unfortunately, learned this lesson with a couple of products that did not exactly meet the customers' expectations.

– Bill Johnson, Former Chairman & CEO – McDonald's Restaurants Canada Ltd.

You need to have a very deep understanding of your customer. If you truly have this understanding, then the customer's decision to give you their hard earned money is easy. Building a business without this understanding would be extremely difficult.

– Tim Fowler, Former Sales Vice-President – Tropicana Beverages at Pepsi Beverages Company

When overly excited about getting a product or service to market, entrepreneurs may make assumptions about their customers' buying behaviours, and build a business around these assumed behaviours. What entrepreneurs should be doing is asking potential customers their opinions on the products or services being offered. Some entrepreneurs substitute friends and family as their base of reference for customers. Of course, it is hoped that friends and family would support the business, but obviously the business needs a much larger number of customers to succeed.

Ensuring that a business will attract enough customers requires a deep understanding of that customer to build a sustainable, profitable business. Done properly, the business's products and services should resonate with the customer, and cause few problems convincing customers to part with their money.

For businesses with an existing stream of customers, there is a danger in making assumptions about their behaviour. Products and services added to a business's existing offerings still need to be vetted through that deep understanding of the customer. Failing to do so may confuse customers, or the new product or service may get a tepid reception. For McDonald's, knowing what the customer wanted, and did not want, was critical to ensure that a product met its customers' expectations.

Bill Johnson started working at a McDonald's location in London, Ontario at the age of 18, flipping Big Macs and wiping tables. Through hard work, dedication, and focus, he rose through the organization, taking on multiple management roles in North America. In 2000, Bill became President of McDonald's Canada, and in the next five years, moved to the CEO position and eventually Chairman, before retiring in 2005. One of the challenges that Bill reflects on from his tenure at McDonald's is making sure that you know your customer, and he shares a couple of examples of challenges that McDonald's faced in this area.

"There was a time that McDonald's introduced breakfast in Canada in the late '70s, and the concept was very well received," he says. "At that time, the doors at each McDonald's location opened at 10:30am or 11:00am, whereas today, it opens at 5:00am. Breakfast at McDonald's was a huge success across Canada, except Québec, which significantly lagged in breakfast sales compared to the rest of the country. And we just could not figure out why. So, McDonald's thought that they would try to 'educate' the Quebec market by using aggressive marketing efforts for the next year and a half. But this did not work."

An outside advisor suggested that McDonald's run some focus groups in Québec to find out why consumers were not buying their breakfast like the rest of the country. The unforeseen issue was that consumers in Québec preferred their eggs over-easy and wanted thick toast. McDonald's changed this overnight, and breakfast sales in Québec rose to match the rest of the country.

The initial failure of breakfast in Quebec highlighted the need to consider that, when launching a product nation-wide, the product may not be successful everywhere. You must be mindful of subtle cultural differences between regions, and integrate that into your product.

Similarly, when Bill ran McDonald's in Mexico, it was suggested that the locals wanted a guacamole burger. Intrigued by the concept, Bill wondered what the product looked like. The product was quite simple – it was a Quarter Pounder burger with guacamole on it. Bill prepared to launch the product with some investment in marketing and product development, and after everything was said and done, only 10 burgers sold.

Bill was shocked at the customer response. He knew that he had to find out want happened, and that the best way to do this would be to ask customers directly. The problem that the local customers had was that when they saw the golden arches, they knew what they were getting in terms of food. The locals could get guacamole and tacos anywhere in Mexico, but that was not the reason they visited McDonald's. The lesson here is once again looking at what your customers want, but in particular, what they do not want.

"The pizza experiment at McDonald's provided another lesson in matching the product to the customer's expectations," says Bill. "Initially, this product was well received and sales took off. A pizza took seven minutes to prepare and customers who came into the location knew they had to wait. At that time the drive-thru business comprised only 25% of revenues. Customers ordering a pizza through the drive-thru had to wait for a longer time compared to ordering other food items."

As the percentage of revenues for drive-thru business increased to 70%, more customers had to wait for their food, either in the drive-thru line or in the parking waiting area, while customers ordering other menu items were able to pick up their food and drive away. It was a frustrating experience for customers expecting to spend the least amount of time from order to payment to receiving food. Clearly, pizza was not conducive to the drive-thru customer experience. Even though pizza was a popular item, the vast majority of revenues and therefore customer experience dictated that pizza had to go.

Not being able to meet a customer's expectations had deleterious effects on both revenues and costs for McDonald's. If the customer does not buy, then the company simply does not collect revenues. With few sales, any marketing or product development costs spent upfront would be difficult to recover. This results in a big hit to profitability which, in some cases, could bring a firm to its knees.

McDonald's had the resources to right the wrong and re-align their products with their customer's expectations. But many entrepreneurs in start-up mode need to get the expectations of their customers right from the start or face the potential for skewed positive financial results, mislaid confidence, or possibly a failed business attempt.

Entrepreneurs often get into this situation due to a strong bias of seeing their particular product as different from similar products in the marketplace. Although being differentiated is a good thing, the entrepreneur needs a solid business plan that explains how this differentiated product will create demand and end up in the consumer's hands. With blinders on, entrepreneurs often use their own needs as a proxy for the needs of typical customers, and then structure a business plan around a phantom customer that will supposedly get excited about the product and buy immediately.

Tim Fowler met such an entrepreneur, who approached him seeking investment capital. Although the entrepreneur had a good knowledge of the restaurant industry he was entering, his business never got off the ground. The problem? He failed to fundamentally understand why customers go to restaurants.

Tim Fowler is former Sales Vice-President, Tropicana Beverages at Pepsi Beverages Company. Before Tim joined this company, he ran another company that provided a matchmaking service between start-ups and investors for a fee. If an entrepreneur presented a viable idea and could articulate the business's value proposition to both Tim and potential investors, the entrepreneur stood a good chance of securing investors for the business. Because of the success of Tim's company, he had an opportunity to see many different business ideas from entrepreneurs.

Tim commonly sees entrepreneurs mistakenly believing that everybody else shares their excitement over their idea, with little validation that their particular product or service is needed or wanted by customers. Hence, the entrepreneur skips the work required to understand whether enough customers will value the product or service being offered. Often, with this lack of information, the misguided entrepreneur takes out a loan and begins to market the product, only to find out that there are not enough customers to run a business.

"Typically, entrepreneurs use themselves as a judge for others," Tim says. "So, I believe X, and therefore others believe X. I then skip the work to find out if there are enough people out there who will value whatever it is I'm offering. And I just assume that they will. And I start chasing down a path and lo and behold I find out that not enough people share my point of view, and I have spent a bunch of time, energy, and money crafting something that no one wants."

One such entrepreneur had an idea for a restaurant that would serve a differentiated product not offered elsewhere in the marketplace. He spent his personal resources creating a design for the restaurant, establishing the restaurant's name, and registering the business. It was clear that he had a good understanding of the restaurant industry. After exhausting his personal resources, he came to Tim's company looking for external investors.

Tim could see that this entrepreneur did have a truly differentiated product. However, this entrepreneur differentiated himself from his competitors by focusing on opening a restaurant that only served one particular product on the menu.

"The major failure was not that he did not understand the restaurant business, because he did understand the restaurant business in general," Tim says. "He knew how to run a restaurant. He knew that your food costs couldn't be too high, and so on. What he didn't understand was a major motivation of why customers choose a particular restaurant. Because most consumers that come to restaurants are families with larger groups, he did not understand that a major motivation of that was variety. And he wasn't providing that. This was a fundamental breach of the reason why people go to restaurants. They don't want one thing. They want variety. What he failed to understand was that the key ingredient to running a restaurant is that customers want to have a bit of choice on your menu. So, while being focused was very good and got him operational efficiencies, he was offering only one product that was not being served broadly anywhere."

When looking for investors, the entrepreneur could not explain to them why potential restaurant patrons would choose his restaurant over others.

"Because the investors didn't understand it, and the entrepreneur could not explain it, he never received one penny from external investors," Tim says. "He was swimming against one of the golden rules of the business that he was trying to enter. So no one gave him any money because everyone saw the writing on the wall. What everybody could see was that he did not understand the business he was getting into."

When putting a business plan together, it is imperative that it include a believable argument that details why a particular product or service meets the needs of a set of customers. This is predicated on an entrepreneur knowing the needs of the customer, and ensuring that the business aligns its products and services to meet that need. The entrepreneur should understand the motivation of why a customer would choose the business's products and services over others.

In addition, the entrepreneur simply cannot assume that there are an infinite number of customers that keep growing every year. In most cases, only a subset of customers will find the product or service unique, and only a percentage of that subset are likely to buy the product or service. With the pricing model worked out, these numbers can then work their way into the financial projections, which are discussed later in this section.

If there are not enough customers to bring in profits, NEVER make the mistake of assuming that one can bump that number up by 10%, or 25%, or whatever percentage to make the business "look" profitable, which I call spreadsheet roulette. This is a sure recipe for business failure.

Various research companies will also tap into the opinions of customers to find out what products or services they are looking for in the market, trying to spot trends. If a trend is found that has high market potential, the opportunity to get into that market may be profitable, creating an initial hype. But the reality is that for a business to be profitable in that market takes time. The advice given by a respected and seasoned entrepreneur, Louis Lagassé, is to not follow the hype.

Don't Follow the Hype

Getting into an industry because of hype generated in size and exponential growth may result in an entrepreneur being extremely aggressive and possibly overleveraging the company. In reality, the actual growth takes time. This was a $30 million mistake for us.

– Louis Lagassé, Chairman, CEO & President – GPV Inc.

For some entrepreneurs, seeing research reports that bombastically announce the attractiveness and size of a particular industry generates excitement. The problem with being entranced with the incredible growth potential of these products is that, yes, the growth does happen, and the size may be attractive, but resulting profitability is more muted with the potential profitability being spread over a longer time period because companies cannot change their business processes overnight, no matter how attractive the potential is.

A classic entrepreneurial mistake, also talked about in the chapter on making realistic projections, is to eagerly look at an attractive industry and assume that the entrepreneur will somehow capture a small percentage of that big market.

For example, in 2010, if an entrepreneur was looking at a study done by IDC[12], it predicted that the mobile application market was to grow from 10.9 billion downloads in 2010 to 76.9 billion in 2014, generating $35 billion in 2014. Fast-forward one year, and lo and behold, in another study by World Mobile Applications Market[13], the mobile application market in 2011 only reached $6.8 billion, vastly different from IDC report. The point of this is not to criticize either research report, but

---

12 http://mashable.com/2010/12/13/idc-mobile-apps-study
13 http://readwrite.com/2011/01/18/mobile-app-market-25-billion-by-2015#awesm=~oeVrXsmzCu933z

to show that a predicted growth size used at one point cannot be solely relied upon to wrap a business around, and that the predicted growth tends to take much longer. Even successful serial entrepreneur, Louis Lagassé, was tripped up by this.

Thirty years ago, Louis Lagassé was the lead investor in a group which founded Les Industries C-MAC Inc., in 1996, and was also a co-founder with the late John Dobson of the Dobson-Lagassé Entrepreneurship Centre at Bishop's University. He is also CEO and President of GPV Inc., a holding company with a focus on communication technology products and services. Louis has received several honours and awards, including the Order of Canada, presented to him in 2003. He is extremely well known for his talents as a businessman and his philanthropy throughout Canada, and particularly in the Province of Quebec where he lives and has his head office.

Louis firmly believes that success cannot happen without failure.

"One of the biggest dangers as an entrepreneur in business is in having a series of great, great, great successes without any failures," he says. "This is very risky because one morning, you will fall on a rock somewhere. It happens to anyone. If one has not had a failure event happen, there may be one on the horizon. Lessons need to be learned from failures to ensure that mistakes are not repeated."

Louis is no stranger to the drastic ups and downs of business. In fact, he faced such a close encounter with failure with one of his first ventures.

In the mid '80s, the town of Sherbrooke, Québec, had a weak industrial economy due to a gradual exodus of major industries. The local government tried to revive this area by tapping on the shoulders of some prominent local entrepreneurs. Louis was one of them.

In 1983, Louis got a phone call from a good friend who was a Member of Parliament and President of the National Assembly of Québec at the time.

"He asked me if I had the guts to put up $25,000 with four or five other people to start a study on creating a manufacturing company in Sherbrooke," he recalls. "The idea was to help create some economic wealth creation activities in the Sherbrooke area. At the time, I had a successful law practice and I had some real estate by the university which was doing very well for me; I felt that I could contribute more to the fundamental wealth creation of the community in Sherbrooke by creating an activity that would generate money. So, I said yes and I was able to get five other people to put in the investment with the intent of creating a company that would manufacture and distribute electronics and provide local job opportunities to local graduate engineers from the University of Sherbrooke."

The Department of Regional Expansion gave the group a grant to do a study to identify electronics products which could be produced that were unique to Canada and also had a tremendous potential for growth. After 15 months, the study pointed to hybrid microcircuits and gate arrays,[14] which were a part of the high-growth microprocessor industry.

At the time, the Canadian giant Nortel, a major user of these products, would typically buy these products from England or Japan. With the idea of opening a manufacturing facility in Sherbrooke, Nortel was a probable customer.

To get the company off the ground, the company needed $10 million for an initial capital investment and $10 million in working capital even before reaching a break-even point, and this made some of the investors nervous.

"The report was sent to the group in Sherbrooke and everyone said that it was not their cup of tea and beyond their financial capability" Louis says. "I was the entrepreneur, and I said, 'Let's have a look. Maybe we can find a way of doing it. Maybe.' With me, there's always a way to do things."

If the investment group was able to raise $3 million instead of the original $20 million required, the federal government had agreed to subsidize the building of a new plant to the tune of $2.5 million and the provincial government guaranteed a number of financial instruments: a $3 million long-term loan for the facility, a $1 million line of credit and $1 million for the training of employees.

"We were close to $11 million and it was a go," Louis says. "We then found a partner which had a small manufacturing facility in Montreal

14 Various components related to the production of different types of integrated circuits and discrete components, typically used in military and communications applications.

called C-MAC Components, a division of Prime Tech Electronics (Prime Tech). For the purpose of the exercise, Prime Tech took a stake in the company and added a bank guarantee of its own[15]."

In February 1986, the construction of a facility got under way and production began in early 1987. But things did not go as easily as expected.

"We came very close to bankruptcy at the end of November 1987," Louis says.

By the end of that year, the company incurred revenues of $2 million but had a net loss of $3 million, and was effectively in a bankrupt situation by the end of the year.

The only assets left on the company's balance sheet was a guarantee from the mid holding company partner, C-MAC, and a $200,000 guarantee from Prime Tech, which was not enough.

Louis visited the bank VP in Montreal to essentially say that there was no more capital available for the venture and that the keys had to be handed over to the bank. Using some harsh words, the bank refused to take the keys; it turned around and loaned $200,000 to Prime Tech that would allow C-MAC to release Prime Tech from its bank loan guarantees.

"This last $200,000 from Prime Tech saved us," Louis says. "It saved us. Then, in 1988, we sold $3 million and we were EBITDA[16] negative by $600,000. In 1989, with sales of $6 million we made $600,000, and in 1990, we started a process of acquisitions. We had sales of $12 million that year with a profit of $1.6 million. And then we started growing there – $12 million to $65 million in 1991, to $150 million in 1992 to $250 million in 1994, with several acquisitions of course. It was quite a progression. Over 10 years, C-MAC raised over $1.3 billion from North American capital markets. Unless your name is Google or Facebook, raising that kind of money does not exist anymore."

Louis has always been a master at making things happen if he sees an opportunity, going back to the creation of the initial wealth at C-MAC. One such opportunity came to Louis in late 1988 with the US

15 Prime Tech provided a line of credit to C-MAC Industries' bank, starting in December 1985
16 EBITDA – This acronym stands for Earnings Before Interest, Taxes, Depreciation and Amortization. It is an approximate measure of a company's operating cash flow based on a company's income statement. It is calculated by looking at profits before the deduction of interest expenses, taxes, depreciation, and amortization.

telecommunications company, TIE Communications (TIE). When this company was looking to build a plant in Canada, Louis was involved in the local Chamber of Commerce and encouraged the company to build the plant close to his, as there were potential synergies between the two companies.

Fortunately, thanks to Louis' presence in the industrial markets in most parts of Quebec, he learned that TIE Communications, whose head office was in Shelton, Connecticut, and with a foreign branch manufacturing facility in Sherbrooke, had made a US acquisition which almost killed them. It was being sued and needed to sell any assets it had to convert that into cash rapidly.

The plant in Sherbrooke cost them $15 million and then they approached C-MAC and its principal shareholders to buy the facility and assets for an incredible amount: $3 million, a significant discount from its market value of $12 million. Although the acquisition looked very attractive for C-MAC and its shareholders, which included Louis among others, the problem was in trying to find out where the company would get the money from.

"We looked at the Sherbrooke Group of partners for equity, then added a first and second mortgage on the property, a line of credit on inventories and receivables, and we got a company from Thailand to give us a contract to buy the products generated from this TIE facility in Sherbrooke," says Louis. "Four months later, a large US chip manufacturer landed a lucrative five-year contract to do end of production tests for microcircuits."

This second business made this acquisition extremely profitable for C-MAC and paved the way for a $6.7 million end-of-year profit in 1991, which was followed by C-MAC's IPO in September 1992 to secure the acquisition of several other properties in Europe and North America.

Louis says that one of the biggest failures entrepreneurs make is to follow the hype and make assumptions that being in an attractive and rapid-moving industry will bring immediate and ongoing profits.

"If this 'hype' is factored into financial projections, they could be too aggressive with a danger of the company overleveraging and over-spending," he says.

Such was the case for Louis when he was looking to purchase a company that specifically sold products using a popular form of wireless communication at the time, WiMAX.

"This company, once a star in Canadian telecommunications technology then operating under court protection, had lots to offer," he says.

The consultants that Louis brought on board looked at the spreadsheets, and suggested that picking up the company at a deeply discounted value of the assets would be favourable.

Blinded by the hype of the increasing growth in wireless communication, Louis failed to ask a simple question.

"You fall in love with the technology: fantastic WiMAX with point-to-point, point-to-multipoint technology, and the whole gizmos and the works," he says. "But, at the end of the day, if you are an operator, why would you need WiMAX? Why should people use WiMAX? What makes WiMAX a product that people should or would need? We forgot to ask ourselves that question. Very basic."

The benefits of using WiMAX as a wireless solution, compared to other types of wireless solutions, were perfectly suited for dense populations such as those in Bangladesh, Sri Lanka, Mexico, Chili and Brazil. Wireless was preferred as it was expensive and extremely inconvenient for these cities to run wires to transfer voice, video, and data.

In places like New York or Boston, which already had well deployed fiber-optic networks, WiMAX would not be needed. There was some potential to have wireless technology around lakes and in off-shore applications for oil-rig platforms, but there were not enough of these situations to sustain a business.

If the majority of North American cities did not need this technology, Louis would have to go overseas to build up sales, which was not what he was bargaining for. But, the hype certainly brought in interest.

"When I bought this company, there was a logbook of very serious opportunities with customers to whom the company had previously sold its microwave communication products, to the extent of several hundreds of millions of dollars," he says. "The new product was coming in and there were $200 million of opportunities which never showed up. But you're here to deliver. And now we're spending $2 million a month in fixed costs. What do you do after 15 months with no sales? Pfft," he says, giving the 'thumbs down' signal.

Louis also states that although the hype may exist for particular market, the predicted growth for that market takes place over a longer time period than suggested in research papers. Such was the case when Louis got into VoIP, or Voice over IP, a way to carry high quality voice over the Internet, a significant change as only data had been transferred over the Internet in the past.

One of Louis's companies, Media5, was formed in 1992 to produce soundcards to allow music to be played on computer systems. Because of its expertise in this area, Media5 experienced rapid growth as it supplied chip designs to large companies such as Yamaha.

In the mid-1990s, Louis's company discovered that it was able to produce soundcards that could send voice signals, which were the early days of high quality VoIP. He had a number of engineers take a look at the opportunity, and people began to tell Louis that with a few engineers and a couple of salespeople, the company would make a killing.

"With the right bright guys in place, then, we started putting in a little bit of money: $1 million, $2 million, $3 million, and we reinvested the profits from the Yamaha side of the business, which added $5-$6 million too," he says. "And then, in 2000, for sure, Gartner and all the mobility research specialists were forecasting that the IP Telephony market would build up and be several billion dollars in three years from 2008. Everybody thought that one morning people would say that products such as Nortel's Meridian phone would be replaced by IP Telephony boxes forthwith. Every single company would need an IP phone network immediately."

Louis knew from previous experience that just because there was hype in the market for a particular technology, it did not mean that everyone would switch to it overnight. The change in both consumer and business behaviour would take a more gradual path.

"It will still take about 20 years to come," he says. "It is like the change from the horse carriage to an engine. Now we see it being popular, but $75 million later in investment in Media5 Corporation, this company is finally succeeding in earning a nice profit every month, but it's not a killing."

One of Louis's customers, a very large Japanese Telecom OEM (JTO), realized in 2012 that the VoIP hype would take a more gradual shift, so they took a much longer timeline to convert their traditional phone systems to VoIP – and the JTO had a lot of phone systems worldwide:

over two-and-a-half million phone systems with each phone system having handsets numbering in the single digits to a thousand phones per system.

"We were selected to migrate their systems to VoIP because we had a great knowledge of Carrier-grade hardware and great knowledge of all the phases of software that goes into the systems," Louis says. "And, they do not want to change all their customers to IP because they've read in the market that their existing phone works. All their customers were only looking for were adapters to make their systems work on IP networks. So, it's not about spending an average of $100,000 per customer, but maybe $15,000 per customer. So even though you have 2.5 million customers, you won't make $200 billion, you only make $1.5 billion or $2 billion."

When Louis looks back at how the predicted growth and size actually occurred, he recalls that to get to the peak of VoIP popularity required several years and $75 million of investment in Media5, as compared to the three-year explosion of growth and an industry size predicted to be in the billions of dollars by research firms.

"People got carried away," he says. "They all thought that because the technology was great, suddenly overnight, companies were making the decision to carry these gizmos."

Louis advises business owners to be patient in business. Time will help solve problems and also present opportunities down the road. A great example of patience being rewarded that Louis provides is one where he supplied VoIP adapters to a company in Ralston, Virginia.

"In 1998, we sent 300 boxes to an agency of the US government for an initial trial," he says. "That's all we knew. Finally we got to know that it was for a very important agency of the government. They wanted to send IP encrypted faxes with our technology. When an important European telecom manufacturer, still the most important customer of Media5, saw that, they said that they just invested in a company from Israel, and they started wanting to offer our product. So we started a long relationship with this customer who has now been there for 15 years, and they are still our largest customer."

After learning from his setbacks, Louis tempered his excitement over the growth of the VoIP market with a practical, down-to-earth approach. Louis's advice for entrepreneurs is to have a cautious attitude when looking at hyped up business opportunities as it leads to a better understanding of how a business case can be wrapped around an opportunity. If an entrepreneur approaches such an opportunity too aggressively, revenues may fall short, and with higher costs, fewer profits are realized.

As Louis' grandfather told him when he was a young man, "You earn your bread from 9:00 to 5:00 and you ensure your future before 9:00 and after 5:00; nevertheless, always be aware of the illusions ("phenomenal forecasts"); they will always kill you."

If an entrepreneur does decide to follow the hype, to see if there really is a business case, the entrepreneur should perform a quick "back of the envelope" calculation, something that Joe Atkins recommends.

Back of the Envelope Calculations

If you don't start looking into the financial realities of getting into a business early, you risk failing and losing your money. By doing a very quick feasibility review, preferably with a qualified mentor, at least you will have a very early sense about the business's viability.

– Joe Atkins, Chairman & CEO – Bowers & Wilkins

In most cases, those looking to start a business are generally looking to sell a product or service that they are familiar with, either from working in a previous firm that sold those products or services, or because the entrepreneur has a related skill or hobby. The entrepreneur then begins to chat with friends and family about the business and everybody starts to get excited. But what is often not discussed, or even analyzed, are the financial realities of opening such a business.

Asking tough questions early on will give entrepreneurs a good chance to think about the hurdles they may face. If they cannot sufficiently answer how they would overcome these business hurdles, then they should go back to the drawing board and re-evaluate why they want to invest in this business idea.

This "step back" may prevent a bad business idea from actually moving forward, preventing the entrepreneur from sinking hard-earned money into a troubled venture, possibly wiping out savings and leaving the entrepreneur overleveraged by maxing out credit cards, draining lines of credit, or risking the home because of a second mortgage that was taken out.

When initially going through the steps of evaluating an idea's merit as a business, it would be fruitful to have conversations with many different people. People with appropriate experience can give some good feedback on whether the idea is financially viable, others can give you a sense of whether you will actually have some customers, and hopefully, someone will ask you to show them how you will make money. Of course, you would have worked something out in your head: pricing, the number of customers, how much money you will make, and a rough estimate of profits, and so on. But having it in your head is not enough because at this point it is still a "thought".

One of the best ways to see if a potential idea has legs financially is to use a quick "back of the envelope" set of calculations that give an entrepreneur a sense of how much money the business will roughly make, taking into account high-level estimates of revenues and costs. The term, "back of the envelope" refers to a series of calculations that can literally be written out on the back of an envelope, but the point is that someone with the right experience can often do it very quickly.

This type of calculation was done for a colleague of Joe Atkins, which saved the colleague, and his potential business partner, from having a sizable amount of their savings wiped out, and was followed by a phone call to Joe thanking him for "saving my life!"

Joe Atkins is Chairman & CEO of Bowers & Wilkins, one of the world's leading suppliers of high-end audio equipment. Due to his business expertise, Joe is often approached for his opinion on business ideas. More often than not, he counsels people to not go ahead with business ideas because he knows the road to success is much more difficult than most would-be entrepreneurs perceive. Although there may be exceptions, those who do not take his advice often end up regretting their decision to start a venture.

Joe's business experience started when he was 13, working in various positions at a small business all through his school years. When Joe obtained his Chartered Accounting designation and entered the insolvency business, he oversaw dozens of failed businesses of various sizes and industries including car dealerships, lumber yards, and manufacturing companies. All in all, he has over 30 years of business experience dealing with hundreds of business owners and operating in the best and worst of economic cycles.

Bowers & Wilkins, a global company and well-established premium brand within the audio business, was founded by John Bowers, an engineer with only one ambition: to make the perfect audio speaker. Originally, Joe bought the North American distribution rights for Bowers & Wilkins. John Bowers died a year later and Joe eventually acquired his shares. Since that time, Joe has continued to direct Bowers & Wilkins and develop the world's leading provider of premium audio products.

During one of Joe's travels to the United States, he was approached by a colleague who wanted to open a small store to sell crystal gift items. Being close to retirement, his colleague was looking to invest a sizable amount of his savings to open the store. The conversation went like this:

Joe: So what's the business idea?

Colleague: A friend and I are looking to open a store to sell crystal gift items. I've asked a lot of my family and friends about the idea, and they love it, and told me that they were going to buy them for themselves once I open the store.

Joe: Have you done any math to see if the business would work?

Colleague: No, I haven't.

Joe: Well, what are you looking to sell these gift items for?

Colleague: I think we can sell them for $45.

Joe: How many do you think you can sell a year?

Colleague: Well, I'm not really sure.

Joe: Give me your best guess.

Colleague: Okay, 10,000. Wow! That means I would make $450,000 per year in sales!

Joe: And how much do you think the material costs in making one of these items?

Colleague: I'm not sure. I think, maybe $25.

Joe: Okay. That must mean that your Cost of Goods Sold is $250,000. How much time do you think it takes to assemble one of these items?

Colleague: Probably half an hour.

Joe: Okay. Are you going to be working seven days a week or are you looking to dedicate some time for family?

Colleague: No. Both my friend and I are going to put in 40 hour weeks.

Joe: Well, to make 10,000 pieces, you're going to need to hire other people. And because you have a little store, there's going to be rent and other associated costs.

Within an hour, Joe estimated that, even if things went perfectly with the business, they were losing money from Day One. In terms of timeline, it took Joe about an hour to show his colleague the financial reality of opening that business.

Luckily, Joe's friend was able to get some insightful advice from a seasoned entrepreneur before making the unfortunate plunge in following a bad business idea.

Many entrepreneurs do ask for advice, but often, it is not from someone who has the appropriate background to give such advice. This was the case in one situation, discussed in Section 3, which resulted in a couple filing for bankruptcy. The advice? Ask advice from those with the right qualifications.

"Because these advisors have been successful, they know what it takes to make it, and they can instantly provide key advice to help someone make a decision to start a business or not," he says. "If someone looking to start a business does not have a plan, and does not seek out the advice of those who have a lot more experience in the same industry, that business is almost certainly destined to fail."

The statistics on business start-ups and associated failures vary, as illustrated in the Introduction, but they all essentially point to one common theme: the majority of businesses fail. Joe estimates that approximately 10% of new starts are still operating after five years. But when looking at the reasons for failure, in most cases, the business may not have failed if the idea had been vetted through a proper mentor.

"If those who ended up in the 90% of businesses that failed would have asked for advice from those who have been successful, ideally in a related business – someone with an unbiased and qualified view – and work through their business idea, and then listen to the feedback, it's probably going to cut that failure number by at least half, if not more," he says. "It would seem that this should be the number one starting point for someone looking to start a business."

Some would-be entrepreneurs fear that, if they do approach a mentor from the same industry, somehow, the idea will be stolen, or the idea will be perceived as very bad, resulting in an embarrassing situation. This often discourages the entrepreneur from approaching a savvy advisor. Without talking to someone who has some level of understanding of the business, then the "back of the envelope" calculations may not be as relevant, or may not even be performed and the entrepreneur may have a false hope for the success of the business.

To start these calculations, generally, one would start with the general business idea, what the product is, how it is priced, and who are the intended customers. Assuming a certain number of customers, one can quickly estimate the potential revenues. If there is a disconnection between the pricing versus the value perception in the minds of a consumer, a red flag should go up. Because of Joe's deep experience in the retail space, he knows that pricing and value perception is critical, especially in the retail sector.

"People who are in the retail business need to answer a couple of very simple questions," he says. "What is your product and who is your customer? For example, if you are in fine dining, make sure that everything you do with your product presentation is consistent with fine dining. Do not have a drive-thru hamburger window in the back of your expensive steakhouse. You will then confuse both types of customers: the person that might come through your drive-thru window will think that you are too expensive, and you will not attract the steakhouse customer who is looking for a high-end dining experience."

Once revenues are estimated and general costs are outlined, a profit number can be estimated. The next phase should look at how the company will grow, and part of that involves realistically estimating the annual increase in the number of customers in each of the next five years. Proceed with caution; many entrepreneurs think that there will be unlimited growth.

"The other aspect of knowing your product and your customer is in determining your expectations on how big your business will be," Joe says. "If you sell a premium or luxury product, then the number of customers that you have will be limited. If that is the case, then there may well be a cap on the potential revenues that you may be able to achieve. Hence, you must be realistic about your growth potential."

With the business mapped out on paper, the entrepreneur can then work backwards to find out how much money he or she needs to start the business. If a mentor is present, the mentor will look at that number and often double or triple the early estimate.

"In my experience, when an entrepreneur starts a business, his or her expectations for the first two to five years will actually not be met," Joe says. "If your five-year business plan says that you need $100,000 in capital, you better have two or three times that much. The entrepreneur puts everything that he or she has in getting a business going and when it inevitably takes a little longer to develop and needs more investment, there is no money to continue. This is where I have seen businesses fail."

A perfect example that Joe gives is when he and his brothers started one of the first Hyundai dealerships in Canada in 1984. They had tremendous success in the beginning selling Hyundai's Pony as they were only $2,500 in price. Nobody had ever heard of Hyundai, but at that price, it did not matter.

For several years though, Hyundai had serious quality problems, requiring significant investment on the part of every dealer to survive. Hyundai eventually sorted out their product and image problems, learning from their mistakes. Today, it is one of the most successful imported brands in North America, but it required much more capital to sustain the business through its developing years than Joe originally planned for.

If an entrepreneur truly has a unique idea, and knows that there are customers that are willing to pay for that idea, doing a "back of the envelope" calculation will ensure that one knows, initially, if the business is a viable one.

There are a million ideas. The difference between an idea and a business idea is huge. The difference between a business idea and a financially viable business idea is again huge. Make sure you are able to cross both of those bridges with some intelligent advice if you want to survive. So, perform quick calculations with a qualified mentor and avoid chasing a dream that just does not make money and puts your own money, and possibly others, at risk.

Once these "back of the envelope" calculations are performed, the next step is to put in the effort to generate realistic projections. Making unrealistic financial assumptions will result in a business suffering; for a non-profit organization, having realistic financial projections is crucial, a task that Deborah Gatenby takes very seriously.

Have Realistic Projections

Because of funding pressures, as a non-profit, we NEED to run like an efficient business and do more with less. Any deviation from this means that we cannot deliver our services. And that means we cannot fulfill our mandate and deliver service to our target market – the people who really need our help.

– Deborah Gatenby, CEO – Hope Place Centres

The euphoria from turning a particular idea into a business idea brings incredible pleasure to not only the entrepreneur, but also to those around the entrepreneur who are engaged in the discussion. With some backslapping and high-fiving, everyone gets excited and urges the entrepreneur to move forward.

After performing "back of the envelope" calculations, described in the previous chapter, the next step is that the entrepreneur should take the time to put together a comprehensive and realistic business plan to map out exactly how the idea will turn into a business, and what the road to success looks like.

A major part of the business plan is the financial projections where an entrepreneur should spend a good chunk of time detailing the short, medium and long-term financial viability of the business idea, ensuring that he or she has numbers that are realistic and achievable. The rest of the business plan should identify how the other business functions will support that growth.

These projections serve as a financial guidepost for not only the entrepreneur, but other stakeholders such as potential investors, bankers, or even friends and family looking to possibly invest in the business idea. If the projected numbers are simply not believable and cannot be justified, the entrepreneur will fail to convince those looking to invest or provide any financing that the business is a worthwhile opportunity.

One common mistake entrepreneurs make is assuming that their product or service is somehow going to be soaked up by the market, and the number of customers will keep growing year-in and year-out. With the business plan showing little marketing efforts and a conservative estimate in annual cost increases, products simply fly off the shelves, and revenues skyrocket. What is not addressed properly is how the business plans to create such a demand that has these customers yearning for more.

Another common mistake is to assume that, by just opening the company's doors, it will capture an initial percentage of a large and growing industry. The entrepreneur explains "If I can capture just 5% of this industry, then I would be making $X in revenues in the first year. And then, I will establish a brand name and I will get 10% in the second year, and 25% in the third year..." and so on. All of a sudden the business has been able to earn millions of dollars in revenues by Year 5. Who would not be impressed?

With rosy growth projections and costs that seem to be relatively flat every year on paper, a business goes from having no revenues to those in line with corporate behemoths who have spent a tremendous amount of time and resources building a strong brand. This style of projection is where the term "hockey stick" projection comes from: a slight dip in revenues in the first year, representing the blade of the hockey stick, followed by an incredible growth in revenues every year, which represents the shaft of the hockey stick.

Pretty impressive. Yes, absolutely. And pretty unrealistic.

And when asked how the entrepreneur came up with this magical 5%, 10% and 25% in addition to asking whether the entrepreneur considered the extra operational, marketing, and sales costs to support the growth, the smile disappears, eyes begin to shift rapidly to try and come up with "something", and the conversation ends with a blank stare.

If the entrepreneur truly believes in this unrealistic growth, then business failure is certain.

When asked to redo the financial projections with some realistic numbers, the viability of the business comes into question. The euphoria disappears, and entrepreneurs start scratching their heads to figure out how the business can succeed now that the projections have had some reality injected in them.

Realistic revenue projections should provide a reasonable guide to the potential financial success of the company. This generates a sense of comfort for those reviewing the financials, showing that the entrepreneur has taken the time to provide a set of dependable numbers and providing a sense of comfort in knowing that the entrepreneur will likely make smart business decisions along the way, despite what hurdles may come.

Realistic financial projections are critically important for non-profit businesses because being inefficient means that funding simply runs out ahead of schedule and staff are left scrambling to try and find money to stay afloat, or begin the arduous decision to cut back on resources. Such a situation has been experienced by Deborah Gatenby.

Deborah Gatenby is past-President of Addictions Ontario and also holds the CEO position at Hope Place Centres, a non-profit organization that provides programs and services for men and women who are addicted to alcohol or other drugs. As CEO, she has found that she needs to address a large business challenge of trying to provide a consistent level of programs and services given a restriction of government funding and a slowing of donations.

"As the economy has shifted, it has created an interesting paradigm for the social sector to provide more services than ever before because of the demand, while the people and businesses I rely on as donors have a disposable income that has also shrunk," Deborah says. "My challenge is how to run a business efficiently and effectively with dwindling resources and increasing demand."

One of the colossal failures that Deborah has seen, particularly for non-profit organizations, is the budgeting process. The government allocates a certain amount of money for a particular non-profit group which generally does not increase from one year to the next. In addition, the government mandates that non-profit groups perform a multi-year budget using zero-based budgeting.

Zero-based budgeting is a process by which budgets are established with no reference to prior years, effectively starting every year with a clean slate. One would begin with estimating revenues from various funding sources, and then begin to allocate costs accordingly. The other type of budgeting is incremental budgeting, which uses the previous year's budget as a reference, and a future budget incorporates increases or decreases to the reference budget.

The danger in the budget process is that one can make a myriad of assumptions, making increases or decreases to certain budgetary line items that may not happen, resulting in an unrealistic budgetary estimate.

Typically, the government leaves the budgeting process to their subcontracted service providers. The problem begins when the government advises the non-profit providers to make increases to the volume of services planned, when in fact these services cannot be increased due to the lack of available funding, combined with a shrinking number of donations, resulting in a "cash squeeze".

"So for Year 2, you have no more money, and your costs will have gone up because your employees want a little bit more, the cost of things such as food, hydro, and gas are probably going to cost little bit more, your auditor is going to want to charge a little more, and everything is going to cost more, including bank fees," Deborah says. "You're suddenly going to produce MORE with LESS. And then for Year 3, guess what? The funding stays the same and the non-profit organizations think that they are going to do even MORE service volumes than they did in Year 2 while still maintaining the same budget, or in some cases growing an employee or two. That is impossible!"

Deborah says that, "People lose sight of this and they shoot themselves in the foot. Now you have committed yourself to doing these increased service volumes, and if you don't do these increased service volumes, the contract with the funding organization dictates that one needs to reduce your funding and your resources. And now you have shot yourself in the foot. And, oh my God, everybody is doing this."

The first year that Deborah became President of Addictions Ontario, she was speaking to a number of CEOs from the residential treatment sector. She asked them, "Based on zero-based budgeting, how many of you have forecasted increased service volumes in Years 2 and 3 of your funding agreements? You know, every single hand went up. I then asked them to mentor me on how that was possible."

They went through an exercise and quickly found out that it was not possible. This resulted in a healthy discussion around reducing resources and service volumes, while still delivering treatment services for recipients for three sequential years on the basis of zero-based budgeting. The only other way to not reduce some of these services was to generate more money.

Generating more money has its own pitfalls, as Deborah has experienced: "Anything that had an 'a-thon' attached to it, such as a walk-a-thon, a skate-a-thon, a ride-a-thon, and so on. Oh my goodness, abysmal failure," she says. "People think that when they do these events, they tell you that they made $6,000, or $8,000, or whatever it is. They have no concept of what net proceeds means. When I came here I was told that they had a rather successful walk-a-thon and a rather successful skate-a-thon going. So they generated $6,000 in proceeds. But what they did not take into consideration is that they had five or six staff members who were being paid to be at the event for the entire day, and they also had a fair degree of staff time invested in the planning and development and coordination of the event before. What was done before is that they started to cross out all the staff hours which people don't consider because they were working anyway. Those staff members weren't really doing their job that they are on the payroll to do. They are doing the skate-a-thons and walk-a-thons. When you add that in, they actually lost $11,000. These were not successful events. This is where we failed. We failed to realize that our time is not free. We failed to take into consideration the cost of the employees that are not doing what we paid them to do."

Deborah says that another classic mistake made by non-profit organizations is simply deciding to run another fundraising campaign because a previous one failed, trying to compensate for the shortfall. The thought process is that by fundraising more, the two campaigns can essentially be combined, when in fact all this does is compound the problem. Deborah calls this tactic "donor fatigue".

"There are so many individuals or businesses out there that are exhausted with the onslaught of requests for donations and sponsorship: buying the chocolate bars for your child or one of the employee's children, someone coming to your door for donations, someone standing in front of the grocery market, the online campaigns, the direct mail campaigns, 'buy a ticket to our charity ball', buying a lottery ticket, and so on," she says. "People get so tired with all these requests for their money."

The only way that an organization can survive this financial pressure of doing more with less is to reduce the volume of services delivered while maintaining the same quality of services, which can only be achieved by being as lean and efficient as you can be, which Deborah points out is much like what a successful 'for-profit' business would do.

To ensure that she has a good handle on the pressure of trying to do more with less, she went through an exercise where she drew concentric circles around the business operations and began defining what the core business was, what the actual charitable purpose was, and what programs would be affected if the organization was to scale down. She then defined the program delivery strategy based on various levels of funding. With more money, there would be more programs.

To counteract the funding pressures, Deborah constantly talks about not fundraising more, but fundraising smart. She suggests building a limited number of signature events that align with the charitable purpose. These events take into account who the individuals are whose lives an organization touches, what services are delivered, and who are the recipients, essentially defining the target market.

All of Deborah's fundraising revolves around creating safe events for people who are new to recovery. That means no alcohol is served at the events and the attendees are able to share their experiences of strength and hope in recovery. Deborah also makes their events affordable because those recovering do not have a lot of money. She tries to draw from donors who have had a similar experience recovering from addiction to underwrite some of the costs of the event.

The other strategy that Deborah uses is to charge user fees to access some of the services.

"There used to be a time when people would be appalled at the notion that a publicly-funded organization would charge clients an extra fee, but it has now become quite common in the non-profit marketplace."

Deborah started charging an activity fee of $50, which went toward recreational passes and equipment. If there were additional programs that would be beneficial, the user fees would be increased to compensate for the additional costs.

One program that caught on was having a stock of fee-for-service beds that are funded privately by major employers whom Deborah has excellent relationships with. These employers are keen on having their employees get immediate access to treatment by making these beds available, restricting them from collecting sick benefits until they are hospitalized or are in treatment for their addiction. This means that the employees are able to access the treatment programs immediately, ensuring that they get the proper help at the right time.

That form of productive enterprise has been incredibly successful.

"This is something that we already know how to do expertly and aligns well with our core business," Deborah says. "We are not professional fundraisers or professional event planners or art auctioneers. We are professional treatment providers. The campaigns have to be treated like independent cost centres, which is what we are doing now."

As Deborah has experienced, the success of her non-profit business relies heavily on efficiency. Too often she has seen, and the public has also experienced, the multitude of fundraisers clamouring for dollars. In addition to donor fatigue, previous donors may also shrink the amount that they donate, getting non-profit groups thinking about yet another campaign.

For entrepreneurs beginning the financial projection journey, it is important to justify each and every number. The more realistic the financial projections, the better handle on the success of the business, and the better the signal to others that you know what you are doing. If the entrepreneur relies on unrealistic numbers that seem to propel the business forward, at least on paper, be prepared to be surprised when the bank account does not reflect the numbers on the spreadsheet. If the entrepreneur is lucky to catch this early, review the financials with a qualified mentor, and listen to their advice. It may just save the business.

Another important set of details that need to be included when creating valid financial projections is ensuring that one identifies all possible costs that may arise. Tapping the shoulders of an experienced mentor will definitely be a bonus. But others simply carry on without doing so, and start the business. All of a sudden, hidden costs become apparent, and the business is at risk. And in some cases, this is the end of the road, as experienced by Menno Meijer and Ambrose Duncan.

Know Your Financials

One of the mistakes we made was that we got excited, so excited in fact that we forgot to properly take into account all of financial details of the business. All of a sudden, we realized that costs were higher than the revenues and scrambled to make ends meet, but it was too late. The end result is that we simply ran out of money.

– Menno Meijer, Photojournalist

What killed me was a very simple cost: the company's payroll obligations to the government, which I kept putting off. That small amount kept growing, and by the time I was forced to pay it, the amount I needed to pay nearly knocked me off my chair. I just could not afford to pay it. It was a significant contributor to the bakery's bankruptcy.

– Ambrose Duncan, Former Bakery Shop Owner

When running financial projections, hidden costs may come up, resulting in an impact to the financial viability of the business. These costs should be taken into account somehow, even listing them as "Miscellaneous expenses", calculating them as a small percentage of revenues or overall costs.

The reality is that most small businesses take in few profits in the first year. In fact, in a 2008 study by the Kauffman Foundation[17], close to 50% of businesses surveyed had first-year revenues of less than $5,000, with close to 55% of businesses experiencing a loss in the first year. This means that entrepreneurs need to be extremely aggressive when

---

17 http://sites.kauffman.org/pdf/kfs_08.pdf

trying to bring in revenues, while at the same time being diligent in accounting for each and every cost.

If this is not done, and the missing cost items are significant, the initial revenues might not catch up to cover them, and the future of the business begins to look quite bleak, a situation that Menno Meijer found himself in.

Many years ago, Menno Meijer was working for a newspaper in Wallaceburg, and came across a friend who worked for a paper in Dresden, Ontario, called the North Kent Leader.

"Both my friend and I were not happy with the papers we were working for," says Menno. "They were corporately owned and were not making money. They were also not producing good local stories concerning the local businesses and politics in the community. The local stories were what people cared about."

Menno moved in with his friend to produce a high quality regional paper, called the Dresden Telegraph, which would highlight local stories. Initially, the paper was to be produced once a month, with the first two issues being free. The first issue was put together in their living room. Menno worked on the photography and writing, and his friend worked on the advertising and design. With the advertising revenues established, both Menno and his friend were able to pay off the printing costs, and each made a little bit of money on that first issue, despite creating it in their living room.

They distributed their paper to the surrounding communities through retail outlets. The pictures and stories in the paper generated excitement and buzz, and after the second issue, they sold their issues for one dollar to put some value on it so that people would not use the paper as a fire-starter. The dollar would be kept by the owners of the retail shops as an incentive to promote the paper. Despite costing a dollar, the paper sold well.

A famous historian contributed to the paper without taking any compensation because she wanted the paper to do well. Menno also attracted a former publisher of his who had previously run a successful column, and convinced him to run the column again for the Dresden Telegraph.

As the advertising revenues continued to flow in, Menno locked in a half-page advertisement on the back page of the newspaper for a national grocery chain, owned by a gentleman originally from Dresden who liked the idea of having a newspaper with stories relevant to those living in Dresden. This was Menno's anchor advertiser. This advertisement paid for the printing of the paper, with any additional advertising revenues helping to pay for salaries and other costs.

With all these people contributing, Menno mentioned that, "people would be knocking at our door asking if the paper was out yet. I would have to say, 'Ah…no… not yet…just two more days! Just wait…it is coming.' We were on the verge; all we needed was a little bit more expansion money. This was our fatal mistake."

Menno and his partner decided to join the Ontario Newspaper Association, or ONPA, for a number of reasons. First, it would allow them access to national advertisers because only members of the ONPA could approach them. Second, it would open up the paper to be submitted into competitions. Menno and his partner were confident they could win these awards because they ran an excellent paper with great stories and a solid base of advertisers.

Although there were great advantages, there were also some disadvantages, which translated into increased costs, something for which they had not planned.

Unfortunately, the ONPA required its members to have office space. So, Menno and his partner took over an empty space, and suddenly Menno and his partner had overhead costs. To increase revenues, Menno and his wife tried to sell fine art prints and other such items by opening up the space as a gallery.

The municipal government was supposed to give all newspapers a half-page or a full-page ad detailing all the municipally related information, and for some reason, this revenue was not given to Menno and his partner. This revenue was crucial to the viability of the paper, and despite having a couple of municipal councillors fight on their behalf, this revenue was not collectible.

"The problem was that we could not generate enough money to pay for the paper, pay for the rent, and pay us," Menno says. "That is where it went south. And we had to be in this position for a year before we could join ONPA."

Eventually, Menno and his partner secured a loan, and this money went to pay off immediate bills, a security system for the storefront, and interior upkeep. The bills piled up fast, and they decided to hire an advertising executive to help generate more advertising sales. She ended up being an absolute disaster.

"We got into a lot of trouble very fast at this point," says Menno. "We had a lot of payments to make. We were at a point that if we were to put out another issue, we were not going to be making one dime. We were just going to break even after paying all the bills. None of us were being paid. I had bought a house very cheap with next to nothing in monthly payments, and I still couldn't afford it."

The final nail in the coffin came when a competing paper approached the large grocery chain with an advertising "steal of a deal". When Menno found out, he approached the owner and told him that the price he was getting was cheap now, but he would pay a high cost later. On top of that, if he pulled his advertisement out of the Dresden Telegraph, the community paper was done.

Menno pleaded with the owner to support the community paper and not make a rash decision. However, the grocery store owner decided to move his advertisement to the other paper, and that was the end of the paper business for Menno and his friend.

"This was most heartbreaking thing I've ever done," he says. "I had a friend who provided, for free, the signs on the store. We had people help us with business cards, and there were so many other people who invested a lot of time and money to help us. My partner was desperate for money and while working on a lucrative contract for the municipality, he ended up pocketing the money himself rather than running it through the business. We needed that money. He got money, but the business got nothing. I was pissed at the time, but in retrospect what could he have done? He needed the money for rent."

The lesson that Menno and his partner learned was clear. With the excitement of the paper being successful early on, they made plans to grow. Of course, there is absolutely no issue with being bigger and growing a successful product, but Menno and his partner failed to consider all the possible costs the business would incur within that one year timeframe. Even after joining the ONPA, there might have been increased costs from traveling to secure national advertisers and other costs related to the competitions they wanted to enter, which needed to be included. If all these costs were considered, maybe becoming a member at that time was a bad idea from a business perspective.

An unforeseen drain on cash which seems to be forgotten are payroll liabilities owed to the government. When paying employees, various liabilities such as personal taxes, pension plan contributions and employment insurance deductions are taken off their paycheques and are held until they need to be remitted to the government at certain times of the year.

What typically happens is that, in the first year or two of the business, whatever cash comes into the bank account seems to be immediately used up by the entrepreneur to pay for any start-up costs that are vital to keeping the business alive. However, at some point in time, the collected payroll liabilities become due, and a cheque is supposed to be written to the government. But because payroll liabilities seem to be low on the priority list, these get deferred until a later time, and then delayed again, and then again.

Despite reminders from the government, the delay tactics continue while at the same time, the balance owing increases substantially as both financial penalties and interest also begin to accumulate on the outstanding balance owed. After a few delays and unanswered requests for the outstanding balance owed, the government begins some heavy-handed tactics to collect what is owed, beginning the procedure to freeze bank accounts and seize assets, which paralyzes the company.

There is no escaping the money owed to the government. If the entrepreneur is not able to pay these obligations, the recourse is simple: a business funeral, like the one experienced by a bakery run by Ambrose Duncan.

After graduating from university with a Bachelor of Commerce degree, Ambrose was keen on working right away. She did not have substantial work experience, going into university right from high school, and she had no preconceived notions of where she wanted to work.

"I was strolling along a particular street in my neighborhood, and stopped in a coffee shop to get something to eat, and to think about what I wanted to do next," she recalls.

Ambrose approached the counter, ordered a large coffee, and perused the sugary baked items that were for sale. She picked a chocolate chip muffin, sat down, and began to think about what type of business she wanted to work in.

"I bit into the muffin, and it was the best chocolate chip muffin I had ever tasted," she says. "I finished it so quickly that I had to go up to order another one. I finished the last one so I decided to try the banana loaf instead. I sat down again, took a bite, and it was extremely tasty."

Ambrose then asked a staff member where those baked items were made because they were so good, she wanted to buy them in bulk to take home. The staff member told her that the coffee shop had a contract with a bakery a few blocks down that made the baked goods for several coffee shops around the city.

"I asked for the name of the bakery and went to go visit it," she says. "I walked in and asked for the owner, who had been working behind the counter along with four other people. Once introduced, I let the owner know that she was making one of the best muffins and banana loaf pieces that I had ever tried, and I want to purchase a few to take home."

After visiting the bakery several times over the next few weeks, she noticed that the workers were always in a rush, so she casually asked the owner how busy she was.

"She pointed to a paper with close to 20 names of businesses on it that were all part of a backlog for that day," she says. "It was clear that she was understaffed and since I was looking for a job, I asked if I could join her company."

The owner let Ambrose know that she was extremely busy and an extra set of baking hands would definitely come in handy. Ambrose began two days later, immersing herself in the baking of a wide variety of items along with the four other staff. Over the next six months, Ambrose was asked to help think of new and innovative baked items to offer customers, and she was proud to help.

After some time, Ambrose became interested in the actual business of the bakery. She loved the baking part, but wanted to understand how successful the business was and asked the owner if she could help on the business side. The owner appreciated the offer and took Ambrose under her wing, allowing the owner to concentrate on getting out of the bakery to generate sales.

After seeing the growth in the customer orders, experiencing how the operations worked, developing new baking products, and reviewing the financials from time to time, Ambrose became interested in running her own bakery. She approached the owner and asked if it was okay to open her own bakery, promising not to go to any existing customers. Although the owner would be losing an excellent resource, she understood the entrepreneurial spirit, and wished her well.

"I knew that I had to be located close to the opposite end of the city so that I had access to a new set of customers," she says. "I took a drive out that way, and saw a really nice place that was close to a number of really small offices. I took a bit of a drive around and noticed some coffee shops in the area. I knew that I could market to both the coffee shops to get them to sell my baked goods and maybe provide the offices with something in the mornings. So I signed the lease on the space, dipped into my savings and also asked some family members to help pitch in, which I would pay back in the first year."

Ambrose started with a small oven at first and began to bake in the afternoons while spending the mornings visiting potential customers. Slowly, over the course of the next four to five weeks, she supplied her baked goods to three coffee shops and also delivered coffee and baked goods to a few offices around her building.

"Things were going well and I was getting busy, but my time was being spent running around trying to fill orders and find customers," she says. "I also needed some help baking as I spent literally no time making new products. So I put a 'Help Wanted' sign in the door, and pretty soon, I had five people come into the store to talk to me about a job."

Ambrose had budgeted for one employee to join her after one year in business, but knowing that she needed more than just the one, she hired three of the five that approached her, putting them to work right away.

Ambrose was now able to spend more time outside the bakery to woo more customers. She signed on a few more offices, but these required more effort because of the time spent delivering the baked goods and picking up the trays at the end of each day. She needed to get more coffee shops carrying her product, which meant that she had to travel more, which increased her travel expenses, including gas and meals. She was also often asked if she had any brochures that she could leave behind, and after saying no several times, she decided to print some flyers so potential customers could contact her right away.

After being pampered with a decent bank balance, she now faced a thinner one as her travel expenses, employees, and marketing expenses began to take a toll on the cash balance.

"I was used to having a good bank balance every month, but now with the wages, it was very hard to write those cheques this month because bringing on those three people really drained the bank account," she says. "But I needed those employees because I needed the business to grow and I needed to bring in more customers, which seemed to be going well. Plus these brochures really set me back and I was starting to see the bank balance get down to less than $500 on some days, and this really worried me."

One of the larger coffee shops in the area made a deal with Ambrose, offering a one-year contract to carry her baked goods every day with the option of paying after 60 days. Ambrose became excited because she had an opportunity to sell a tremendous number of baked products to a busy coffee shop, bringing in much-needed cash. Thirty days later, a lot of inventory went out the door to the coffee shop, but the cash from that coffee shop was still 30 days away.

"Yes, I did see a big increase in revenues and lots of baked goods going out the door, but the problem was I still had to wait another 30 days for that money to hit my bank account," she says. "Meanwhile, I'm sitting here writing cheques for rent, wages, utilities, flyers, and a whole bunch of other expenses here and there. My bank balance was now around $500. And then, I got a form from Revenue Canada that I had to fill out for submitting the deductions from the employees. I generated a report from the accounting program, and I looked at the amount that I needed to write a cheque for, which did not seem like much, but there were other priorities that I needed to pay first. And it wasn't like I wasn't going to pay the government. I was just going to pay them a little bit later."

Delaying the payment to the government is exactly what Ambrose did, but that "little bit later" ended up being 12 months later. In the meantime, because of the increase in the number of customers, she financed a larger oven in addition to other specialized baking equipment. A couple of months went by, and Ambrose received another notice to remit her payroll liabilities.

"I got this notice again, and I knew that I had to issue a cheque for all the monthly payroll deductions that I kept putting off," she says. "So I generated another payroll deduction report from the accounting system, and when I looked at the amount that I owed, I nearly fell off my freaking chair! It was so HUGE! There was no way that I could afford to pay that amount to the government. I was already tapped out because of the bigger oven that I was leasing and paying for every month, on top of all the other cheques I was writing."

Once again, Ambrose decided to delay paying the payroll deductions for another few months, hoping to get that one big customer, accumulating more deductions in the meantime. Then, Revenue Canada called.

"I saw on my call display that there was a call from the Government of Canada," she says. "I picked up the phone, and the gentleman said that he was from Revenue Canada and was wondering where the payments were for my payroll deductions. He also reminded me that I was accumulating interest and penalties on top of what I owed every month I was late. Honestly, I got very nervous, and froze. I asked him if I could delay it a little bit, and he reminded me that I was already several months past due and reminded me that if I did not have a cheque to Revenue Canada within 30 days, then I may be facing some legal action."

Ambrose put the phone down, sat back in her chair, and thought hard about what to do next. She got in her car and drove around to potential customers, thinking that this would calm her nerves, but she kept replaying that conversation again and again. She wondered how, with no money in the bank account, she could possibly pay the government, the monthly finance payments for the bigger oven, wages, rent, and all the other small expenses that she put on her credit card. She became dizzy.

"I felt like I was in a fog. I started sweating and pacing and looking at the bank account online and going back to my spreadsheet to see if there was anything I can do," she says. "I went to go talk to some family members to discuss the situation, and they gave me a dose of reality: I had to throw in the towel. There was no way I could make those payments. What was even worse, which made me sick to my stomach, was that there was no way I could pay back my family immediately. The only way I could do that is to go out, get a job, and pay them whatever I could."

Ambrose tried putting the bakery up for sale by putting an advertisement in the paper as well as a sign on the door, but when a few people phoned in asking about the business in general, they never phoned back. Finally, one day, Ambrose stepped out of the bakery, turned around, and locked the front door for good. She then went home and called closest bankruptcy trustee to begin the proceedings to file for bankruptcy.

"I lost it all. I kept putting things off and the amount that I owed to the government just kept getting bigger and bigger," she says. "And it was not as if I could just ignore the government. They were going to get their money at some point. I guess I didn't grow the business fast enough. But now I have an incredible learning experience. I hope there are others reading this story that will learn from it."

Ambrose eventually went to work for another company unrelated to the baking industry. She was a natural salesperson and continues to do well in that role today.

In both of these case studies, not being able to identify unforeseen costs played a major role in the closing of the businesses. Menno simply could not generate enough revenue to cover the operational costs, despite trying to generate cash in different ways. Ambrose kept putting off her payroll deductions, and after accumulating those over time, and having to meet all her other financial obligations, the cash being deposited in the bank account never covered the costs.

Adding these unforeseen costs into the financial projections is essential. The entrepreneur can then move onto the other areas of the business plan to ensure that the rest of the business supports the projections.

Depending upon what industry the business happens to be in, there may be stakeholders that could be problematic if their concerns are not addressed. Mapping out these concerns and the strategy in how to appease these concerns is an essential part of the business plan, if relevant.

If these concerns are not properly identified, this can throw a wrench in the business's success, as experienced by both David Monty and Doug Wastell.

Provide Value to Stakeholders

We did not get full buy-in from the one stakeholder group that was the ultimate decision-maker for the project. Because of this, we had to shut the project down after two years.

– David Monty, Director – Dobson-Lagassé Entrepreneurship Centre

As builders, we get so frustrated by an ever-changing land development process that City Hall has us experience. We are trying to work with them to try and define a smooth process, but in the meantime, the constant changes result in delay after delay, and that is costing me money.

– Doug Wastell, President – Wastell Homes

One area of a business plan that does not seem to attract much attention compared to the other sections is stakeholder analysis. In the process of running a business, there may be stakeholders represented by individuals, groups, or other businesses that may be indirectly affected by, or have a concern toward the selling of a business's product or service. Identifying these stakeholders allows their concerns to be defined, so the entrepreneur can then outline how the business will mitigate each concern.

Entrepreneurs need to consider stakeholder analysis because some of their products or services might affect the stakeholder in a negative way. If that stakeholder has some power or influence, such as a government entity, a regulatory body, or a prominent activist organization, the stakeholder could assert its power or influence to create hurdles for the business and stop it in its tracks.

Although stakeholder analysis should always be performed, not all businesses need to go into an in-depth analysis. For example, the products offered by a grocery store or a retail clothing outlet generally cause few issues for any influential stakeholders. But for businesses in areas such as pharmaceutical products or oil and gas exploration and mining, an in-depth stakeholder analysis will definitely be required as there would be a number of powerful stakeholders whose concerns need to be addressed.

For those who neglect to address the concerns of stakeholders, a business that has a project with a strong business case and community need may still be shut down because the stakeholders were not involved from the get-go, or they do not understand the value that the business and its offerings bring to the community. Such was the case for David Monty.

David Monty, an entrepreneur at heart, is involved in entrepreneurship at Bishop's University and is also Executive Director of the Dobson-Lagassé Entrepreneurship Center. He has been instrumental in getting entrepreneurs to answer tough questions to make sure they fully understand the value that their product or service brings to every stakeholder. Prior to his academic pursuits, David was involved in a number of start-ups.

He recalls a project started in 2006 where a number of high-profile entrepreneurs were looking to start a direct flight from Sherbrooke to Toronto because of the demand from the business community, which would also enhance economic development in the region. David was keen and volunteered to lead the project. The entrepreneurial group had put in a sizable amount of money and looked to the government to have political funds added to the pot, without which the project would not go ahead.

Because David and his group needed to involve politicians, one of David's roles was to ensure that the political groups understood how the project would add value to the business community and future development for the city of Sherbrooke.

"I was a keynote speaker at the Economic Development Association of Canada, and presented this project to over 200 economic involvement officers from across Canada," he says. "The attendees loved the idea of private businesspersons getting in, putting money in, and getting the project going. Although conceptually there was excitement from the political side, getting the political groups to understand the value was a problem."

A member of the provincial government had agreed to put in some money provided the project start before the fiscal year end, as the government funding had to be allocated before a new budget was being announced. This was a problem; it was difficult to guarantee that the project would be completed within that timeframe given all the inputs necessary and analysis required to ensure the project went ahead properly.

Another issue was that the government officials at the City of Sherbrooke, who managed the airport, did not understand or clearly see the political value and payback of the air service. For example, city officials discouraged the Montréal air service subcontractor from supplying his own cheaper fuel out of Montréal. The City of Sherbrooke airport management wanted to sell their own fuel to the operator, which was more expensive and would negatively impact the project economics. This created additional costs for the carrier, who was more interested in investing in the long term success of the service and would eventually take over the air service as an ongoing business. This was a classic case of making short-term decisions rather than taking aim at a more attractive longer-term view.

"That project was very successful from understanding the customer's needs because we were the customers," David says. "But the political community really didn't see the FULL value of the investment required. So after two years, we shut it down. The major problem, or failure, was the fact that we really didn't have buy-in from all the groups. And that buy-in was the ultimate failure."

In David's case, the group should have received buy-in from all of the political stakeholders before moving forward. With the City of Sherbrooke being a major stakeholder, David and his team worked closely with members from the economic development office, who were great supporters, but the overall political support was not there.

Even with a positive relationship in place, a stakeholder could still make life difficult for an entrepreneur by using delay tactics or changing some of the rules in a given process. This was the case for Doug Wastell, who had nothing but frustration when dealing with representatives of the City of London, Ontario.

Doug Wastell is President of Wastell Homes, a builder of residential homes in the city of London, Ontario. This company started as Wastell Builders Group in 1979 by founders Garry and Elaine Wastell, Doug's parents. Doug took over the business, and has been running it for the past 18 years.

Doug changed the name from Wastell Builders Group to Wastell Homes to begin establishing a certain brand name and brand presence in the local market. This brand recognition has resulted in the company winning several builder awards and being respected as a quality builder of homes in the London area. Doug leads a team of sales and service professionals who embrace the importance of placing customers in homes that meet their needs.

One of the stakeholders that Doug absolutely needs to deal with in order to get approval to build homes is the City of London. Dealing with the City, he has found differing agendas as to where development needs to take place.

"In our industry, the main thing is in having land in the proper areas, where you want it, which is where the market demand is," Doug says. "That's all we're trying to do is fulfill the demand, right? People want to live where they want to live for their particular reason, which, we don't really care, that's where they want to live."

This seems simple enough, but, as a developer, Doug needs to maintain positive relationships with staff at the City of London, and dealing with them has not been easy.

"A lot of our issues stem from City Hall in dealing with certain staff that are there, and in making sure that we want our lots where the market is demanding, that's all were trying to do," he says. "The City wants them to go in different areas for their own reasons. So they try and open up and free up areas where people don't want to live. This is one of the number one things that we have to deal with. Another issue is in timing. At City Hall there is no clock, there is no time. Your project gets released this year, or next year because they have to take more time to do a little bit more work, and it doesn't really matter to them. Meanwhile, I'm sitting there with millions of dollars laid out, tied up for one year. That's a lot of money, which ends up going to the final purchaser anyway."

Doug is also president of the London Home Builders Association (LHBA) and sits in on many of the meetings with representatives of the City of London. He finds encouragement in these representatives trying to improve the affordability of housing for Londoners. Doug always points out the need to cut red tape, or even set up a simple process whereby, if city officials ask developers to attend to a certain number of issues on a particular development, and the issues are completed, a stamp of approval is given. He feels City staff should not keep asking for more issues to be worked on.

"Just set up a process where, if you tell us to do these 10 things, or 20 things or 100 things, then let us just do those things, and then stamp it, and say 'Here you go, here's your piece of land, your parcel, you're ready to go,'" he says. "Then at least we have a process to work with. Now, you already know historically from the jobs that you have done, that you go to them with pretty well everything done, and they come back with 20 more things for you to do. And so you go away, you work on those 20 things, and you think that that would be it. You go back to them, and there are five more things. Well, wait a minute, where were those five things that I could have been doing before? We've burned six months. Why did you not give me those five things before? So you go away and attend to those five things, and then they come up with a new process, and now we have two or three more things that we have to do. And now, here we are a year later asking what's going on. It's tough. That part of it is tough."

For Doug, this means that his large investments in land are sitting idle with no return for a minimum of one year, delaying any return on his investments and affecting the project financing.

By asking for improvements in the process, Doug says that developers are not looking for favours, but more of a structure and a system. The builders need some certainty in a process, and a one-time comprehensive list of what needs to be delivered, rather than continually facing cycles of seemingly never-ending updates. To help City Hall realize that the process is taxing on developers, resources at the LHBA are looking into the land development processes at similar Canadian municipalities to showcase the efficiencies that other municipalities have incorporated.

"We look to other municipalities to see what they have done," explains Doug. "We compare ourselves to places like Hamilton, Niagara, Ottawa, not so much Calgary and Edmonton, maybe Winnipeg. We are in Southwest Ontario and we are in the hub of everything being right between Michigan and Toronto, so we have our pros as well. It's a thing that we've been working on for a while, and is not an easy thing to do."

All Doug and other builders want is a proper system in place with a set process such that he can cost his developments more accurately. With inefficient processes, more work is required on Doug's end, which means that he incurs more cost. To maintain a set profit margin on each property he sells, this increased cost flows down to the end customer.

"These extra costs flow to the end customer which impacts affordability," he says. "Affordability is something that City Hall pressures developers to keep in mind. If one looks at a typical $300,000 home, the taxes alone could make up $150,000 of that home, which should be shown to City Hall. These costs, combined with the long approval process, seem to go against the idea of affordability."

Because of the long, drawn-out process, Doug has had to reduce his staff, which certainly reduces his ability to sell properties. He has also had to run the business lean, particularly in current economic times. However, these efficiencies have allowed his company to weather the storm, which was not the case for a number of other builders in London.

Hopefully, through ongoing discussion with City Hall, there will be an improvement in the approval process to ensure that building a house addresses both the affordability perspective and return on investment for the builder to make a win-win for both parties.

Funny enough, the two case studies illustrated above deal with a stakeholder that happens to be a government entity. However, there are a multitude of stakeholders that an entrepreneur must identify, which is dependent on the business, and its products and services. Ensuring that stakeholder concerns are mitigated can only produce a positive outcome and a great relationship between all parties. For an entrepreneur, this is a desirable outcome when trying to build the business from the ground up.

With the concerns of stakeholders mitigated, the entrepreneur should not begin the business until all major business risks are also addressed. If they are not addressed properly, these business risks will become major business hurdles that an entrepreneur will not see coming. If proper planning is done, as in Mate Prgin's case, then the business will not fail; without proper planning for risks, the business could easily fail, as in John Scaliani's case.

Preparing for Risks

Being in the telecom industry, I need to pay incredible attention to the risks I face. If I don't, my business is done even before it starts.

– Mate Prgin, President & CEO – Avvasi Inc.

I opened a business without clearly thinking about ANY of the business risks that hit me, and hit me hard they did. These risks killed the business. I was finished in less than one year and my partners and I lost all our money.

– John Scaliani, Former Owner – Chicago-Style Pizza

There will always be risks in business, no matter what product or service the entrepreneur decides to wrap a business around. To prepare the business for these risks, an entrepreneur should be able to articulate what risks the business will face well before the business is off the ground. Once these risks are identified, a realistic and convincing mitigation strategy should be paired with each risk to outline exactly how the business would tackle them.

A failure to identify potential risks should be a major cause for concern for both the entrepreneur and those reading the business plan, such as banks or potential investors. Another red flag would be providing unrealistic or weak mitigation strategies to be employed if and when those risks come to fruition. In either case, the business may be hit hard, and the entrepreneur would have to shift resources and spend time away from growing the business to tackle these hurdles, which could have been prevented.

For Mate Prgin, being aware of the business risks was crucial; not knowing them, based on his industry, had a simple result: no business.

Mate Prgin has a 15-year history of building infrastructure for video delivery over DSL[18], cable, and satellite networks. He started his career working for a start-up company called PixStream, where he held engineering responsibilities for key product lines. In 2000, this company was bought by Cisco, which gave Mate his first exposure to a successful venture-backed start-up acquisition.

Mate started another company called VideoLocus Inc., a semiconductor company that developed the default video standard for Blu-ray and broadcast TV, among others. This company was eventually bought by LSI Logic Corporation. While at LSI, Mate completed his MBA, and in 2007, he left LSI to start Avvasi Inc.

"I started Avvasi to take advantage of where the future of video streaming was going," he says. "YouTube and Netflix were becoming popular, and the iPhone was just released. The bet was that video was going to be very prominent in the mobile space. When Avvasi was started, video on mobile phones was nonexistent, whereas today it is over 50% of the traffic, and so the industry had made good on my bet."

Avvasi has an advantage from giving telecommunication companies, who already provide voice and data, an ability to carry premium video quality on their existing networks with no increase in expensive infrastructure to carry the video service.

"The carriers never imagined being video providers as they were concentrating more on being voice and data providers," he says. "The benefit my company gave the telecommunications companies was that they did not have to replace billions of dollars of equipment to run video on the cable system. All they needed to do was to retrofit their towers with Avvasi's flagship product and provide video service to the

---

18 A digital subscriber line (DSL) is a medium for transferring data over regular phone lines and can be used to connect to the Internet. A DSL circuit is much faster than a regular phone connection, even though the wires it uses are copper like a typical phone line.

customers. This would give its customers a good experience and the telecommunication companies would be able to monetize this easily."

Because video on mobile devices is rapidly becoming a primary requirement for most users, many of the Tier 1 wireless carriers understand the need for video. This has provided Avvasi with multiple opportunities to have its flagship product deployed and tested with many of the top multinational wireless carriers in their various global footprints.

One of the largest business risks that Mate faces is the long sales cycle, typical for Tier 1 carriers. These carriers lag in efficient decision-making processes, with the shortest sales cycle being one year from initial engagement to purchase order, and the longer ones being two years in length. Because of this business risk, Mate faces another business risk: obsolescence.

"Within these two years, technology is changing very rapidly which may result in a danger that the existing technology may become obsolete," he says. "That means that we must have a mature product, developed, tested, and ready to go before beginning the sales cycle."

Avvasi also needed to consider the capital requirements of not only developing the technology, but also running a company during a period with few revenues due to the sales cycles.

"Given the time in ensuring a product is ready to be deployed on top of a long sales cycle," Mate says, "the venture capital required to successfully launch such a telecommunications firm is in the range of $40 million to $50 million if done right and operating very lean, and if operating inefficiently, up to $100 million!"

But finding money is a constant challenge. Just because an entrepreneur has developed an excellent product for the marketplace, one cannot assume that the money will start flowing through the door, especially in the telecom sector.

"The ability to raise additional capital for a company in the telecom space is difficult," says Mate. "Venture capital money seems to be chasing companies like Instagram and others in the social media space whereas there is less money available for backing telecommunications firms, particularly in Canada where there has been a shrinking of venture capital in the past 10 years. Luckily, Avvasi has a good history in the space, and I have a proven technology. Even though Avvasi has a great story, it must be run very lean as everything takes longer. Even though Avvasi is under 50 people, it must go global from Day One based on the technology that it is developing. If you don't, the competitors will encircle you, and you'll be done."

Another business risk that Mate must deal with is in the sales and marketing area, where specialized skills are needed to demonstrate his technology. Because of this requirement, Mate has trouble finding an appropriate sales resource, despite the attractive opportunity with his technology.

"Despite doing trials with extremely large carriers around the world, there is a limited sales force," he says. "A challenge in building out a sales organization is that a lot of salespeople will have excellent relationships with one or two accounts, so I may need to hire 20 of them to get global reach. It is hard to find people that are able to leverage their skills from their existing relationships and apply them to new relationships. I went through a number of resources through trial and error, starting with consultants, and experiencing a lot of failure. I tried going through partners and distribution channels but the problem with this is that the partners do not want to do the trailblazing work in the early stages of a new market. They will easily lineup for a $20 million deal, but when faced with a two-year sales cycle and a $500,000 deal, they shy away."

With little talent at his disposal, Mate needs to personally travel to meet with customers.

"I need to find out what they need, when they are ready to buy and how close they are to a decision," he says. "If it seems to take too long, I will pull my resources back. I look for the early adopters, those with the shortest sales cycle, or those with a real pain point, and I try and gather a lot of intelligence along the way in addition to networking and building relationships. Once I see a pattern that works, then I can build a sales team and replicate that pattern."

Despite having a technologically superior video solution for Tier 1 telecommunication companies, Mate has had to think about a number of risk factors for his business just to ensure that he has a business to operate. But for John Scaliani, his inability to take into account any business risks led to his business closing its doors within a short 10 months.

In the mid '90s, John Scaliani had plans to open a take-out style pizzeria, named Chicago-Style Pizza, with two other partners in Calgary, Alberta. John had no experience in the pizza business, but ran a number of small business ventures before. Of the other two partners that were brought on board, one of them had no experience in the pizza business, but helped finance the company, whereas the other partner, Mike, had been a manager of a local pizza franchise that was part of a large multinational pizza chain, giving him some operational experience.

John wanted to separate Chicago-Style Pizza from the rest of the take-out pizza competitors by offering a 3-for-1 pizza deal. It was thought that this would give potential customers even better value than others, most of whom only offered a regularly advertised 2-for-1 pizza deal. For customers to take advantage of the 3-for-1 deal, they would only have to pay an extra $3.00, on average, to get three pizzas instead of two.

"We thought that this was a very attractive offer, and anybody trying to order pizza would only order from us because they got so much more pizza for their money," says John. "This would force the others in the area to shut down, and we would be the only ones in the area offering pizza."

John purposely located Chicago-Style Pizza in a low-income area where residents would consist of those on social assistance, students, and seniors. Locating in such an area would also result in a reasonably low lease payment.

"The rent was cheap and we knew that twice a month, most of the residents in this area would get a cheque from the government because they were on social assistance," he says. "There were also a number of seniors in the area, and once a month, they would also get a big cheque from their pensions. We knew that this would attract a lot of business around the dates that they got paid."

The owners wanted to start the business lean, with most of the initial investment going toward minor leasehold improvements, inventory, and second-hand equipment. They were going to rely on word-of-mouth marketing to initially get the business off the ground. Mailing flyers out to residents in the area seemed quite expensive at the time.

One of the first business risks that John admits to was management not having the appropriate background or experience in running a successful pizza business location. Although Mike had some experience managing a franchise location, he was never responsible for the overall finances. All of the owners made assumptions that running the business would be easy.

"I ran small businesses before, and so did [the financier]. But we needed a third person who had some pizza experience," says John. "So we picked up Mike. He is a really nice guy and easy to work with. Because he managed a previous pizza location, I hoped that he would know about keeping costs low and making sure that customers were happy."

The doors to Chicago-Style Pizza opened, and, as planned, many residents in the area strolled in to ask about what the 3-for-1 offer meant. Regular customers were quickly established and many began spreading the word about Chicago-Style Pizza. A few companies in the immediate vicinity started to place corporate orders. With a growing number of customers, daily revenues also started to grow.

To keep costs low, Mike and John were the only ones involved in the business operations: opening the pizza location, getting everything ready, preparing pizzas for the customers, delivering pizzas, closing down, and paying bills, all of which made for long days.

Operationally, Mike set up the location to mimic the pizza franchise he previously managed with one exception. There were no scales to measure the weight of toppings or instructions on how to put toppings on certain pizza orders. This practice resulted in another business risk – not having a firm handle of the overall profit on each pizza and also the overall profits of the business.

"One of the risks in offering a 3-for-1 deal was that we should've had a handle on how much each pizza was costing us," John says. "But we just never thought of that. We used some rough estimates from Mike, who gave some numbers from the pizza location he had worked at, and we thought that if we were smart about costs, then we should be able to do well. What we should have done, even before we opened the doors, was to actually use a scale to weigh some of the toppings, like cheese, bacon, or ham. And we should have been able to count the number of pepperoni or Italian sausage slices to put on certain sizes. We did not want to be too strict because we wanted our customers to know that they had a nice pizza to eat with a good amount of toppings. But with every pizza being handed to a customer, we had absolutely no clue how much profit that particular pizza was making us. We just started rolling out the dough, putting on the sauce, and then began sprinkling the toppings. And then we collected the cash. That was it."

John also explained that they were so busy that he had no time to sit down to properly analyze the finances of the business. Every month, he just looked at the money that came in from the pizza sales and the bills he had to pay for that month, and subtracted the two figures.

"Well, I knew how much we bought our toppings for, and the good news is that we were getting better at reducing our prices there," he says. "I also know that after I paid my bills, there was money in the bank account. The only time I got nervous is when I had to buy some newer equipment because the older ones seemed to break."

In the first three months of operation, as predicted, the largest influx of customer orders came two times a month: when the government cheques would be mailed to seniors and social assistance recipients. However, after some time, the consistently high number of daily orders started to die down, and for close to 10 days each month, pizza orders were very slow. John did not think about this happening as, once again, assumptions were being made that there would be a consistent level of sales, and so he had to begin thinking of getting a marketing plan together.

"We never thought about this risk because we assumed that the customer orders would just come in all the time," he says. "Mike and I kept thinking that, because we were cheaper per pizza than the other pizza joints, people would keep ordering from us. But it looked like this wasn't happening. We needed to do something. Mike suggested that we print flyers as this seemed to increase sales at the previous pizza company he worked for. My concern was that if we had to continuously print flyers, this added to costs which I was not comfortable with, but I had no choice."

John contacted a local printing shop, which designed the flyers that would showcase all the different sizes of pizza, the toppings available, and associated coupons. He then hired a number of young students to go around door-to-door within a five-block radius to deliver the flyers. The orders started picking up, and the bank account started increasing again. John had a beaming smile on his face until he realized that his regular customers were redeeming the coupons, but not increasing their order amount or frequency.

"I never thought about our regular customers also using the coupons," he says. "Now I was losing maybe two dollars per order every two weeks with each one of our customers, which was about 10% in cash, gone. And that 10% was VERY necessary for us to survive."

Despite running various promotions, Chicago-Style Pizza hit a revenue ceiling. Unfortunately, these revenues were not enough to carry the business forward for much longer, and neither of the owners put any more money into the venture. Ten months later, the doors were closed for good.

"It was clear that we had no real plan, let alone a business plan," John says. "Our attitude was just open the doors, and it should work. And it might have worked if I would have thought about all of the things that would have prevented us from moving forward. Who knows?"

Properly identifying the major business risks is a good sign that an entrepreneur has a handle on where the possible hurdles may be. Once these risks are identified, the entrepreneur can detail how these risks would be mitigated, and assuming that the risk mitigation plans are realistic, the business has an excellent chance of overcoming these risks, which was the case for Mate. However, not being aware of these risks may have dire consequences as the entrepreneur becomes consumed in the quest to tackle the onslaught of business hurdles, taking valuable time away from the business. If the risks are too great to mitigate, then the results could be the end of the business, as it was 10 months later for Chicago-Style Pizza.

FAIL FAST SUCCEED FASTER

PART 3

Do You Have the Right Team?

Success is the ability to go from failure to failure without losing your enthusiasm.

–Winston Churchill

Once a business plan has been properly prepared, the entrepreneur should think about what resources will be needed to move the business forward. There are two groups of resources that need to be looked at: the first are those that help with the management and operation of the business, which would normally include business partners, management, and employees; the second provide a supportive role, such as professional services, advisors, and mentors.

For the business to move forward successfully, the entrepreneur needs to take the proper time and effort to select these resources carefully, bringing them on at appropriate stages in the business life cycle. For example, it may not be necessary to add management and employees right away as the entrepreneur may be able to build the business alone initially, but eventually would need help. However, when the business has customers and is looking to expand, management resources and mentors, both with the right experience, should be added to the team.

If the entrepreneur decides to bypass the use of these resources, substitute them with those that lack the required experience or bring on resources at the last minute as a knee-jerk reaction without proper due diligence despite the obvious need to move the business ahead, then there is a real possibility that the business will face additional and unnecessary hurdles, taking attention away from growing the business and wasting time and effort to overcome the hurdle.

The best situation is to have a proper plan in place and take the time to select the right resources for the business. If this is not done early enough, the business will stall, or in some cases, even crumble.

The stories in this section shed light on problems interviewees faced by not bringing on the proper resources, which created a number of challenges for their businesses.

Never Sacrifice Your Core Values

The times that I have compromised on my core values when hiring or partnering, it has resulted in a waste of time, energy, and a lot of money. I never let that happen to me now. By sticking to what I believe, the businesses that I invest in have a much greater chance of success because they resonate with my values.

– Bruce Croxon, Co-Founder – Round13 Capital and Former Co-Founder – Lavalife

When assembling a team to help a business grow, an entrepreneur needs to put new resources through a hiring process that will ensure the resources brought on contribute to the culture and core values of the business right from the start. Although the process will never be 100% efficient because individuals sometimes slip through the cracks, compromises made by the entrepreneur will open up a possibility for rogue resources to take the business in a different direction, detrimental to its success. To eliminate this from happening, the entrepreneur must stick to his or her core values right from Day One. For Bruce Croxon, making compromises resulted in a project burning a lot of hard-earned money.

After co-founding Lavalife in 1987, Bruce Croxon served in many roles with the company – as partner, chairman, and CEO – guiding it to the position of category leader and achieving revenues of close to $100 million prior to its sale in 2004. Bruce currently runs Round13 Capital, a company dedicated to incubating and investing in digital start-ups, including Sprigg Software, Walkaway Canada, and Round Assist. He also pursues investments in the health and wellness sector; he currently owns Vida, a chain of high-end holistic spas on Canada's West Coast.

Bruce is adamant about bringing people on board that resonate with certain core values that he continues to uphold in his business dealings.

"Core values cannot be shaped overnight. They take time to build," he says. "When forming these values, one would have to go through a number of iterations, allowing experiences, both good and bad, to shape them, which in turn would shape one's gut feeling about any situation."

Two core values that Bruce talks about are teamwork and open-mindedness.

"Teamwork is an overused term in and of itself," he says. "If you break it down, and you really understand what it means, I think people that think they are team players don't fit my definition of what a team player is. For example, the "not invented here" syndrome[19] – how willing are you to hear all sides of a discussion that might not be aligned with yours, and change course based on the logic presented and then support the outcome? These are relatively rare individuals. There are a lot more people that consider themselves to be team players when they are not."

Open-mindedness is defined as being receptive to new and different opinions or ideas. Bruce says that often times, open-mindedness and teamwork overlap.

"In terms of open-mindedness, the infighting or the politics or the egos become so important that logic and alternative ways of doing things are not viewed on their merit," he says. "That, to me, would be overlapping the teamwork and open-mindedness values."

Adhering to these core values was paramount to Bruce and the rest of the senior management team at Lavalife, so much so, that it became critical to their hiring process.

"We developed a whole recruitment, selection, and hiring process around making sure that the people that we brought into the company possessed qualities that lined up with our definition of teamwork and open-mindedness," he says.

---

19 "Not Invented Here Syndrome" (NIHS) is a slightly tongue-in-cheek name for the tendency of both individual developers and entire organizations to reject suitable external solutions to software development problems in favour of internally-developed solutions. Closely related to the "let's re-invent the wheel" syndrome, NIHS can be seen in intensities ranging from a mild reluctance to accept new ideas all the way up to a raging software xenophobia. (http://www.developer.com/design/article.php/3338791/Overcoming-quotNot-Invented-Herequot-Syndrome.htm)

Bruce has come to regret situations when he failed to adhere to his core values, and quickly points out an example.

"I found, in my career, that the mistakes that I've made have inevitably been made when I have compromised on core values," he says. "This happened once when I prioritized technical skill – I don't mean technology, I mean technical competency – that was compromised over core values. An example of that would be when we underwent a large technology transformation at Lavalife, which was a critical project."

At the time, Bruce was running Lavalife and brought a team on board that was technically competent to move the technology transformation forward, but with less focus on adhering to core values.

"I found that the team, although very technically competent, got sidetracked into issues that involved ego, the antithesis of open-mindedness when trying to problem solve," he explains. "Really, in hindsight, for a good number of months, we were getting updated at the board, being told that everything was on track, and everything was fine. But in fact it took us a while to figure it out that everything wasn't fine and the project wasn't on track. A large part of that was a lack of transparency and unwillingness to look bad in front of the board, right? And it was a lot of blaming between team members and why it was not on track – all the things that would add up to he opposite of working as a team."

Because of this dysfunction, the team wasted a lot of time having unproductive discussions, resulting in them being unfocused on the original goal – completing a technical project on time and on budget. This lack of focus cost the company a significant amount of money.

"The budget for the project was supposed to be $20 million over two years, and it turned out to be $42 million over four and a half years," Bruce says.

While this project was going on, Bruce was living in Whistler, British Columbia, and would fly back to attend board of directors meetings, where information being shared gave him a sense that something was not right. The situation reached a tipping point and one day Bruce got a sudden call and had to fly back.

"The board called me up one day and said that we were burning $1 million a month and you are coming home," he says.

Bruce did not waste any time making resource changes and took steps to turn the project around.

"I came back to take the helm at the request of the board and I fired the entire senior team in one day," he says. "The leadership to get us out of the mess came from within the company. This person had some opinions on what was going on, but no one would listen to him. When I came back, I listened to him. He said, well, listen, this is what we need to do, and he was right. And it was a quick turnaround after that. The old leadership were too caught up in the politics and ego to believe that a mid-level resource could have the answer when all the high-paid consultants that we were burning the money on did not."

Sacrificing these core values was a mistake that Bruce vowed to never make again. He now has a high bar when it comes to trusting somebody's ability to execute as an entrepreneur.

Bruce's core values were also tested when he and his team were looking to raise a round of capital for a large project requiring a significant amount of investment to complete. The company would have been able to provide its own capital to move the project forward, but Bruce and his team were seduced by a short-term opportunity into pocketing some money for themselves once the investment came in.

Bruce and his team went to look for investors, and found it difficult at first because of the risky nature of the company's product. This was further compounded by venture capital groups seeing a misalignment between Lavalife's product offering and the portfolio of products that the investment required. Eventually, Lavalife did find some capital, but Bruce had reservations with one of the investment groups as "something" just was not right with them.

"The person that led the investment group was scary smart, technically so astute using terms such as 'financial' and 'exit' and this and that," he says. "A lot of it was new to me. But I had real reservations about the core value overlap. We spent a lot of time at the board, him and I, going head-to-head, wasting a lot of time."

The ongoing suggestions that this individual was making were clearly not resonating with Bruce's core values. Bruce had to stop, rethink and then realign the discussion to ensure that the investment group understood what Bruce and his team stood for. This resulted in a lot of back-and-forth discussions.

"The end result is that you're sitting with a partner now who is making a suggestion at a board meeting and instead of it being a one step process, it's now a two-step process. Okay, let me get this straight. He is making a suggestion and so let me figure out what's in it for him, and whether it's in the best interest of the company, or is there another agenda going on. So, it was a two-step process every single time he made a suggestion. This was an incredible waste of time and energy, and detrimental to the growth of the company. Lavalife was a success, but it could've been a monster. I don't look back and I don't have regrets, but it's learning."

Bruce went through a stage as an investor not long after he sold Lavalife, when he had some significant capital to distribute. He was very approachable and, because of that, many people came up to him with ideas. In some cases Bruce liked the idea and told himself that if he could be successful, then the other person with the idea should also be successful.

"I underestimated what it took to be successful," he says. "If I could do it, then anybody could do it. Here you go. Go to it. But it turns out that this was not the case, which leads to my talk about the life of an entrepreneur in that it really is not for everybody. People think that they might be able to execute and deal with the 49% that goes wrong, but they can't. My gut told me that this person could do it, but my gut was wrong. It was wrong gut, bad gut I've learned about what my gut has told me. The bar is now higher for me on the people side."

Bending on core values can easily result in trouble, and in some cases, failure. But you learn from your failure, iterate, and reshape or strengthen your core values. Bruce sums it up well:

"There is an interesting thing about failure. If you spend too much time wallowing in the regret of it for the sake of wallowing, it could paralyze you. You can spend too much time looking in the rear-view mirror. Take the learning, get it articulated, and make sure you have squeezed every last little bit of juice from the learning lemon, and then move on."

For Bruce, his core values provide a screen for all potential investment candidates. By doing this right from the start, he can rest assured that the people he invests in will help grow the company in a way that maximizes its potential. For entrepreneurs looking at bringing on resources such as advisors, employees, investors, or even partners, screening them using a set of core values will ensure that the company grows in an efficient manner. By taking a chance and compromising on these values, entrepreneurs face the real possibility of never recovering from the business going sideways. A simple mistake ends up creating a complex problem.

Bringing on resources that adhere to your core values should be an obvious requirement for the business, but one also has to ensure that resources are brought on to compensate for an entrepreneur's weaknesses. If not, the business will either lack in certain skill sets, or there will be too many resources with one particular skill set, which is ineffective. Irene Chang Britt needed an "ah-ha" moment to help her compensate for her weaknesses.

Compensate For Your Weaknesses

*Unfortunately, it took an embarrassing 'ah-ha' moment
to make me realize that I needed others on board.*

– Irene Chang Britt, President – Pepperidge Farm, Senior Vice-President
– Global Baking and Snacking, Campbell's Soup Co.

Not everyone will have all the skill sets required when starting a business. Every individual has strengths, and of course, weaknesses. To make sure that you start your business right, it is important to assemble a team that makes up for your weaknesses.

If not, you may find yourself in a precarious situation if your business suffers a hiccup in an area that is not being properly managed. Of course, sometimes these situations provide enlightenment for hiring for your weaknesses. Such was the case for Irene Britt.

Irene Britt currently holds the position of President, Pepperidge Farm and Senior Vice-President, Global Baking and Snacking, Campbell Soup Company. She has worked for many large consumer goods companies during the past 27 years and has held a number of positions with increasing C-suite responsibilities.

"Thirty-one years ago, I started as an entrepreneur," she recalls. "One of the failures of many entrepreneurs is that they often do not realize early enough in their careers what they are good at, and what they are not good at. Furthermore, they might not surround themselves with those who can counter deficiencies, or short-comings in their skill sets.

Irene had this realization during an incident when she directed a business unit at a large paper company.

In the late '80s, the company had developed an innovative dispensing system which featured value-added technology designed to take the paper industry out of the commodity arena. This system was going to revolutionize how commercial customers, such as hotels, healthcare, and businesses, bought regular paper towels and bathroom tissue.

Traditionally, commercial customers ordered boxes of regular paper towels and bathroom tissue, kept them stocked in an inventory room, and distributed individual rolls when needed. The new product controlled the "portion" of bathroom tissue or hand towel available for use, thereby eliminating overuse and waste, and provided some regularity in inventory management for those particular items.

"The dispensing system literally changed the discussion, going from asking, 'How much is a case of bathroom tissue or hand towels' to 'How do we get a hold of this product that has a dispensing system,'" says Irene.

Irene quickly fell in love with the concept and the value that it brought to commercial customers and was eager to showcase the product at a national sales meeting. However, at THE critical moment, in front of hundreds of people, as she reached to pull a towel from the dispenser, the product failed. Red faced, Irene apologized to the audience, hurried through the rest of the presentation and quietly kicked herself. In her enthusiasm for the game-changing potential of the new product, she had overlooked doing her due diligence to check that the prototype actually worked.

This was an important 'ah-ha' moment for Irene, and has shaped the way she has led and built teams subsequently in her career. She knows she is 'good' at looking ahead and creating a compelling strategy for a business. She also knows that others excel in executing the details necessary to developing plans to deliver that vision, and recruits accordingly. This becomes incredibly important when moving the strategy for a business forward, also known as strategic intent.

When defining the strategic intent, Irene works with her team to visualize the strategic pathways required to achieve breakthrough growth or transformation. She then unleashes her team members to chart the best way of reaching this intent. They are responsible for developing and executing plans and processes necessary to transform the business and help the organization realize its potential. Irene's role is one of vision and leadership, ensuring that the team stays focused on the end game. When conflict or disagreement arises while implementing these strategic paths, Irene steers her team to the founding principles they signed up to when the strategic intent was initially set.

For Irene, it was important to bring in team members that complemented her skill set and have distinct roles and responsibilities allocated to each of the team members as a whole. This ensures that all aspects of a business are looked after by someone qualified, helping the business move forward.

For entrepreneurs that are starting up, there is a perception that they should be doing everything. This makes sense if there are restrictions such as a lack of start up financing. However, given the chance, entrepreneurs should think about spending some money on areas in which they are weak, or bring in some help with an appropriate compensation package.

Failure to bring in these resources often results in a business stalling and without a growth plan because the entrepreneur is constantly working IN the business and not ON the business. This also may allow competitors to come in and overtake the market that you were hoping to secure.

To help entrepreneurs with advice on what resources to bring on, or for overall general business issues, it is extremely advisable that an entrepreneur make the investment to seek the advice of a qualified mentor, one who has the proper experience and qualifications to provide key business advice. The entrepreneur should make the investment upfront as typically, the value in not making that investment is realized after the venture has failed, as can be attested by Bill Kenward and James Edwards.

Seek Advice From a Qualified Mentor

*Perhaps a mentor would have talked me out of the
idea and/or steered me towards a feasibility study.
In either case, I may not have pursued this idea and
not suffered the financial losses that ensued.*

– Bill Kenward, Former Juice Franchise Owner

*I asked the wrong people about my plan to get into
another business. I should have asked a qualified
mentor for advice. The result? We went from a house
with a nice pool to bankruptcy court to a one bedroom
apartment for me, my wife and my two teenage kids.*

– James Edwards, Former Convenience Store Owner

Generally, advisors are tapped from time to time for their advice. But entrepreneurs may want to seek out a personal mentor to ask for advice even before starting the business venture. The danger is that some entrepreneurs do not want to spend the money on a qualified mentor, one with the appropriate level of experience to provide sound advice. Either the entrepreneur consults others that lack the appropriate experience, or the entrepreneur pushes ahead with little to no advice.

Interestingly, the value of that qualified mentor will only be realized when the business gets off its rails and begins to fail. Bill Kenward and James Edwards both realized, after their ventures failed, that a qualified mentor would have been a valuable investment.

In 2003, Bill Kenward of London, Ontario contemplated getting into a franchise that he thought would be interesting and had a lot of potential. After some investigation, Bill became interested in juice franchises as these types of franchises seemed to be on the upswing, and he enjoyed the healthy aspect of the product. After visiting some franchise shows, he decided on one particular brand popular in Western Canada that was beginning to establish a brand presence in Ontario.

"In 2003, there were only four of these juice franchise locations in Ontario," Bill says. "I went to the one in Kitchener and tried some their products, and it was very impressive. It was situated in a mall beside a gym and so there was a natural flow of clientele. I was looking to put a franchise in [a large local mall]. As I recall, the juice franchisor tried to deal with the mall before, and it had fallen through, and had it come up again. So we have the perfect storm here: this place is SUPPOSEDLY, and I emphasize supposedly, a great location in a large mall, and me looking for a business, a location in London."

Bill received some general financial data from the franchisor and spoke to other franchisees in Alberta and British Columbia, who all had successful locations in food courts with supporting financials. Looking back, Bill now realizes that the financials he looked at were not applicable to his situation.

"It was not in my best interest to rely on financials from those in Alberta or British Columbia because, in Ontario, the juice franchise was an unknown quality out here, relatively speaking. Unless I had a solid brand name behind me, business would've been extremely tough."

Bill did get advisors on board, but these were professional services, not really in the business of advising people on business matters outside of their expertise.

"In terms of advisors, I had an accountant who looked at the estimates and said that these all looked good," he says. "I had a lawyer who looked at the legal aspect of it, but he was really not in a position to evaluate the business. However he did tell me that these people, that is the franchise owners, tended to put a really good shine on things when they weren't necessarily that good."

Bill was afraid that he would have to do a business plan in order to get a loan from the bank, which he asked the accountant to do. The accountant was not comfortable drawing up a business plan for him, but as it turned out, the bank had prior dealings with the juice franchisor and was familiar with the juice franchise's brand name and loaned the money to Bill without requiring a business plan.

Armed with the interviews, the financial estimates from the Western Canada locations, and franchise information, Bill made the plunge and opened up his franchise location in December 2003.

"When I opened up, the mall was very busy – peak shopping season. It was in the New Year 2004, that I found that the mall was very quiet. This trend continued for the first three or four months of that year. There were days when I went there, and you could shoot a cannon down the hallways and not hit anything or anybody," he says. "And every month was a losing month. If you looked at the profile of the people who patronized that mall, there were seniors there with limited incomes, you had poorly paid mall employees who also had limited incomes, and teenagers and young people."

Concerned, Bill chatted with some of the other retailers in the mall. They told him that since 9/11, fewer tour buses came to London, with fewer shoppers.

Bill also found few shoppers showed any interest in spending a large amount of money on a healthy smoothie.

"What I did notice, that was conspicuous by its absence, was a large number of people who were health-conscious," he says. "If you look at the food court on any given day, probably three quarters of the people that are sitting there eating, they are probably drinking gallons of [a cola] and eating French fries and things like that. What they're looking for is lots of food for low prices. Therefore the idea of spending five dollars on a high quality smoothie such as what we had did not appeal to very many people. And a lot of people did not know who we were, as we were relatively new in Ontario, and they could not differentiate what we were selling versus the smoothie from [a competitor in the mall]. I don't know what the ingredients are in that smoothie, but it is probably a lot of sugar and ice, and I don't know what else, whereas we had a breakdown in terms of calories, fibre, protein, and a list of ingredients."

The ongoing business losses were certainly not due to Bill's lack of effort.

"I went to virtually every business in the mall and offered discounts," he says. "We were very active in the food court, walking out and talking to people, and tried to do something like the Nazi soup kitchen guy, but in a more positive way. I would literally talk to people as they are going by saying 'Hey, you're approaching the fat zone', and things like that to try to get people's attention and encouraged my staff to do that too. We tried all kinds of things. I had a couple of really good staff who knew much more about restaurants than I did. It wasn't due to lack of effort, it wasn't due to lack of advertising; it was kind of like having a Cadillac dealership in a Lada neighborhood. Too expensive for most of those blue-collar people, and it was not a very large audience of health-conscious persons."

The falling sales and continued monthly losses resulted in Bill closing the location down in nine months, losing about $130,000 in the process.

One of the surprising issues that Bill finds is that despite his experience, he has not gotten one call from either the franchisor or a potential franchisee wondering what happened.

"The franchisor should have provided any persons looking at the business clear access to me and my experience, without putting any spin on it. Given that I heard from no one, I doubt that this information was made available to prospective franchisees. If so, definitely an incomplete picture!" he says. "Of course, from the franchisor's perspective, it would most probably want to paint the best picture it could."

After the business had failed, Bill met a former work colleague who had a comprehensive feasibility study done.

"In my opinion, either having a business study done or utilizing a mentor/business consultant may have changed my decision to purchase a franchise."

Some entrepreneurs do ask for advice, but commonly seek advice from friends or family, or even other colleagues. The problem with asking friends and family is not so much that their opinion is not valued, but more that they may lack the background or experience to provide relevant advice. Some will ask insightful questions based on logical thinking, but there are more comprehensive questions that need to be asked about the business, that can only be asked by an experienced mentor. Not doing so cost James Edwards his business and his lifestyle.

James Edwards and his wife operated a convenience store and gas bar as a franchisee for a number of years. This particular gas bar was at a popular intersection and attracted a tremendous amount of traffic, which provided a healthy profit for the franchisor and a steady stream of income for James and his family. With this income, James bought a house with a pool in an upscale neighborhood, both his children attended private school, and the family took lavish holidays from time to time.

There came a time when the franchisor struck a deal with another major company also operating several gas bars in the city. Because the other company already had franchisees signed for all their locations, James did not get the opportunity to continue on and received a substantial cash buyout.

"We took a well-deserved vacation together, and it was during this vacation that me and my wife began to discuss what the next chapter was in our lives after the sale," he says. "What instantly came to our minds was that we were able to run a very profitable convenience store, and knew the products that sold very well, and those that did not sell as well. So, why not just take the money that we received and open up another convenience store? We both loved the idea."

Thinking hypothetically, they worked out how the profitability of the venture would look. They estimated how many customers would buy from them every month, how much the sales would be based on their previous experience at the gas bar, roughly what the operating costs would be, and the eventual profits.

"The money that we would make was very attractive, and the best part of the business is that we would not have to pay our franchisor the 4% royalty payment forever," he says. "That was money in our pockets. And we couldn't wait to tell our friends what we were planning to do."

Excitedly returning from their trip, James and his wife got together with a couple of close friends to tell them the good news and ask their advice. Neither of the friends had any experience running a business, but they listened intently to the logic that James and his wife had worked out while on their vacation. Of course, everybody was excited, and the only question that came up was where the location would be.

"We knew that we had to try and keep our costs low and so we would have to find a reasonable place to locate the business," James says. "Also, because we knew what the customers were purchasing, we can try and encourage them to buy additional products that may go hand-in-hand with their original purchase."

James quickly found out that all of the locations with heavy traffic flow were expensive, so he decided to move to a more industrial location with cheaper rent, thinking customers would come either on their way into work or on their way home.

"We then signed a five-year lease and spent $100,000 on leasehold improvements to make the shelving, and purchase the register and the software and other such stuff," he says. "Then we spent another, I think, $50,000 on getting our inventory in, and ordering our inventory was quite easy as we knew the suppliers before. We had to pay a little bit higher for the inventory because we were no longer attached to the franchisor, who had negotiated cheaper rates because of the volume of purchases, but a few cents here and a few cents there did not really matter."

James and his wife ordered essential items such as colas, bottled water, milk, juices, energy drinks, beef jerky, chips, gum, candy, and had space for a coffee machine. When considering some of the upsell items, James and his wife thought that customers would love knick-knacks such as key chains and funky T-shirts.

"We also thought that we needed to keep small items like bread, jam, cookies, cereal, and other food items because we knew that customers may want to grab these on their way home," he says.

James and his wife then worked out a schedule with James opening the store in the mornings at 6:00am and his wife closing the store at midnight to make sure that they were open long enough. They had a small ribbon-cutting ceremony with their two children and other friends and family, and the convenience store was now open for business.

For the first couple of months, there was a nice uptick in customers that came by because many had just noticed that the convenience store was open. Some customers were happy the store was there because, in emergency situations, they would be able to pick something up.

But soon after, the number of customers became sporadic. There was always a small bubble of customers in the morning as people went to work and a small bubble of customers in the late afternoon as people went home, much like what James and his wife predicted, but the number of customers was nowhere close to what they predicted on vacation.

From Day One, they simply were not making enough money to cover their costs, and they lost a tremendous amount of money every month.

"After six months, we were tapped out financially, and we had lost all our savings," James says. "Finally, I had to declare personal bankruptcy, moving from our dream home into a one-bedroom apartment. We were really ashamed. I really had no experience and, funny enough, I went to work for somebody else in a grocery store just to pay the bills."

James believes the major lesson to take from his failure is, above everything, that he did not ask the right people for advice.

"I was very upset initially at my friends because nobody asked me any questions that would've given me any warning," he says. "But then, my wife told me that it was not our friends' responsibility to answer these questions because they did not know any better. All they knew was to really support us, which they did very well. So really, I was upset at myself. In the excitement, I never asked a proper person who could ask me the tough questions and really get me to think about the problems I would have in the business. Not doing that one VERY SIMPLE step had dashed all our hopes and dreams for us and the kids. And now look at us," he says, tearing up. "All I had to do was ask one person, one intelligent person who would've saved us from what happened. And all I can think about now," he says, tearing up again, "is what my kids are going to think. We live for our kids, you know."

James's sad story, unfortunately, is one that many looking to get into business experience. A qualified mentor would have pointed out to James and his wife that the customers coming into the convenience store at the gas bar were buying gasoline for their vehicles. Buying chips or coffee was not the main purpose of their visit to the convenience store. A better gauge of the number of customers would have been those that were truly walk-ups who had no gas purchases but came to buy groceries. Knowing this, James would have never opened up the convenience store, putting his money to good use somewhere else.

Unfortunately, situations where entrepreneurs sidestep finding a qualified mentor, or ask those with little relevant experience their opinion on the business idea, happen too often. Challenging questions that reveal whether the entrepreneur has planned for difficult situations get missed.

Entrepreneurs may not like the fact that a qualified mentor challenges an excellent business idea. The idea is not to tell the entrepreneur that the idea has no legs, which it may not; if the idea cannot stand up to scrutiny, then maybe there is not a business to be had, or growth will not be as aggressive as projected, or unforeseen costs have not been taken into consideration, for example.

Investing in a qualified mentor will help the entrepreneur answer all the challenging questions with honest, realistic answers, and determine if their idea can become a viable business. Not making that investment could result in what happened with the two case studies illustrated in this chapter, a wipeout of $130,000 of savings and a personal bankruptcy. There are many more stories like these out there that result in the egregious failure statistics for businesses.

Once a qualified mentor is found, the entrepreneur needs to be sure to listen to the mentor's advice. Failing to heed the mentor's advice, as seasoned mentor Chuck Allen has experienced, can lead to a business collapse, or an inefficient business model, such as that of Doug Bourgoyne.

Listen to a Qualified Mentor

A qualified mentor is brought in to help entrepreneurs realize the business hurdles coming that may prevent the business from growing. One company ignored my advice, and 30 days later, poof, it was gone.

– Chuck Allen, CEO – Giyani Gold Corporation

When I look back at all the mistakes that I made, most of them were because I was told by other very experienced entrepreneurs not to do them. I just didn't listen.

– Doug Burgoyne, Co-Founder – FROGBOX

Entrepreneurs reap huge benefits by seeking experienced advice from a qualified mentor. What makes mentors qualified? They have the appropriate depth of knowledge and experience to ask tough questions and provide frank advice to an entrepreneur. This may not make for a popular discussion, but it is better to spend the time and money being warned about the pitfalls in opening or running a business rather than scrambling much later to try to ensure the business can jump over the hurdles that the qualified mentor might have mentioned. By listening to the advice, and acting accordingly, entrepreneurs are sure to save themselves a lot of headaches, allowing them to concentrate on the business rather than fight preventable fires.

Despite having an experienced mentor, some entrepreneurs decide to ignore the advice mentors give, feeling that they are better positioned to move the business forward by themselves. Taking this route may still end up in success, but, for the most part, ignoring this advice drastically increases the odds of the business stalling, and in some cases even failing. Chuck Allen, a seasoned business mentor, shares a few examples.

Chuck Allen is CEO of Giyani Gold Corporation and also serves as a Cleantech and Technology Advisor for MaRS Discovery District in Toronto, Ontario, mentoring many start-up companies in the clean technology space. His extensive background includes filling senior executive roles, and he has an impressive track record of growing businesses or business units in North America, Europe, Latin America, and Africa by focusing on building strong relationships with clients and using innovative management, leadership, accountability, communication, and process-based skills to create corporate and revenue growth, operational efficiencies, and support stakeholder objectives.

Among Chuck's many accomplishments, he used a combination of organic growth and strategic acquisitions to grow Oneworld Energy into a diversified international renewable energy company with 10 offices world-wide. Under his guidance and leadership, revenues grew from $2.7 million in 2008 to over $25 million in one year, with expectations that those revenues would more than double in 2010.

Chuck has mentored many entrepreneurs, and on some occasions he sees an attitude that entrepreneurs just do not want to listen to advice. The business becomes personal to them, and receiving critical advice does not sit well.

"What you see out there is that the entrepreneurs start to feel that it's their idea, it's their business," Chuck says. "What you also see is lots of ideas. The idea is great. There are lots of people with great ideas but never went anywhere with them. You'll see people with lots of money that have burned it into the ground and have done nothing with good ideas and bad ideas. There's a reason for that."

In one particular case, Chuck was an advisor for a company with a promising technology with applications to a number of industries. The anticipation surrounding this technology drew many early offers from investors with sizable amounts of money.

The entrepreneurs wanted to paint a wide swath and apply the technology to every relevant industry sector at the same time, which was not recommended. Chuck advised them to do well in a couple of industry sectors, prove the success of the technology, and then move to the other sectors. Going after multiple industries not only spreads the company too thin in terms of resources, but more importantly, it requires heavy funding. The conversation continued:

Entrepreneur: Chuck, I just won't do it. To do that would limit the possibilities, and the possibilities are endless.

Chuck: But you don't have the money, and by doing that, nobody's going to give you the money. And you're not creating success in any two sectors because you're not focusing on this. Maybe you have to license this to somebody else and let somebody else run with it.

Entrepreneur: Oh, but then I'd only be getting a revenue stream.

Chuck: You know what, what's wrong with a revenue stream?

Entrepreneur: But I could be making so much more!

In the end, the entrepreneur did not take Chuck's advice and failed to understand what it took to be successful. The entrepreneur decided to move on, and, not surprisingly, there has been no news from him or the business. This is typical of most entrepreneurs who push aside experienced advice because it is advice they do not want to hear.

Generally, businesses experience a ramp up in revenues until they hit a ceiling. For some businesses, the entrepreneurs are fine with reaching this ceiling and continuing on. Often, mentors are needed when entrepreneurs look to push through this ceiling so the business can keep growing.

This was the case for one particular company that was in an attractive industry, run by two intelligent individuals with marketing backgrounds. Not only did they market the product effectively, but they also developed the technical aspects of the product well. In a conversation with one of the entrepreneurs, Chuck asked him how he wanted to grow his business.

Entrepreneur: We know that if we want to grow, all we have to do is spend more money on marketing, but we really don't want to do that. So we are going to try and find other ways.

Chuck: Well, what are the other ways?

Entrepreneur: We're hoping that viral marketing will help us.

Chuck: If one of your largest clients took this on, and, you know, want you to double, triple, or quadruple the order, are you ready for that?

Entrepreneur: Well, there's the other reason that we don't want to do this, because we're not ready to do that.

Chuck: So you guys are happy doing this, and not being able to grow your business because, to grow your business means you have got to do things that you're not doing right now, so you'd rather not do them?

Entrepreneur: That is the essence of it.

When an entrepreneur is ready to move outside their comfort zone to grow the business and break through a revenue ceiling, new resources need to be added to the team. If those with the right skills are brought in at the right time, the business will move forward; however, too often these new resources are added too late to make a difference.

Often, founders balk at the advice given to bring in additional key team members because they believe they can wear multiple hats to fill in various roles and still have the organization grow. The reality is that talent is limited. Even with one or two extra resources, there is still a limit to the talent available to grow the company. This lack of talent stunts any possible growth, reducing opportunities to monetize the business idea, no matter how much promise the idea holds.

"If you truly want to try and create success, you really need to understand what your needs are and what challenges you have to bring to the table," says Chuck. "If you don't have all the talent you need, and not very many of those mom-and-pop type shops will, some will be able to rise above it and to develop the kinds of skills that are required, but sometimes you need to bring people in from the outside. A couple of them made that decision probably much later than they should have. But, when they brought people in, they weren't prepared to truly integrate these people into their businesses."

Adding talent takes sacrifice, but many entrepreneurs find it difficult to give up equity in the company when the going is good to add high quality resources to take the business to a greater level. Unsurprisingly, many entrepreneurs want to keep everything for themselves rather than add resources to make the business more money.

"It should be easy for people to understand that it's better to have 15% or 25% of something incredibly large rather than 100% of something that's worthless," says Chuck. "So many of these people are so deeply and madly in love with the business and feel that this is going to be a monstrous opportunity and all of a sudden we see the Gollum effect[20] – it's mine, all mine. As a result, they can't get beyond that. Logically, they should be thinking that 'if you do this, and, you know, we bring in this team, and we share this wealth'. Share is an operative word; it's good for all of us."

If the business has excellent growth potential but requires an injection of capital from an investor for it to grow, entrepreneurs tend to either drastically overvalue the company, or feel they can go ahead without the investment as the Gollum effect takes over. The consequences of not sharing can come fast and furious.

"I was part of one business where I found the money for us to be able to grow, and we were going to split the shares of the business amongst ourselves," says Chuck. "An investor was going to take a big chunk of this, and [the founders] were not prepared to do it. And the thing collapsed 30 days later. This was part of a dream that this family wanted to run for a very long, long time."

While Chuck can provide many examples of cases where his advice was ignored, with poor results for those entrepreneurs, Doug Burgoyne is able to share some insight into an entrepreneur making the mistake of not listening to good advice.

Doug Burgoyne is Co-Founder of FROGBOX, a company that delivers re-useable moving boxes and supplies to those who are moving, picking these up when the move is over. The company has relied on word-of-mouth, similar to Seth Godin's definition of tribes[21].

"In Vancouver, we are 27% word-of-mouth and 18% repeat business, and when you think about when people move, it's not very often," Doug says. "Once we get a customer, they absolutely love the product."

The idea for FROGBOX came to Doug when he and his business partner looked at opening a business that was simple to operate. At the time, both had full-time jobs, with Doug working in high-tech sales.

---

20 A mythical creature featured in J.R.R. Tolkien's trilogy, *The Lord of the Rings*, who is obsessed by hoarding ownership of a particular ring.

21 Seth Godin defines a tribe as a group of people who are connected to one another, a leader or an idea.

"Every two weeks, we would select businesses that we admired and we really cared about, and wanted to get behind, not just for financial purposes," Doug says. "We talked about businesses such as Patagonia, lululemon and Whole Foods, companies like that, and we tried to find out what we liked about all these companies."

They came up with a number of characteristics that they wanted their business to have. One was ensuring that they had a good brand. They also wanted the business to be eco-friendly or "better than the alternative" for the environment. The business had to have a wellness aspect to it. Scalability was also important as they wanted to do one thing only and do it well. The business had to solve a problem that they both had experienced, and had to be one lacking in customer service so that the business could thrive on word-of-mouth advertising.

After putting all these qualities together on paper and thinking of an industry that had the least customer service exposure, they came up with the moving industry. However, they knew that they did not want to be movers because this was labour-intensive and a tough business to run. So they began thinking about associated services connected to moving that they could offer, and they came up with plastic reusable bins that they could rent out.

They knew they had a large market because in North America and Europe people often move themselves, especially with the high cost of hiring commercial movers. Providing moving materials such as boxes, paper, and packing tape was not a unique business as there were a couple of companies in Vancouver already providing such a service. In fact, Doug looked at buying one of these companies. He came close to finalizing the deal, but he soon realized that re-creating the whole brand would require a tremendous amount of effort, which did not make sense for Doug and his partner, and they walked away from the deal.

After speaking to a few people, Doug and his partner decided to test the business out.

"We bought some cheap boxes and a 1970s milk truck, and started a cheap website to test the idea out," Doug says. "We both had full-time jobs at the time and hired somebody from Craigslist to help with sales. He is now Director of Sales and part owner of the Toronto franchise, which is his biggest market."

While they did not make much money, the concept began to take off in Vancouver. Customers loved the service, and Doug and his partner had a strong sense that this would grow. They were not interested in making this a local regional business, and decided to try the model in the US to make sure it would work. They secured a small amount of funding and opened a location in Seattle where Doug had to monitor it full-time, and hence had to quit his full-time job. The new location also did well.

Despite the incremental success, getting customers to think about renting boxes from FROGBOX was quite tough.

As Doug states, "When people move, it's such a special time, and moving boxes are not the first thing the people think of. So when they move, they usually say, hey I've got to get cardboard boxes. How you change that customer perception and that decision is really hard. It is a slow and organic growth process."

Doug also comments on his commitment to being customer-centric and delivering exceptional customer service.

"We said that we needed a great brand and we needed to make people have FROGBOX as top of mind when they are thinking of moving," he says. "So we look at two things: brand and absolute focus on customer service. If there's any problem whatsoever, we just give people their money back. We are really in the early stages where we need them talking about us with their friends."

Doug had been involved with a company that constantly acquired franchising companies. This experience had opened his eyes to what should not be done in franchising. He saw many companies with great ideas that immediately thought about money coming in through the selling of franchises. However, these companies had not proven their business model. They assumed that they could collect the franchise fees, which would be allocated to perfecting the franchise system, which would then work out profitably. But this simply was not the case.

Given the experience, Doug initially decided to run a number of corporate stores before franchising the business. Franchising the business would be easy because it differed from the typical high capital upfront cost franchising model, which would mean franchisees need a higher amount of upfront investment. For a typical FROGBOX franchise, the upfront fee required would only be $30,000, a low investment for a high margin business, with a relatively quick payback if the franchisee sold aggressively.

Doug and his partner appeared on the Canadian show, Dragon's Den, where two of the Dragons, Jim Treliving and Brett Wilson, came on board as investors. Their appearance on this popular show also had the company's phone ringing off the hook as the number of requests for franchises exploded.

Because of this sudden surge in franchise opportunities, Doug created a list of criteria that would help him select what type of franchisee he felt comfortable bringing on board. The first criterion was that the individual had to be from that particular city. This would ensure the franchisee would have existing local contacts to leverage for potential business opportunities. Second, they had to have a strong values alignment as FROGBOX required the franchisee to commit on paper to donating 1% of revenues to environmental causes. Shaving that 1% from revenues would be tough for potential franchisees to think about, but this was important for Doug and the brand that he and his partner were creating.

Next, he needed someone who was well-capitalized and had some business savvy. With low franchise fees, a potential franchisee would not be putting his or her entire life savings on the line.

Finally, he needed hungry people who needed to generate a lot of profit from the business to feed their families. This would ensure that the franchisee would put the maximum amount of energy into making that particular franchise successful. Without that hunger, potential franchisees could shift their focus away from FROGBOX to their real job and wait for the FROGBOX franchise to take off.

Doug knew that he needed more time to perfect the business model but he had gotten excited at the number of requests for franchises after being on Dragon's Den. He went ahead and began to franchise, and soon realized that he had made a mistake.

"The biggest mistake I made was in franchising too quickly," he says.

The company continued to be strong in larger markets such as Toronto and Vancouver, but did not fare well in some smaller markets, mainly because the franchisees had other sources of income and were not putting 100% of their effort into FROGBOX. Doug felt that the press generated from their appearance on Dragon's Den and the momentum from opening lots of franchises would be beneficial enough to build the brand to outweigh the negatives of franchising early.

"I had known that you can't live off your franchise fees," he says. "But, you know, I can literally sell one hundred franchises in the US right now this quarter. There's something about our brand that people like. We don't have a history of the financial performance to back it up. But, people really want to buy our brand."

Another problem arose from franchising too quickly: without a perfected system, Doug and his partner took the focus away from increasing revenues from the Vancouver business and perfecting the business model to getting the franchisees up and running. But Doug knew this as he had been given some advice from a well-respected franchise expert.

"I was told by a very well-respected individual with tremendously deep experience in franchising to wait and not franchise yet," he says. "And I just didn't listen. He kept reminding us to perfect the model, perfect the model. You're almost there in Vancouver. At the time we owned three corporate stores, one in Vancouver, one in Seattle, and one in Toronto."

After coming on board as an investor, Jim Treliving also suggested that FROGBOX was too early in its development to franchise, especially in the United States. Jim knew this well; he had spent a few million dollars trying to expand in the US, and Jim's company, Boston Pizza, still had a ways to go. Given this expensive experience, Doug was advised to slow down.

Finally, Doug listened. He completely stopped entertaining calls from potential franchisees so that he could focus his attention on perfecting the business model and being a much bigger company, rather than trying to accelerate the business.

The hard part for Doug was realizing the opportunity cost[22] in slowing down. He estimates that he could have sold 20 franchises in a period of six months, not to mention the PR exposure that would come along with this expansion. But with hindsight being 20/20, he is not

---

22 Opportunity cost is the opportunity that is lost, financial or otherwise, by taking a certain path. For example, by taking one path, a business earns $100,000 in revenues. However, if it took a different path, it would have been able to earn $150,000 in revenues. By committing to the path that it did, the business actually forgoes the opportunity to earn $50,000 more in revenues, the calculated difference. This $50,000 difference represents the opportunity cost.

sure if having those 20 franchises come on board would have made a difference.

"I don't know if I would have been better prepared to take on an extra 20 franchisees, or if it would have even made a difference. That's a tough one," he says. "Hindsight is 20/20. But by taking our time, we also have the benefit of having a franchise that people love working in. People like it because of the environment, and people like it because of our product. If it was purely a franchise based on financial performance, I think my franchisees would be a lot less happy."

Doug now knows that the success of his business is not about selling hundreds of franchises just to make a short-term financial gain, but more of putting all the resources back into the company to make a typical franchise the best investment possible for a franchisee.

Entrepreneurs looking to franchise generally focus on the upfront collection of revenues from the franchisees, when they should focus on the recurring revenue. This makes it much more attractive for franchisees.

Doug does a quick calculation to illustrate his point.

"If you do the math, if you have a $30,000 franchise fee, and sell 200 franchises, then you have $6 million in franchise fees to play with," he explains. "So, you can sell them now, or perfect the model and attract high quality franchisees. With higher quality franchisees, although you will defer the $6 million upfront franchise fee, you will have a better chance to live comfortably off the 7% royalty."

To properly wrap one's thinking around the upfront franchise fee, Doug suggests that it be treated as an investment in the franchisee.

"The upfront fees should almost be written off, and should be put back into things like training," he says. "The model seems so simple where it's a high margin process and all you have to really do is train somebody. But what you really want to do is set that franchisee up for success. You can blow all the $30,000 on training and give more to that person. At the end of the day, if that franchisee is not making money, you are also not making any money and they may even sue you. You also have to think about giving them your most valuable possession, which is your brand in their city."

Ultimately, Doug raised money through the issuance of shares rather than franchise fees, and perfected the system.

The $6 million will still be there; it will just be $6 million in franchise fees that are collected later. But these will be collected from high quality franchisees and with a perfected franchise model. FROGBOX now has partners for life.

Holding back and refocusing has certainly helped the growth of FROGBOX. When Doug and his partner started in Vancouver, they experienced 100% revenue growth. After deciding to franchise, growth slowed to 22% that year and 20% the year after as the focus shifted to development of the franchisee. After delaying the acquisition of franchisees, Doug and his partner refocused on Vancouver and grew it by an additional 40% and they now look to grow it by another 50% this year.

"It's hard to get these things into people's minds that it's not the right thing to do to just open one store in one city and then start beginning to franchise," Doug says. "If you don't understand franchising, it seems like a get-rich-quick scheme. And what's funny is that I knew that it wasn't, from my previous experience. And I still went out and did it. It's a hard way to make a living."

Chuck and Doug illustrate the ramifications of failing to heed the advice of mentors. Knowing that the business will face continuous hurdles, listening to the advice of others who have gone through these hurdles themselves is an absolute must. From the mentor's perspective, Chuck showed that not listening to his advice has resulted in companies stalling, and in one case, closing its doors within 30 days. From a company's perspective, Doug began to make the mistake of franchising too soon, despite the advice of a mentor, resulting in a weaker franchise model. The results are common to both: the business suffers.

One of the pieces of advice that qualified mentors seem to commonly give is being cautious when hiring family and friends. Although they may share in the excitement of starting a business with an entrepreneur, they may simply lack the appropriate skills and talent required, and during times of disagreement, an entrepreneur may not want to engage in difficult conversations for fear of losing the relationship. In some situations, the entrepreneur might have to choose between the relationship and the business, as was the case for Bill Charles and Samuel Chandler.

Be Cautious When Hiring Family and Friends

It is very difficult to criticize the CEO when the members of the board of directors are all friends and family. In my case, this lack of ability to challenge the CEO almost resulted in the company going bankrupt.

– Bill Charles, Vice-Chairman – Major US Manufacturing Company

To my shock and dismay, my father brought his girlfriend into the company as a partner. She did not help the company in areas where it was needed. When I asked why she was even there, I was asked to leave the company.

– Samuel Chandler, Entrepreneur

If there is a single piece of advice entrepreneurs hear time and time again, it is to exercise caution when thinking about hiring family or friends. Of course, they may be your biggest supporters either emotionally or in some cases financially, but involving them in the business may seem easy at the beginning when the business is looking to take off and everything is rosy.

The problem starts with improperly evaluating why you want family and friends as resources to help your business move forward. The most common mistake involves asking them to join the company in a certain capacity and fill a role that "seems" appropriate for their background and experience, regardless of how directly that experience relates to the role being filled.

Friends and family may generate excitement and ideas for the business, but that does not necessarily translate well into satisfactorily delivering in a certain role. So, having "some" marketing experience may not be sufficient to properly fill a position that requires extensive marketing skills.

Properly filling these roles is crucial to getting the business off the ground. The entrepreneur should first look at the skill sets the roles in question require, and then match those skill sets with the appropriate resources, without making exceptions for friends or family members. Obviously, if they have the right amount of relevant experience and skills to move the business forward, given the stage that the business is in, then, by all means, they would be appropriate hires. But the entrepreneur needs to be 100% confident that this is the case.

Another consideration, often missed by entrepreneurs, is the difficulty of addressing conflicts with the family member or friend, whether due to sub-par performance or a general disagreement on issues. Worse, if the entrepreneur has to let a relative or friend go, entering the room, closing the door, and starting that conversation would be agonizing for most of us. Not only is this a difficult conversation to have, but it may spell the end of that particular relationship.

Often, family and friends become involved as advisors to the firm. Although they may have excellent backgrounds, they may not be able to provide unbiased business advice, which can be critical. Such was the case for Bill Charles.

Bill Charles is Vice-Chairman of a major US manufacturing company and has been involved in a number of start-ups as investor and advisor. He has tremendous experience as a board member for various organizations in addition to having an extensive network of contacts who also serve as board members.

"As a member of the board of directors, one of the duties is to ensure that the CEO is adhering to the outlined strategy put in place," Bill explains. "If there is deviation from this strategic plan, the CEO needs to tell the board of directors why this has happened, and how the company can get back on track. The board of directors will usually give some time for the CEO to realign the firm, and if not, then a change at the helm should be a strong possibility."

When friends or family sit on the board of directors, personal friendships tend to prevent them from raising business concerns and challenging the CEO on issues. This leads to certain business issues being avoided altogether. Over time, the number of issues being avoided could be significant enough to seriously affect the business in a negative way.

Another avoidance tactic may be to raise critical issues in a passive tone. This downplays the critical nature of that issue, and the CEO may not give the proper time and attention to the issue. In this scenario, the CEO may continue operating down a faulty path, possibly putting the company in harm's way. The board member would not have done his or her duty of properly advising the CEO.

"Many years ago, my brother-in-law had started a private company, and gathered a number of friends and family, including myself," says Bill. "I was elected as Chairman of the Board, and met with the other board members on a quarterly basis, many of whom were personal friends of my brother-in-law, the CEO. None of them were prepared to challenge the CEO."

The company grew successfully, but there came a point in time when the brother-in law's strategy was steering the company in a bad direction and revenues suffered.

"At some point in time, my brother-in-law had been implementing a strategy that had gotten the company into trouble, one that many of us on the board felt was not in the best interest of the company," Bill says. "Normally, some sort of monitoring controls would have been in place to alert both the CEO and the board of directors that something was not right. But because of the close friendships around the board, we failed to implement these controls. Also, because he was my brother-in-law and he was friends with all the board members, how could we challenge him?"

The revenues continued to decline rapidly, and soon the company was close to bankruptcy. Bill had to make a decision, not only because he was Chairman of the Board, but he had to think about the reputations of the other board members. If the company went bankrupt, all of the board members would have this as a black mark on their professional careers. As senior executives well known within their industries, this was not a good situation.

After some tough negotiations, Bill convinced his brother-in-law that he needed to step down. Once a new CEO was put in place, the company's fiscal picture brightened and bankruptcy was avoided. The new CEO brought a sense of independence between him and the board of directors, which made raising issues less challenging than before.

"There are three lessons to be learned from such a situation," Bill says. "One is to make sure that there is a degree of independence between the CEO and the board of directors. This allows proper controls to be put in place to monitor the CEO's progress with no bias or undue influence. Any deviations to the strategy can properly be questioned and corrected. The second lesson is to ensure that there is a good relationship between the CEO and the Chairman of the Board as the Chairman of the Board has to chair board meetings, set the agenda, and address key issues. Therefore, chemistry is crucial. The third lesson is to ensure that a company has directors with experience and knowledge in similar companies, and that they are prepared to challenge the CEO. This background ensures that relevant questions and issues are discussed during board meetings rather than having board members try and learn the business while trying to provide opinions on the direction of the company."

As Bill's story demonstrates, a board of directors that includes friends and family of the CEO can have difficulty articulating problems to the CEO. Not only should board members be able to express independent thought without hesitation, but they must also have some relevant experience and knowledge to give proper advice.

Difficulties can also arise when friends or family join a company as management or employees. For Samuel and his father, Rick, tensions and frictions started to happen when Rick brought on a close friend who had little to no skills in moving the company forward. In fact, she sadly broke up the father-son management team.

In 1993, Samuel Chandler and his father, Rick Chandler, both with backgrounds in mill work and framing, were looking to purchase a company in the manufacturing area when an opportunity to purchase a door manufacturing business from a gentleman who was retiring came up. The business was quite healthy with a modest client base, four to five employees, and 6,000 square-feet of manufacturing space.

The business manufactured high-quality custom doors and door frames, a niche area that ensured that it did not compete with the larger companies. Samuel and Rick decided to purchase the company and began to work on improving the business right away with the father, Rick, owning 75% of the company's shares and Samuel owning the other 25%.

"Through sheer hard work and long hours, my father and I were able to have an immediate impact on the business operations, adding tremendous value right away," says Samuel. "Within three to four months, the business had really taken off. Our company moved to a larger 10,000 square-foot building, added more employees, and continued delivering the niche custom work to our current clients. I mainly looked after the sales and marketing end of the business, and my father made sure that we had good relationships with the existing clientele and helped in the administrative functions of the company."

In 1996, much to Samuel's surprise, his father, who was divorced at the time, sold a small portion of his shares to his girlfriend, and tasked her with helping in the sales and administrative functions of the company. Samuel was already helping in the sales area, and he was not aware of any shortfalls in the administrative function area. Despite this, Samuel went with the decision and decided to work more in the manufacturing end of the business to get more exposure in that area while still working in a sales role.

This dual function helped Samuel expand the company's product offerings, driving revenues that were in line with the business's competitors. With additional growth, the company needed to hire independent sales representatives throughout the country. This further propelled business revenues and cash flows, and the company had to triple its space requirements, going from a 10,000 square-foot building into a 35,000 square-foot space.

With this expansion, the order book was healthy, but the operational end of things became messy. The focus shifted to getting the products out the door over operational efficiencies. Because of this, proper controls were not put in place to evaluate costs of asset purchases and production costs, both of which were high. Not having these proper controls in place affected the business significantly, especially during the dot-com crash in 2000. The order book receded and the business was still saddled with expensive inventory and production costs, shrinking profits significantly.

"When we entered the recession, I really began to think about why my father brought in this other partner," Samuel says. "She was supposed to work in the administrative area and help sales, but outside of seeing her fax some documents and make some calls I did not see her help in the sales area at all. It soon became clear to me that she did not have much experience. So I wondered what that heck she was doing there."

From time to time, Samuel would casually bring up his concerns about the third partner. However, his father would insist that he needed her in the office. When Samuel tried to find out what her exact duties were and how much time she spent performing those duties, the conversation was shut down. Samuel started to seriously question why this partner was even a part of the company.

"I let my problem with the third partner go for a few years, but at some point, I had to take the gloves off," he says. "I really had to get to the bottom of what this partner was really doing, as it was definitely affecting me personally and the company as a whole, in which I was partner. When I told my father that this partner was just not adding value to the company, despite me having some very clear arguments, I couldn't believe that he threw his blind support behind this person. I just couldn't believe it. This was my own father. After trying to bring this topic up over the next few months, my father finally insisted that if I didn't want the partner in the business, I would have to buy her out. This was really a slap in my face."

Samuel decided to back off and concentrate on the business. The business faced another recession in 2009 and sales fell off drastically with a rapidly disappearing backlog of orders the company relied upon. The stress of the financial situation got to Samuel, and finally, he had had enough with the partner's inability to contribute to the company and began the process of buying her out.

"I approached my father and told him that I was ready to buy this other person's shares," he recalls. "I'm not sure what happened to my father, but the most bizarre thing was that he said that if I was going to buy her out, I would have to buy him out as well. I really did not know what was going through my father's head at the time. So I scraped together whatever money I could to move ahead with the purchase of shares. I approached my father with the financing all arranged and he then turned around and wrote me a cheque for my shares! At this point, I really did not want to stir up too much and made the decision to take the money and leave to help save whatever relationship I had with my father."

Samuel took a year and a half off after working 60 to 70 hour weeks, finally getting a chance to spend some quality time with his family, but still had a yearning to get back in the game. He kept in touch with his father's company as, oddly, his wife was still working there. The company's problems continued with falling sales providing little to no profit each quarter. Neither Rick nor his partner were in touch with the production, the sales, or the customers, and accepted manufacturing jobs with no clue as to whether these jobs were profitable.

Because retail cabinetry was in his blood, Samuel started up his own firm. He gathered some financing, purchased all-new state-of-the-art equipment, hired key people with the proper skills and experience, and quickly gained sales. Although in the same business as his father, Samuel was not in direct competition with him as he manufactured low volume, high margin custom work, whereas his father manufactured mid-margin, higher volume products. In fact, 75% of the revenues from Samuel's company came from manufacturing custom products for his father's company, although he was in a much better financial position than his father's company.

After experiencing operational problems with the previous business, Samuel learned to grow his new business at a slow and steady pace, making smart business decisions along the way. When he started, he ran the business lean, without an order entry system, a scheduling system, or an order tracking system. At the time, he simply did not have the volume of orders to justify those investments and wanted to ensure that he did not grow too big and too fast like his father's business.

Today, Samuel has doubled his square footage and has invested in an order entry system as well as plant tracking and scheduling software. He has also increased his sales volume enough to justify bringing on an independent sales representative. From a personal standpoint, he carries an excellent reputation in the industry, and on the business front, he is comfortable with the slow and steady approach as it fits with the business model of doing custom work and delivering products on time and on budget. He does not want to be everything to everyone.

Rick and his girlfriend ended up selling the company at a significant discount. The new owner has continued the business with the small number of customers it currently has, and is currently looking for a buyer to take over. Surprisingly, some of Rick's current customers want to switch their business orders to Samuel, but he cares deeply about the employees who are still working there, and will not accept this new business unless the company successfully gets sold, and the employees are taken care of financially. Once that happens, Samuel estimates that he will have enough of a backlog to bring on those employees. As of now, Samuel estimates that with the current level of business, his father's former company can only survive for another 12 to 18 months.

In both of these stories, having friends and family within a firm or in an advisory role created business challenges that affected the business's performance. Bringing in friends or family members will not always affect the business in a negative fashion; certainly many successful businesses employ friends and family members as advisors or employees and they continue to do well. There are benefits to having someone you know and trust work within your company, but only when their experience matches the position and when their roles and expectations are clearly laid out. So, it can work, but an entrepreneur needs to make sure that there is proper justification in place.

Some entrepreneurs think that money could be saved by finding somebody with lesser qualifications required for a position commensurate with a lower hourly rate, assuming that things will work out. In some cases, things do work out, but there could be a risk that the resource produces sub-standard results at a time when the business needs all the help it can get with whatever limited resources it brings on. The resource might also begin to feel overwhelmed due to the pressure, or overloaded due to the lack of experience, with a good possibility of leaving. This restarts the hiring process once again, and yet another resource is brought in at similarly low hourly rate, and the cycle continues.

Did you really save money?

Entrepreneurs should think about the possible gains the business would have had, financially or operationally, had the right resource been hired.

The result of a bad hire?

Wasted time, effort, efficiencies, money, and, in John Sparling's case cutting corners in HR resulted in all of his employees leaving, shutting the doors of his business for good.

Don't Cut Corners in HR

*I thought that I could save costs by getting rid of a
manager and cutting hourly rates for employees. But this
backfired. Because of that, I really pissed a customer off,
and created an embarrassing situation in the store for me.
I also lost credibility from my own staff, and I had to close
doors because nobody would work for me anymore.*

— John Sparling, Former Video Store Owner

When positions are being filled within a company, it is
vital to ensure the resources filling those positions have
the appropriate education and skill sets to be effective in
that role. If this is not done properly, the desired outcomes
for that position will simply not happen. This affects the business
because it still lacks those outcomes, and at some point, the business
could slow down and possibly stall.

If corners are cut when trying to hire resources, the entrepreneur
takes a risk in doing so. Every resource will need to perform to the best
of his or her ability at the most crucial time for the business: the start-
up phase.

The business now has resources that are under-qualified that could
result in them being overwhelmed or overloaded, adding stress. Some
resources are asked to manage people through promotion when that
resource has no management skills whatsoever, which could result in a
caustic work environment, as is the case in the next chapter.

Now you have even more employees unhappy, and all of a sudden,
an entrepreneur's attention shifts from bringing in much-needed revenues to reviewing resumes again, re-interviewing, re-training, and so

on. And if the cost-cutting lesson is not learned the first time, another under-qualified resource is brought in, and the same issues begin to percolate.

A focus on cost control is essential for the entrepreneur to grow the business in a conservative fashion, a piece of advice that Som Seif provides in the next section. The entrepreneur may not have the capital to begin hiring right away. But realize the risks and trade-offs that need to be made in employing resources that do not have the proper skills and qualifications for a particular position. The business needs all the horsepower it can get right from the start.

John Sparling filtered his staffing requirements through a cost-saving lens that cost him his reputation among the staff and eventually the whole business.

In the early '80s, John Sparling owned and operated five video stores in several malls in Vancouver. He had no previous experience in the video store market, nor was he a movie buff, but he was encouraged by a friend who had shown him the profitability from a number of video stores that the friend had owned in Toronto. Seeing these great numbers, John decided to open some video stores of his own. He arranged for financing and signed a 10-year lease agreement with one particular mall.

Of course, there was a tremendous amount of competition around the mall, but John decided to employ a strategy to offer paid memberships that allowed customers to get 10% off rental fees, every 10th video rental free, and exclusive reservations for new titles.

To start the first store, John needed a manager to take over staffing, stocking, and ordering of video titles so that John could concentrate on opening other stores as well as managing the company's finances. Luckily, John was able to source a family friend, Tim, who had previous experience managing several video stores, and brought him on board.

Tim advised John that to properly run a video store location, each one required a manager, and one full-time and two part-time employees. John told Tim his plan to expand video locations into other malls, and advised him that when hiring, the employees should be paid minimum wage and the manager a dollar per hour higher.

"Because of my insistence in keeping my wages low, Tim and I got into an argument right away," he says. "He wanted to pay a much higher rate for employees than I wanted to pay, especially for managers. For the regular employees, I thought the position required someone with little to no skill sets which meant that the position was really worth minimum wage. But Tim tried to tell me that by paying slightly more, he would not have to constantly worry about the turnover when managing staff. Someone working for minimum wage would have absolutely no allegiance to the company and I thought that this was ridiculous as we were giving somebody a job."

Then came the discussion about managers.

"What I was paying Tim was an exception because I needed him to start the business," he says, "but I suggested that the other managers be paid less. Tim said that this was unfair and that the other managers would find out eventually, putting Tim in a very uncomfortable position. If Tim was going to be running the team, all managers had to be paid equally. If Tim was to hire somebody at a lower rate, then Tim knew that he would be spending more time training this person than having this person actually run a store from the get-go. After seeing that Tim was quite steadfast, I relented, although I was not very happy with the decision."

The business opened its doors with a full complement of staff thanks to Tim's help. The customers found out about the membership fees, and the tremendous value offered, and revenues began to take off. Over the next six months, John opened four other video stores also located in malls and business started to pick up in those locations as well.

Despite strong revenues, John was still bothered by three particular line items on the financial statements: lease expenses, inventory costs (the videos themselves), and wage expenses. John also knew that he carried a heavy debt burden, and wanted to pay that off quickly.

John could not change the lease agreements, but thought that he could lower his wage expense by trying to lower the dollar per hour rates of the employees. He approached Tim to see if he could convince the employees to take a cut in their wage.

"When I asked Tim about trying to save a dollar per hour for the employees, he gave me a very stunned look," he says. "Of course, Tim was not willing to do that and I knew that this would become an issue again and again. So I began losing faith in Tim. I also noticed that Tim seemed to order the more expensive videos from our supplier. I took a closer look at what Tim actually did and in my mind, it seemed quite simple: schedule and monitor staff, order videos, and make sure that the cash balances of the end of the day."

John began to calculate that if he could take over Tim's role, and somehow get the other employees to increase their responsibilities, then Tim would not be needed and the business would be able to save a significant amount of wages every month.

"I thought to myself, I can schedule staff and order the videos," he says. "I can also train the other staff to balance the cash as it was quite easy. Confident that I could take on this role, I thought I would test it out in one location first, so I let Tim go. And I got excited because I just saved myself several dollars per hour! If I get good at this job, then maybe I can manage two stores at the same time, and I can double my savings. That means more money in my pocket."

The news of Tim being fired traveled fast to the other stores as he had gained a significant amount of respect across all the stores. Of course, John was not open about why he let Tim go, stating that things just did not work out. But the business moved forward.

John found that managing the employees was quite easy as the schedules were generally set by the employees themselves, filling all the available shifts. At the top of the month, it was time to order videos for that month, and John looked over the video titles.

At the top of the form were two featured new releases, *Under the Volcano* and *Rocky III*. When looking at the price points, he noticed that *Rocky III* was considerably more expensive, and he was not impressed with the description of a movie about a boxer. *Under the Volcano* was much cheaper, and the description seemed more thrilling. So he ordered only one copy of *Rocky III* and 10 copies of *Under the Volcano*.

Posters went up notifying the members of the new releases that were soon to hit the video shelves, and a high number of members began reserving *Rocky III* on a first-come first-serve basis, with no waiting list for *Under the Volcano*.

When the videos actually came in, the employees were shocked that only one copy of *Rocky III* was ordered, and assumed that because of the popularity of the video, more copies would be coming in the mail at a later date. But they never did come in, and members began to get angry at the staff, and the staff began to get angry at John.

Despite his hesitation at paying a premium price, John was forced to order another nine copies of the *Rocky III* video. It was clear to the employees that John simply did not know what he was doing when ordering videos. This lack of product knowledge resulted in an embarrassing situation for John.

One of the complaints that the store often received was that there were not enough videos for children, and John decided to tackle this problem on his own. John had heard some rumblings about a cartoon movie called *Fritz the Cat*. He assumed that because people were talking about this cartoon movie it was quite popular, and approached his video supplier, but the supplier told him that they did not carry such videos, which confused John as it was a cartoon.

John put a notice in the store to see if any of his customers were able to find copies of this cartoon. A week later, a box was left on John's desk with a colour picture of a cartoon cat with the *Fritz the Cat* title. John immediately put the video out into the children's section, with a note that this children's movie was now available.

That weekend, a parent came in asking John for his suggestion of a good children's video for a birthday party. John proudly pointed to his sign saying that he was able to secure the *Fritz the Cat* cartoon. The parent had not heard of it, but took John up on his suggestion, paid for it, and went on her way.

The next afternoon, the same parent came back to the store fuming mad. The conversation went like this:

Parent: Where is that damn person that told me to rent this video?

Staff Member: I'll go get him.

John: Hi Ma'am, how can I help you?

Parent: Do you remember me from yesterday? You told me to rent this video.

John: Yes, I did.

Parent: Do you know what type of video this is? Why did you have it in the children's section? Did you not know that it is not appropriate for children?

John: I don't understand. It is supposed to be a popular cartoon is it not? That is why I ordered it.

Parent: It absolutely is a cartoon. But it is a cartoon porn, you idiot!

The parent threw the video at John and stormed out of the store, vowing never to come again, and ensured that she told as many people as possible not to come to the video store ever again.

"I was so embarrassed," John says. "I clearly did not know what I was doing. So I appointed one of the other store managers to take over ordering the videos from that point forward."

However, John's obsession with cost-cutting continued, keeping only one or two pens in each store and asking staff to not use as much paper. Eventually he made his way back to wages and began asking each employee to take a dollar per hour cut in wage.

"One person had reluctantly taken the cut in wage because he needed to pay off some debt, but it was clear that he was not thrilled with my decision," he says. "But then, I got excited as the second person looked at me with a big smile on her face and said, absolutely, no problem. I couldn't believe it. This was very easy to do. She never showed up the next morning for her shift."

News of John's cost-cutting measures traveled fast, and soon, John started losing more staff. He scrambled to rectify the situation by placing ads in the paper and also in the local Human Resources government office, but at minimum wage, there were no takers. John began working in the stores as much as possible to make up for the lost staff but this was not sustainable, and he called all the employees that had left, including Tim, to request that they come back to the video store at the same wage, and a small bonus for the inconvenience. But there were no takers.

"I just could not believe that I was being called cheap by the employees who left. And they also told me that they didn't trust me," he says. "But I don't think I was cheap, I was just trying to run a tight ship. But what got me thinking was when I called Tim, who still refused to come back. He made me realize what my mistake was. He said that I had everything in hand – happy employees, smooth operations, and returning customers. And for a dollar per hour, all that came crumbling down. For just ONE DOLLAR PER HOUR! When Tim repeated that statement, it hit me really hard. With the lack of trust, nobody coming back and nobody coming onboard, there was only one way that the business was going."

The house of cards came down quickly for John. The employees stopped believing in him as he was wishy-washy and he clearly thought more about saving money than the welfare of the individual. One-by-one, employees started to leave the company and John had no choice but to shut down all but one of the video stores. That store survived for a few more months, but it did not generate enough money to pay down the outstanding debt obtained to open up the five stores. Six months later, John shut the business down for good, and his company filed for bankruptcy soon after that.

The only way a business can grow is when those helping to run the business are working efficiently and producing the proper outcomes. These outcomes can only be achieved when the resources in those roles have the right knowledge and experience to produce the results that the business needs. By saving money on wages and placing individuals in roles that they are not suited for, although the short term financial gain may look good, the ability for the business to move forward is hampered.

Of course, when starting up, it is not as if the entrepreneur has a high bank balance to work with, and so he or she needs to be creative in filling these roles with individuals that may have a partial skill set. But by focusing on keeping compensation at a low rate, the business will only attract individuals with misaligned skill sets. In these situations, entrepreneurs need to think of the opportunity cost, and not just the bottom line.

In John's case, cutting corners resulted in the failure of the business, but for Chris Griffiths, putting a resource in a position that did not have the appropriate skills did not make for a happy department.

Match the Skills Required
With the Right Person

*Having the skills and managing those with the same skills
are not compatible at all. Those are two different skill sets.*

– Chris Griffiths, Director – Fine Tune Consulting

When hiring from within, many entrepreneurs assume that those at a junior-level position should be able to manage a senior-level position within the same department.

Performing tasks and managing people who perform those tasks are two different skills with completely different training required. Promoting someone to a management position who has little to no managerial experience could be disastrous for that particular business area. Mismanagement could result in a disruption of culture, unhappy employees, and possibly mistrust in overall management, which leads to a considerable impact on performance.

If a bad hire is made, and the person does not have the capabilities for the position hired, instead of letting that bad hire go, this individual is sometimes put into another position where there still is a mismatch in skills. The right thing to do, which is difficult for some, is to let the person know that his or her services are no longer required. But instead, the original problem with the bad hire has a chance to resurface in the new position.

Finding this out was painful for Chris Griffiths.

Chris Griffiths started his first business when he was 19 years old, opening a guitar repair and custom manufacturing shop with 400 square-feet of space and with $30,000 to finance it.

"I was 19 years old, barely could pay rent, and did not understand anything about accounting," he recalls. "I mean, really, I was one of those people that had a skill. I thought because I had a trade that I could be a business because the business part would be easy. The trade was the proprietary piece. Running a business should have, in my mind, been the generic piece that everybody else had figured out so that I could figure it out to. So, that is how I got into business. I had a skill, I saw a market opportunity, and I had no job."

Chris quickly grew his passion for guitar building, which developed into a passion for business. Chris also became enamoured with accounting, which he recommends all entrepreneurs be familiar with because knowing the numbers will reveal much about your business.

The first year, Chris made $24,000 in sales and paid himself $781. He had to sell his 1984 Ford Tempo to keep the rent paid so he could even have a business. He took public transportation every day and believed that if he made sacrifices upfront, it would pay off down the road.

Chris was working a hundred hours a week before he learned how to delegate effectively. He hired a number of employees who were physically in the building running the business, sharing best practices and moving forward with Chris's vision. This allowed Chris to pull himself away from that business to start a guitar manufacturing business, while still being involved in the overall management of his first business.

Chris started the second business to try to manufacture a unique guitar which used a patented Griffiths Active Bracing System. Essentially, this innovation took the dozens of individually machined and individually installed wooden internal braces or struts on the inside of the acoustic guitar, and replaced them with a single unit of injection-molded glass fibre composite. Not only did this reduce manufacturing time from up to 30 minutes to just 90 seconds, it also benefited the sound of the guitar.

Manufacturing the guitar with this approach resulted in improved quality as well as productivity because having all the braces as a single unit transferred the vibrations of the guitar within the guitar's body more effectively, adding to the overall volume and sustain[23] of the instrument.

Chris spent six and a half years trying this new enterprise, with funding coming from the first business. With an increased requirement for money because of patents and prototypes, the first business could not fully fund the second business, and Chris found himself on the brink of bankruptcy.

Thankfully, because he kept in contact with angel investors over time, he was able to raise $250,000 from them. This money went toward finishing off the prototypes, paying off the patents, doing some marketing, and getting him to the world's biggest trade show for musical instruments. The response from the trade show was incredible, and within four months, Chris raised $4.2 million from investors. Seven years later, his company was acquired by the largest guitar company in the world, Gibson.

Chris has seen entrepreneurs make a classic mistake where, instead of finding someone perfect for the business needs, the entrepreneur identifies a person and tries to fit the person into the business. This "fitting" is usually also done with employees that were hiring mistakes. Someone is hired with all the best intentions, and eventually there is a realization that, despite best efforts, it does not work out. Instead of letting that person go, which is an extremely difficult decision for anybody to make, the business owner begins hunting around for another place to insert the bad hire in the business.

"If there is a legitimate opportunity, everybody deserves a chance," says Chris. "But sometimes it is taken too far and employees are forced into positions where they do not have the skill sets to be there in the first place. The business owner is not strong enough to do something about it, and the employee, unfortunately, is dependent on the paycheck. And maybe, in a personal situation, employees have to wake up every morning knowing they have to go to do compromised work in a compromised position, which they don't have all the tools they need. But they need to do it because that is how they support themselves."

The most common problem when promoting from within is assuming that because somebody is good at certain tasks, services, or

---

23 A musical effect that prolongs a note's resonance (http://www.merriam-webster.com/dictionary/sustain)

responsibilities, they are automatically good at managing other people with the same responsibilities. Chris has made that mistake as well.

Chris's situation occurred in the manufacturing facility where there was a skill set needed in a part of the process of building a guitar where wood needed to be bent. This particular aspect of manufacturing required someone with a deep skill set because, when not done properly, the wood breaks. Costs due to waste could add up quickly if not done correctly.

Although this part of guitar manufacturing involved some science, with some machinery to help, Chris ultimately needed someone with a good skill set. Chris had a small department of people doing this, and within this group, there was one employee who was absolutely stellar at bending wood without breaking it.

"I couldn't explain it. It just came naturally to her with no training or anything like that," he says. "So it came time to hire a team leader for that department, and gosh, she could bend wood like nobody's business. She should be the team leader for the bending department. And so we made her team leader, and it was horrible."

She did not like it, and the rest the team did not like it. She lacked the managerial skills necessary to do that work, and Chris learned that lesson painfully fast. Chris put her back in her old position and hired somebody with leadership skills from outside that department. Once that hire was made, the department ran smoothly.

The implications of not only making a bad hire, but also making a bad placement, go beyond the actual individual. Sometimes, business owners are too busy to make that change, or cannot step up to the plate and address the situation.

An effective business owner should be able to take the lead and make the changes necessary for the good of the company, and the rest of the employees. If not, not only will it affect the culture of the company, but it will create a caustic workplace environment, affecting the performance of other employees, possibly increasing absenteeism, and resulting in some turnover.

One must ask the question: What is the cost of removing or replacing a bad hire compared to all the costs associated with not making that decision?

The way to fix bad hires is to get rid of them at the interview stage. In some cases, those trusted with making the hiring decisions simply do not have the appropriate training to recognize when a bad hire is in front of them. On paper, and in the interview, the person makes it through with some standard interview questions. And in some cases, with the best of intentions, a resource is brought in to try and fix a particular situation. If that resource is not working out, it is imperative to let that resource go early. Not doing so disrupts the business. Just ask Loretta Smith, Jim Graham and Stan Winslow.

Let Go of Bad Hires Early

I had failed in hiring. I was, and am, in the business of helping companies hire the right people, and yet I had failed miserably in hiring for my own business. My mistake? I assumed! I assumed I knew the individual.

– Loretta Smith, Founder – Genesis Executive Management Inc.

I made the mistake of hiring somebody from a large company when I needed someone with a small company mentality, and should have let him go much earlier. Not only did he put in processes that we really didn't need, he disrupted the culture by creating silos amongst the teams; that was not good for the company.

– Jim Graham, CEO – TryRecycling

I strayed from a game plan when doing hiring and I didn't think it through properly. That was my main failure. And you need to fail and you waste a lot of time and energy and it doesn't look good on you, especially when you're in a small market.

– Stan Winslow, Senior Vice-President, Leasing – Major US Real Estate Company

One of the biggest decisions that a business can make comes when hiring proper resources. Each position will have a certain set of requirements that will need to be met so that the resource coming on board can excel in that particular position, and move the company forward.

Letting go of a resource that fails to fulfill the requirements of the position can be particularly difficult. Normally this resource is given a number of warnings, but if the same pattern continues to repeat, steps are needed to let resource go. If this is not done in a timely manner, the business and possibly the culture may be negatively affected.

When giving a resource a second chance, generally, things do work out and both the employer and the employee (or contractor) come away from the situation happy. But if the entrepreneur rests on a hope that the employee will get back on track with no real evidence that this will happen, the process wastes time and energy, as was experienced by Loretta Smith.

Loretta Smith owns and operates Genesis Executive Management Inc., an HR consulting company located in London, Ontario with a world-wide client list. Loretta set out with a specific goal in mind – to be the best she could be – and is currently accomplishing this as a successful business owner, but she certainly had some failures and challenges along the way.

Loretta had previously worked with a firm in the recruiting industry, and left that firm to start one of her own. With her experience to guide her, Loretta knew exactly what the key factors were for her business to succeed.

"We were in a candidate short market, so every candidate presented to a client had to be a true 'head hunt'," she says. "That was the business I had started – that was the vision for the company – to 'head hunt', develop relationships with A+ talent and be able to fill and maintain a pipeline. I did not want our business to be sifters of job board applicants."

Loretta's passion and incredible work ethic paid off almost immediately.

"The business of recruiting, like so many other businesses, is all about building relationships and I guess I had been successful in doing that as a contract came my way within a month of starting," she says.

But being a one-person show had its limitations, and with one large contract coming in, these limitations soon came to light. Loretta needed somebody else to help move the business forward.

"There was so much to do and to get done and I found myself in need of help," she says. "So I went out to the market and hired someone. I believed this person had the same goals in mind that I did. My firm was in essence "me", so when hiring someone I needed to ensure that this person reflected my beliefs, my culture, my goals."

Loretta hired someone she thought she knew from the criteria that she had used, and needed this resource to begin working right away to help generate more business. After three months, although a lot of work had been done, Loretta found herself in a state of frustration.

"The individual I had hired was not proving to be capable of stepping up to the actual hard work of supporting the business," she explains. "The person came in wanting to be able to prove that this person was a capable and dependable recruiter – a head hunter recruiter. We set up weekly meetings. Every Monday morning we reviewed what happened the week before and planned for the coming week. It became obvious that in the review we were falling short....accomplishments were falling short."

The Monday morning meetings were important for both Loretta and the new hire as these were reviews to talk about the ongoing progress, important to estimate potential sales.

"The weekly meetings were to discuss the state of the pipeline and to discuss who had been added," she says. "Yes we were looking for specifics, but the broader specific was A+ talent for now and future client needs. Each Monday was greeted with great anticipation, but three months in, I grew to dread Monday's meetings. The pipeline was filling, but the effort was mine and not much was coming forward from the person I had hired."

Excuses started to appear. With Loretta being in the recruiting industry and with the business being new, when every ounce of effort from all resources needs to count, this would have been a clear sign to let this person go. However, Loretta kept this person on.

"One excuse came after another, and all of them were pointing at me being at fault – I had not spent enough time with them, I had not provided enough time, training, ideas, money, etc.," she says. "I spent more time, provided more training, tools and money, even to the point of listing out individuals we wanted to build a relationship with and add to our pipeline."

Finally, Loretta had had enough.

"The day of reckoning for me came with a simple little shrug when the individual finally realized the state of worry and, yes, frustration I was in," she says. "This person looked me straight in the eye and put a hand on my shoulder and shrugged, 'It's okay Loretta, if you run out of money for this business, you can always take money from your family business to support this one'. It was a clear statement of total misunderstanding of what a business is. How can you help a client build their business if you don't understand the essence of the business you are actually working in?"

At that moment, Loretta realized that she had failed, and ironically, in the same industry in which she was an expert.

"That was when I realized just how much I had failed," she says. "I assumed this person had the same vision, culture, and drive I had. I assumed that the individual was driving to build a business. I had failed in being tough in the interviewing process – I did not ask the tough questions I coach my clients to ask. I had failed to dive deep into asking was this the right place for this person to work and was this the right person to help build my business and help my clients build theirs."

The damage had been done, and the worst part was that it took away too much time and money from the process, both crucial resources for Loretta's business.

"It took me another three months and a considerable amount of money to let this person go," she says. "From the time I recognized I had made a mistake until I ultimately let this person go, I agonized and I tried to make it right. It shouldn't have taken me that long. It was a huge lesson."

Incredibly – and worthy of respect – Loretta is able to tell the story to others, putting aside any uncomfortable feelings, and allowing people to learn from her failure.

"I have never forgotten it and I tell this story to my clients now," she says. "It is our job as leaders to get it right. Peter Drucker[24] says that

---

24 **The Essential Drucker: The Best of Sixty Years of Peter Drucker's Essential Writings on Management**, Peter Drucker quote: *"Executives spend more time on managing people and people decisions than on anything else, and they should. No other decisions are so long-lasting in their consequences or so difficult to unmake and yet, by and large, executives make poor promotion and staffing decisions. By all accounts, their batting average is no better than .333. At most one-third of such decisions turn out right; one-third are minimally effective and one-third are outright failures. In no other area of management would we put up with such miserable performance."*

hiring right is the most important function of a leader, but the reality, as he states it, is that we only get it right 1/3 of the time. That's not good for any business. I still have people that work with me and for me – now I ensure they truly are the 'fit' for what the business is all about."

In Loretta's case, giving her resource a second chance despite seeing a pattern of inactivity was a mistake which led to the business stalling. But in Jim Graham's case, a resource was brought on board while Jim's time and attention were focused elsewhere and he was not able to properly monitor the caustic resource. Unfortunately, he started to see his rising profits fall.

Jim Graham runs TryRecycling, the largest recycling company in Ontario. His industry is so new that there is no real competition or experience in recycling the type of material they do. Every time they take a new direction or engage in a new product, there is always a risk and a calculated opportunity that must be made.

"I bought the business from my father and his partners 16 years ago thinking that I could resell it quickly," Jim says. "What I quickly realized was that there was a real neat opportunity with the company because there was really nobody doing what this company was doing, and there was a strong management team in place."

As the previous group was operational in nature, Jim began crafting a business plan, which had not been properly done before. With Jim's guidance, the company grew organically from $2 million to $9 million in revenues within five years. For Jim, this was fun.

Because cost control and cost management were critical to the success of Jim's business, he needed to get the existing operationally-focused team with a background in the construction industry to understand that the company needed to focus on sales and marketing to expand beyond its regional geographic footprint. After making sure everyone understood the direction the company had to go in, Jim took on the sales and marketing responsibilities.

Jim was successful in doing so, establishing strong relationships with municipalities and getting involved in many "Public-Private-Partnerships", or 3P projects. Marching forward, Jim was the only resource doing business development while at the same time he had to manage the business. On top of this, he became Chair of the Ontario Waste Management Association (OWMA), putting further demands on his time, and Jim began to burn out.

"I needed another resource to manage the day-to-day operations of the business, or a COO, a Chief Operating Officer," he says. "I thought that I was being smart in hiring very slowly, going through a number of candidates before making a selection. In the end, I hired somebody that was a polar opposite of me – he was very detail and process-oriented, an engineer by academic background and a cost consultant."

Jim and his advisory group thought this new hire would offset Jim's entrepreneurial nature because he had come from a large company atmosphere, which might help establish some business processes. This individual was hired as the COO and Jim began spending more time away from the office. In particular, his duties with the OWMA went from spending one day a week to several days a week in Toronto, and he was not able to pay close attention to the office. This did not bode well for the company.

"Within six months, this individual had done a lot of damage to the morale of the team and created silos within a group that had really worked well together on challenges as a team," Jim says. "In addition, rather than looking at opportunities, this person unnecessarily dove really deep into the corners of the business, putting aside culture and putting in place a system that was more concerned about the nuts and bolts and inventory items, and was far more complex than the business needed. He also instituted a new accounting system which made it difficult to obtain information on key scorecard measures."

The COO presented Jim with numbers in a format that was too detailed and complex for the requirements of the company, yet the COO assured Jim that this format would help prepare the company for its growth. Jim decided to allow the COO to carry on, thinking that this could be what the company needed.

After 18 months, the COO lost control of the key areas of cost, crucial for Jim's business. Because he had also broken up the teams into silos, problems were not being identified early because the various teams did not communicate. With such inefficiencies introduced into the company, cash was not being used effectively, and the cash surplus that had been budgeted to help develop strategies had been burnt through, in addition to falling revenues.

The yellow light went up when the COO tried to adjust specific inventory numbers that would make the business seem like it was healthy, when in fact it was not, clearly indicating that he did not grasp what he was doing. Jim approached his original team and tried to find out what was going on, but with the teams kept in silos, there were different stories from everyone.

"By the time I got my hands back into things, the fiscal success of the company was at risk," Jim says. "It took myself getting very hands-on again, doing 80 hour weeks and bringing the core team back together and focusing on back to basics."

Jim fired the COO – and realized he should have done so much earlier – and then spent more time in the driver's seat. The fiscal decline levelled off and negotiations with financiers were done to shore up the cash flow for future years to pursue opportunities that might come up. It took a full year to refocus on the core business and get back to a place where Jim could start looking for opportunities.

"It was very strange for me to let go of things, I let go of them too far," he says. "It certainly underlines the requirement of leadership, even as a small company like TryRecycling."

In hopes of bringing a mature, process-oriented approach from a larger company to a smaller company such as TryRecycling – although the strategy is an excellent one that is generally recommended – this individual went too far. The approach required too much process and too much detail for an entrepreneurial company. In addition, all of the teams should have been involved in understanding and implementing the process together. Certainly, an individual who fits into the culture helps bring the people together rather than establish silos, as the COO had.

Jim also learned that his leadership was necessary to move the business forward, and he has since taken steps to put processes in place, and effectively promote from within provided that the appropriate skill sets are there. By hiring from within, Jim has a more cohesive unit that understands the business and where it is going. Now, he can continue to work "on" the business rather than "in" the business, continuing its growth.

Businesses may also experience problems when the hiring decision-makers stray from a set of criteria for a particular position. If the reasons for moving away from the criteria are valid because of an outstanding candidate, and it helps the business move forward, then, by all means, hire the person. If not, then there is a misalignment between the resource and the requirements of the position, which will generally end up in a bad, wasteful situation, as Stan Winslow experienced.

Stan Winslow is Senior Vice-President, Leasing for a major national US real estate company, located in New York City. He is not only responsible for local commercial real estate needs, but he is also tapped when national or global accounts are looking for commercial real estate in the New York area. Previously a lawyer, he graduated with an MBA in the early '80s, and was offered to join this company upon graduation, and has been there ever since.

Stan has generated a reputation as the go-to person for those looking for a career change or looking to get into the business of real estate.

"If people are looking at a career change or to get into the business, mostly young people or career changers, they find their way to me," he says. "I like to talk to everybody because you never know, you know, who you can resource or where they may end up later on. I am very open to that."

Stan's main target market is essentially corporate users of office, industrial, or retail space.

"Everybody uses space, a commodity, so we get it for them and we negotiate on their behalf," he explains. "We're brokers. We consult, find the right space, we negotiate the transaction, whether they want to lease or purchase. We handle the user's space requirements from A to Z, and even if they want to get rid of the space afterwards, or they have too much space, they hire us to sublease it or get them out of the contract.

Sometimes tenants become buyers because they don't want to lease anymore, they want to buy a building. So we will sell them a building. In a nutshell, we represent the users of premises, whether it be office, industrial, or commercial stores, or retailers. So we handle all facets of commercial real estate."

Stan has had extensive experience interviewing people, adding anywhere from five to ten people every year, mostly young graduates, who want to get into real estate. He prefers younger graduates because they can be molded into effective real estate agents, based on Stan's requirements.

"I usually hire brand-new 'out-of-the-box' people where they start as my assistant, and with mentoring, they become junior agents," he says.

Stan was looking to expand his team for two reasons. The first reason was that he needed to bring on more junior people because the existing junior resources were being promoted.

"We were expanding the team. It's always been a pyramid type of team, me at the top," he says, "and now, as my younger salespeople are reaching more senior positions, it's flattening out a little bit at the top in terms of the organizational chart and we still want to grow the bottom layer. So I wanted to turn it from essentially what was a pyramid to more of a flat organization chart."

The second reason was that he was seeing a shift in the gender demographic for existing and potential clients.

"You read about it in the Wall Street Journal. There is an increase in female decision-makers and not enough CEOs, but that doesn't matter as they could be CFOs, they could be facility managers and so on. So, there are just more and more women that I'm reporting to as clients," he says. "They are my clients. Okay, so they may work in the real estate department of a large firm, not necessarily being the CEO, but they may have a facilities person that's a woman."

Stan thought that if he brought a female resource on board, then he would be better able to establish more of a comfort level with female clients.

"I thought it would help us deal better with female senior managers, you know, because there are more and more of the female demographic in senior management positions, and it's better if you have somebody of that demographic on the team," he says. "It's not that we would fail because we didn't have that. We thought that it would expand our scope and our horizon for clients as there are many more young women, who are taking charge as entrepreneurs."

In addition, because the sales team was primarily from New York, he wanted to bring in a female resource that came from the western part of the United States, which meant that this person had to be sourced from a state such as California, to help increase business.

"My team is very much an East Coast team, but sometimes we deal with people from the West Coast, and they somehow feel easier dealing with someone from that part of the US. It precludes us from getting invited to a pitch, or getting to second base, that kind of thing. That was the thought process," he says.

Because many of his clients, both current and potential, had more senior roles, Stan also thought that if he brought a female resource on board, he would prefer to have a more seasoned salesperson that might be able to establish a better rapport with those in senior positions.

After a search, Stan found a perfect match: a bright, intelligent, seasoned female Californian, with a real estate background, although it was in residential real estate. Stan brought her on board, and began the mentoring process.

There was a sizeable difference between residential real estate and commercial real estate, which Stan had to ensure that the new resource understood to be successful in her position.

"The commercial real estate is more of a professional target audience," he says. "You're talking to entrepreneurs, CEOs, CFOs, and real estate professionals versus lay people who don't really understand real estate. Now, you're dealing with people that want answers immediately. They want you to be available 24/7. You need to have a crisp response, you need to understand your product, and you need to understand the financial implications of everything. When you're dealing with residential real estate, you're dealing with people who don't know better. So if you're delivering stuff, whether it's good or bad, in the commercial business, they know what they want and what they are expecting. So if you can't deliver it, you'll never survive."

Residential real estate also tends to be easier as the typical client does not have as many requirements as a typical commercial real estate client may have, Stan adds.

"I'm not trying to belittle residential, but anybody can sell a house," he says. "But you cannot sell an office building to an international giant like Walmart without having a good grasp of everybody's balance sheet items. You really need a business background, a business degree, and a good understanding of financials and some sales skills."

Within a month, Stan knew that things were not working.

"There were a lot of 'deer in the headlights' looks as it wasn't clicking," he says. "Then we thought we could turn it around, maybe we can work with her, maybe we could educate her, maybe she'll grab it, but it just got worse. She really didn't understand the business."

One of the biggest issues for Stan was her experience; being a seasoned real estate professional in the residential market actually went against her. Trying to get her to "un-think" residential real estate and "re-think" commercial real estate proved incredibly difficult.

Reflecting on that time, Stan realizes that he moved away from key criteria he had relied upon when hiring resources, the major criterion being hiring someone young to mentor and train.

"In our zest and excitement at looking at someone who fit the demographic, we really didn't pay attention to things like education and finesse. We did not do a thorough enough background check, which is what we would normally do with a new person coming on," he says. "We were clouded by the fact that this person hit the three demographic points so neatly and was also very presentable and who would be perfect on the team. But we forgot to peel back the layers of the onion, or the veneer, a little bit and really see if this person had the wherewithal and capacity to learn, and be challenged, and work hard, and keep up, and whether she was comfortable enough to do a deal."

What irks Stan is that his competitors were more successful bringing on a younger demographic with more relevant experience.

"My competitors always follow me, and a couple of them followed and did a better job hiring, which pisses me off," he says. "You know they saw where I was going. They were able to get female resources that had a commercial background, which were inexperienced and so they were able to better train them right out of the gate. They hired better than I did, and then I say to myself, s**t, I should've had a V-8!"

Stan puts his lesson from his failure this way:

"We failed. We brought this person on, she was never able to ramp up to a certain point, you know, and we agreed to part ways. The lesson to learn is, you know, I guess you should never cloud your judgement, or never get away from the game plan. You need to stick to your game plan, your guns, your criteria, everything that you had used to be successful with your team. You should never get away from that because of other ancillary, you know, exciting issues, I guess."

His mistake acknowledged, Stan still needed a resource, so he used criteria that he relied on for many years, hiring a recent university graduate.

"We retooled. Instead of going back and rehiring a more seasoned salesperson, we went back to hiring recent graduates so that we can mold them right out of the gate and train them properly, not necessarily female," he says.

There is an old adage that the best time to get rid of a bad hire is at the interview stage. Of course, this is practically impossible to perfect, and bad hires will slip through the cracks. But it is vital to let go of these hires if they are not performing up to standards. As seen in the three cases above, bad hires resulted in complications for the business. According to an article in Inc. magazine[25], a whopping 75% of hires will fail. For businesses that are starting up, these complications could cause irreparable damage.

Entrepreneurs should take the time to properly evaluate the criteria for the position they are looking to fill. Spend some time monitoring the resources, and if they do not seem to work, take steps without delay to let the resource go. What should be done next is to fix the process that resulted in the bad hire, and use the new process to make a proper hire.

Ensuring that there is a fit between a resource and a position does not necessarily need to happen at an employee level. In fact, the same criteria should be upheld for management positions, with even higher standards when it comes to bringing on a partner that will have an ownership stake in the business.

When deciding to add a partner, or looking to join a company as a

25 http://www.inc.com/drew-greenblatt/three-out-of-four-hires-fail.html

partner, one should perform a thorough evaluation of who the other partner is. If there is the slightest doubt about how effective the partner will be when working together, it might be best to ask more questions, do more due diligence or simply walk away as there could be difficult legal and financial implications, not to mention emotional upheaval, when things go awry between partners.

Brad Geddes wished he had been more careful when coming on as a partner, although going through his problems with a partner ultimately allowed him to run a company on his own, with the business success being solely due to his own management capabilities. Such rosy situations are a rarity.

Selecting the Right Partner

There were some early warning signs that I should not have ignored about my partner. But because I let it go, I was put in a situation where I was terminated from my role as president and guards were hired to prevent me from returning to the company I had rescued. I suddenly found myself with no source of income and without funds after my partner seized all the money I had loaned the business. I should've acted on my gut instinct much earlier.

– Brad Geddes, President – Zucora Inc.

In some cases, a business owner will need to bring in a partner who can help move the business forward. It could be that the business has grown, or the owner simply needs somebody else to tackle different business areas so the company can operate more effectively.

Typically, the owner looks for someone with a skill set to complement his or her own abilities. If done properly, both partners will have separate roles so as to minimize overlap.

While each partner's background and experience is important, oftentimes, a partner's personal values or individual traits may be overlooked in the interest of pursuing a business opportunity. If these personal values are misaligned, it is highly probable that undesirable issues will need to be dealt with at some point in the future.

For Brad Geddes, his sense of ethical, honest, and trustworthy behaviour was out of sync with a partner who only looked to line his own pockets, without regard to the potential impact on the business.

Brad is President of Zucora Inc, Canada's largest provider of home furnishing protection plans and customer care programs. Zucora was founded in 1979 and previously operated as Magi Seal Corporation until shortly after it was acquired by his family's holding company, Zeubear Investments Ltd.

Brad had previously bought, sold, and operated several successful high-tech companies in Toronto, and returned to his home in London, Ontario to become involved in other entrepreneurial pursuits. A mutual acquaintance introduced him to Magi Seal, which was in financial distress.

"I was invited in as a consultant because the owner had told me, 'I have a problem and I don't know why,'" says Brad. "I had worked with a number of companies by that point and so my mutual acquaintance thought that I could offer some advice to help the owner of the business."

Brad looked at the company, and although he did not initially understand the business, he recognized that it had a broken business model. After digging deeper, he also discovered a number of poor business practices that were creating losses. However, he also saw the potential for growth and he suspected that if certain things were turned around, then the business might have a chance to survive.

"After consulting for the company for several months and making some recommendations, I was asked to continue on to implement many of the suggestions to help improve the business," he says. "Following some initial success, the owner approached me about joining the company as its president."

Brad initially resisted the offer as he was busy with other projects, but was asked again a few weeks later because the owner was now looking to exit the company. After thinking about the company's current revenue stream and growth prospects, Brad agreed, buying 40% of the shares of the company in 2004, with the understanding that he would eventually acquire the entire business, while the founding owner would take on the role of silent partner.

A shareholders agreement was put in place, which took two years to complete, and was finally signed in early 2007. What was missing in the agreement was how the remaining 60% of the shares would be purchased by Brad to eventually assume full ownership of the company.

Brad was too trusting of his new partner's assurances that this process would be smooth.

Despite the lengthy delay in completing the shareholders agreement, Brad began to transform the company from a broken operation into a well-oiled machine. He hired additional management staff, cleaned up internal processes, and changed the focus from avoiding serving customers to embracing customers while focusing on how the company could bring greater value to its retail partners. Brad added more than 320 new retail partners by establishing excellent relationships with them from the start. In fact, today, five out of the top six Canadian home furnishing retailers are customers of Zucora.

With this growth, the company became financially stronger, and profits began to improve. Seizing the opportunity, Brad's partner, who was still a majority partner, started taking the liberty of dipping into the bank account.

"When I first assumed my role as President, I soon discovered my partner, the majority shareholder, had not been acting in good faith with customers, refusing to honour legitimate customer claims, and was pocketing cash sales generated by the business," Brad says.

His partner would ask the company's technicians to hand over any cash payments they collected from customer service calls. Of course, this cash never ended up in the corporate bank account. One of the technicians was unhappy with this arrangement, and notified Brad. Brad had a stern talk with his partner, and convinced him to stop this behaviour as it was illegal. His partner agreed.

Despite his partner's assurances, the practice continued. But this time, he asked the technicians to split the cash, giving 50% of the cash to the accounting department while pocketing the other 50%. The partner also told the technicians to not advise Brad of the arrangement.

Brad subsequently found out and was forced to put new financial controls in place, and once again warned his partner about the legal and tax implications of his behaviour. Brad was extremely concerned because, as the president, he would be associated with this illegal behaviour despite being an innocent "bystander". He also assured the partner that there was much more money to be made from the growth of the company, and he would be able to draw money as a shareholder legitimately.

Once again, the partner agreed to stop and Brad continued driving the company to even greater growth and profitability, expanding the company tenfold.

In 2009, seeing the explosive growth and improving bank account, the partner decided to take a more active role in the company and began making additional financial demands as well as re-asserting himself as the CEO to gain better access to the company's cash.

"In late 2009 he came to me with a demand for a substantial amount of money from the company," Brad says. "I don't know what it was for, or what the reasons why he needed the money were, and it was not my concern, but I challenged him at the time. I said I can't do it for two reasons. First of all, he would breach the shareholders agreement that we had between us because it's very clear that neither one of us can take money out of the company without unanimous approval between the two of us. More importantly, we had bank covenants that restricted either one of us from taking money out of the company. I didn't want to impair our relationship with the bank. His response was quite surprising when he told me that he did not care about the shareholders agreement and he certainly did not care about the bank. He just wanted the money."

At this point Brad seriously thought about his future with the company. He felt he could no longer be a part of these potentially unlawful circumstances in addition to the distraction these matters were causing while managing the business.

Brad consulted a couple of advisors who were friends of his partner, while telling his partner that he did not want to be drawn into situations where his personal integrity was at stake or the company's responsibilities to its bankers were not being respected. Brad let the partner know that if this behaviour continued, he would need to reconsider his future with the company.

Brad came from a background of strong ethics and integrity. He believed in the need to be honest in business dealings – which were a direct reflection on his personal reputation. Clearly, the partner did not share the same principles. At this point, Brad learned a valuable lesson: he should have been much more wary of his partner's set of values. Although Brad thought he could manage his partner, it was clear that he could not fix his partner's personal flaw, no matter how much he tried.

Four days after the meeting with his partner and the company's advisors, the partner entered Brad's office, and the conversation went somewhat like this:

Partner: I've accepted your resignation.

Brad: Hold on here, I haven't resigned.

Partner: No, you have, because I'm going to announce your termination as a resignation.

Brad: Well no, because, first of all, I haven't resigned, and secondly, I'm required to give you a written notice of resignation, in accordance with our shareholders agreement.

Partner: I don't care about agreements. They mean nothing to me.

Brad had never been in this position before. "I started to think, well, this is not going well. And before I knew it, I was directed to leave the building on December 1, 2009," he says.

In addition to this shock, two of Brad's children who had been working at the company for several years were let go two days before Christmas, which once again breached the shareholders agreement, which contained a provision that protected the employment of either of the partners' children who were working with the company.

Brad's personal financial scenario was now at risk. Not only was his income immediately stopped, but the majority of his personal savings were tied up in a loan he had provided to the company. His partner had decided to apply financial pressure by withholding funds owed to Brad. It appeared that the only way Brad would be able to recover these funds would be through litigation.

With a company advisor serving as an intermediary, Brad offered to purchase one of the company's under performing divisions, which his partner flatly refused. He also tried to exercise an arbitration provision in the shareholders agreement to resolve the situation, but his partner refused to respect the process that they had previously agreed to – which was intended to be used in the event of a disagreement between the two partners.

Instead, the partner triggered a shotgun clause[26] in the shareholders agreement, thinking that Brad would not be able to raise the money

---

26 A shotgun clause is an offer from one shareholder to purchase the shares of one or more of the other shareholders who are listed in a shareholders agreement. The other shareholders must then either accept the offer, or, within a very restricted time frame, raise enough capital to buy the other shareholder out by purchasing his or her shares at the same price per share. Generally, the clause can be enforced at any time, but is usually enforced when there are signs of trouble between the shareholders.

needed to buy the partner's majority shares. In fact, the partner structured the amount that Brad would be paid for his shares to such a precise amount that Brad would end up with absolutely nothing if he had to surrender his equity position.

What his partner did not know was that Brad had been planning to trigger the shotgun provision but for twice the value of the shares than what his partner had offered. But because the partner triggered the shotgun provision first, Brad did not have to pay this premium value for his partner's shares. Instead, he quickly raised the funds needed to purchase his partner's shares in accordance with the shareholders agreement – much to the shock and dismay of his partner.

"I still remember the day, February 12, 2010, when I walked in and delivered my acceptance of his offer to buy his shares," he says. "I said to him, 'Congratulations, you have just become London's newest multi-millionaire.' As the blood drained from his face, he looked up at me, and said, 'You're not buying my f*****g company.'"

The partner refused to acknowledge Brad's acceptance of the offer. Despite this, Brad advised the partner that he was going to immediately return as President, which further angered his partner.

"Over the weekend, he hired guards to prevent me from coming in the building," he said. "I was now physically excluded from the company. My kids were excluded from the company. And my partner directed that my youngest daughter, who had still been working for one of the business units at another location, to be fired immediately."

Because his partner claimed that Brad's acceptance of the offer was invalid, the parties had to resort to litigation to resolve the matter. Confident he had adhered to the precise terms of the shareholders agreement, Brad and his lawyer were shocked when the court delivered a decision in favour of his partner.

"I was done. That had to be the lowest point in my entire life. I was completely numb. I had no income. I had no money. My career had been taken away from me. And now, eighty percent of my family was unemployed and I somehow had to figure out how to get on with my life," he says.

Brad was immediately advised to appeal the decision because his lawyer strongly felt that the original decision was fundamentally flawed. Unfortunately, Brad had no financial resources to support an appeal.

However, his lawyer felt so strongly about trying to correct the error in the court's judgment, he agreed to undertake the appeal.

Several months later, by unanimous decision of the Ontario Court of Appeal, the three-judge panel, which included the Associate Chief Justice of Ontario, ruled that Brad's acceptance of his partner's offer was indeed valid. The Court of Appeal directed that Brad be returned to his position and also determined that Brad had the right to purchase his partner's shares.

However, despite the court's precedent-setting decision, Brad's partner still refused to provide him with access to the company's records in an effort to thwart his attempt to complete the purchase transaction. A year had elapsed since Brad had been forced out of the company before he finally gained access to the company's books. After completing a review of the financial records, and with little surprise, he discovered his partner had withdrawn more than half a million dollars from the business during Brad's absence – including the purchase of four tires for his partner's new Bentley!

Despite all the challenges he had endured, Brad was extremely fortunate because his partner's low-ball offer, combined with the subsequent removal of company funds, resulted in lowering the purchase price of the company, permitting Brad to buy the business for less than 30% of the appraised value.

The management team, employees, and customers were delighted that Brad had returned to the helm of the business, and Brad resumed his focus on growing the company. Soon after, Zucora was generating more business from just one customer than the amount Brad paid his partner for the remaining shares.

The lesson that Brad learned through this experience is that he should have paid more attention to the early warning signs in the relationship and not to settle for a set of values that was substantially different from his own. There was a clear cultural conflict, and the integrity-based values and vision just did not resonate with his partner.

"It is the leader's responsibility to ensure that the vision is shared, in my view, and understood by all those that are part of it," Brad says. "My experience has been this: People leave an organization for one of two reasons. One is because the skill set does not match the organization – oftentimes, because they are in over their head. Or, sometimes, the culture no longer fits with them. They don't see things the same way. They don't believe in the vision. They don't share the passion. So to me, integrity, transparency, and honesty are significant values that have to be in place because, frankly, they draw most people. My partner did not fit that model."

When Brad reflects on the whole situation, he says that he has come up with four major lessons that he learned:

1. Be wary of irresponsible people who are motivated by greed. For his partner, it was all about keeping the golden goose (the company) for himself without regard to the people who helped it become a success.

2. It really is possible to right an injustice. Things are not always as just as people would like them to be and sometimes it's necessary to challenge the system.

3. There are professional bullies who will take a position simply because they are being compensated for it, or because they are blindly loyal to a personal relationship. When professionals abandon their principles, they undermine their personal integrity and reputation. This was the one lesson that bothered Brad the most.

4. He who wins last, wins. Persistence does pay off.

"I've had a lot of people say to me, 'How did you manage to get through it all?'" he says. "If it hadn't been for the strength of my family and friends, I don't think we would have made it. I was living my passion while growing this company. I really believed in this business. I believed in what we were doing. And to have to walk away from all of that because of somebody else's selfish desire … it just didn't sit well with me."

Despite the early warning signs, Brad continued on because he cared about the whole business and the people who shared his vision. And while Brad had ensured there was a solid shareholders agreement in place that should have protected him, no amount of negotiation would have protected him from having to deal with a partner who held dramatically different personal values.

For an entrepreneur looking to invest in a business, it is worth spending the extra time to uncover any red flags that may come up from previous experiences or business dealings with a potential new partner. If an anomaly is found, then the entrepreneur should continue to look for another opportunity. Fail to do so and you could end up with a partner with a questionable background. Once the contract is signed, it is difficult to fire a partner. Most likely, unless a breakup situation is extremely amicable, litigation may be required, and that is just throwing money out the door. This could be avoided by doing some homework at the beginning.

Of course, this is not a perfect process, and the entrepreneur needs to be practical about how deep he or she needs to delve into a potential partner's past. By asking questions not only of the partner, but others from previous ventures, the entrepreneur may be able to find red flags that would save some potential headaches in the future.

If red flags are found, do not compromise. Spend the time to find another partner as this will save time, money, and resources. Spend time on what counts and urge the growth of the business, rather than on what does not count: a rogue partner.

Not doing the proper research when bringing on an accountant and lawyer, known together as professional services, could also cause headaches for the organization.

The level of professional services needed is dependent upon how complex the business structure is or where the business is in its lifecycle. If one is careful to invest in the proper legal and accounting advice at the right time, then these professional services can save headaches in a number of areas, as Ian Gray experienced. But not being able to find proper professional services could end up in a disastrous situation, as Bruno Barban experienced.

Use the Right Professional Services

There was no way that the complexity of the deal could have been performed without the right type of lawyers and accountants. I was staring at two boardrooms full of three-inch thick binders and stacks of papers at my lawyer's office, and my accountant was able to save me $200,000 in tax credits. That alone was worth their fees in gold.

– Ian Gray, President – Buying Group Services Inc.

I hired a lawyer that was learning as we went along, and I brought on board an accountant that not only had the projections all wrong, but did not see that a key piece of our financing was not going to be available. I was done. The bank called in the loan and I had to declare personal bankruptcy soon after.

– Bruno Barban, Former Owner – Construction Company

An area that some entrepreneurs rarely think about until absolutely required is sourcing a good lawyer and accountant, collectively called professional services. They are often afterthoughts. Lawyers are needed when a legal issue comes to the forefront, and accountants are tapped typically during tax time. What gets missed by delaying the sourcing of these professional services is a good legal and accounting road map that helps entrepreneurs understand what issues they need to deal with in the short, medium, and long-term.

A good law firm can advise the entrepreneur on how to put proper contracts in place, and make the entrepreneur aware of any future legal complexities that may need to be taken into consideration such as shareholders agreements, employment contracts, issuance of future shares, dividend policies, and other such issues. By not having these types of legal issues addressed early, the entrepreneur opens the business up to uncomfortable situations such as shareholder disagreements, employee theft, unprotected ideas, and other such matters that, without proper legal advice or documentation, may result in the business going through difficult times, not to mention the time taken away from actually running the business.

From an accounting standpoint, if the business is simple the accountant will be able to provide excellent advice on common mistakes entrepreneurs make that may result in paying too much tax, or worse, being audited by the tax agency. If the business grows significantly, proper accounting advice may be able to find savings in both personal and corporate taxes by introducing unique corporate structures.

Hiring professional services is expensive as the hourly rates are not low. But, with the type of training and experience these individuals or firms have, and the associated advice they offer, their services are definitely worth the price. Some professional services will be higher in cost than others, and so the entrepreneur needs to engage professional services with the right level of experience and expertise for the stage that the business is at.

For example, a start-up company with one owner and a simple business model may not necessarily need professional services that specialize in complex business matters, whereas a company with multiple partners looking to acquire a company or sell a portion of equity will probably need to engage the services of a more senior level of professional services who have tackled such issues, and are familiar with where problems may occur.

The question is not necessarily in the size of business, as Ian Gray found out. For Ian, despite owning a small business, the complexities of the transactions he was involved with could only have been done by more senior level professional services.

Ian Gray is President of Buying Group Services Inc., which specializes in the formation, development, and operation of buying groups and purchasing co-operatives across North America. Ian has been lucky in his entrepreneurial ventures; he has never failed and has never abandoned any opportunity, but he certainly has come across some incredible challenges.

In 1991, he joined a company called Dimension Retail Automation Systems, a company that sold point-of-sale systems to lumber yards. There were two partners in the business and Ian was brought on to help them grow. Because Ian was doing well, the owners of the company financed his Executive MBA and gave him a 10% equity stake, which they financed through a promissory note.

"After some time the two major partners fell out of favour with each other, and the one partner approached me to buy out the other," says Ian. "I then bought the shares of the third partner using personal guarantees with the banks, which left me with 18% of the company and the other partner at 82%. After some time, the majority partner began challenging me on areas of my responsibility and started making decisions without me. I got the feeling that the majority partner was looking to push me out of the company as well."

Soon enough, one year after the third partner had been bought out, the majority partner decided that it was not working out with Ian and enforced a shotgun clause in the shareholders agreement. Essentially, the tactic was to take Ian out of the company, leaving him jobless, and with no value in his shares.

"Not only would I have nothing to show for my participation in the company, but I would have been saddled with a personal debt owed to the bank from the buyout of the third partner," he says. "This was all happening when I was married, had a two-year-old and another one on the way. This left me devastated both personally and professionally."

The shotgun clause in the shareholders agreement stated that Ian had only 30 days to come up with the money to buy out the other partner. It was impossible to raise that kind of money in that timeline. But luck was on Ian's side.

"I was lucky because the majority partner told me three to four months ahead of time that he was going to 'pull the trigger on the shotgun clause', rather than the 30 days which was specified in the contract," he says. "This timeframe was my lifeline, as 30 days would not have been enough time to come up with the funds to reverse the shotgun and would have wiped me out, leaving me with nothing."

Ian knew that if he was able to raise the money, then he would own the company outright. But he did not have any money as his personal funds were tapped out. So he looked to see if there were any buyers for the company who would provide him with the money to buy the majority partner out and satisfy the shotgun clause.

Ian approached his main competitor to see if there was any interest in buying the company, and Ian's luck struck again. The main competitor was pitching a venture capital group for a possible purchase of its own company, and so Ian approached the venture capital group to offer his company as well, which would give the venture capital group a larger customer base, increased revenues, and higher market share. Ian just needed the funds in advance to counter-offer the shotgun clause, and the company would then be his, which he would then turn around and sell back to the venture capital group. After discussions went back and forth, the venture capital group agreed.

"The venture capital company ended up acquiring both companies, so they funded my buyout with [the majority partner]," says Ian. "I ended up with a significant amount of cash in my pocket and [the majority partner] was out of a job, and the venture capitalist now owned the business and I was kept on to run the division."

To ensure that this complex transaction went smoothly, Ian made sure that he chose the right set of professional services to tackle the sale. He knew that he needed an experienced senior legal team to do the complex transaction.

"I ended up going to Harrison Pensa. A normal small lawyer could never have handled that transaction," he says. "There were two transactions, right? There was the buyout of all the assets from the first partner, and then there were the assets of reselling it all to the other [venture capital group], and it had to happen almost at the same time. I remember going into Harrison Pensa's big boardroom, and there were piles of paper this thick," he says, showing a seemingly large pile with two hands, "which went down the table and around and back in one room, and that was for the one transaction. And then we went down another floor to the other boardroom and it was basically another series of transactions. Even though this is just a small business, you know, as revenues were approximately $2 million and about 30 employees, the complexity of the deal could only have happened with that type of legal advice. Lesson number one is to make sure that you have good legal advice. Most law firms, the smaller ones, can't handle that transaction."

Integral to this transaction happening in the best possible way, Ian also used a senior-level accountant.

"You've got have good accountants," he says. "They have to protect you from what's out there, and there's a lot out there that you can screw up easily, not intentionally, but just screw up. For example, in that transaction, we ended up bringing in a fairly senior tax guy and we were able to structure the deal that, even though it was just a roll over and flip, I was able to take advantage of my lifetime capital gains because I had proper legal counsel and proper accounting to do it. And that added to the complexity of it because you want to structure the deal in a certain way that would hold up to challenges that I didn't in fact hold all the assets for the correct period of time. And so there was a way to structure it properly. There is an example that likely saved me $200,000 of tax. So it was a significant thing to do."

Ian's example illustrates that hiring more senior professional services is not necessarily restricted for larger businesses as it really is about the nature of the transactions. But those simply starting up a company could find themselves in a trap of using professional services that do not have the right experience. When the entrepreneur is faced with a set of recommendations that may not be the best for the business, the company could get into a lot of trouble, which Bruno Barban experienced.

Bruno Barban, a resident of Sault Ste. Marie, Ontario, owned and operated a successful construction company in the early '80s. Sault Ste. Marie had a bustling industrial sector which employed a large number of local residents, which fueled the growth in the housing market. This growth kept Bruno's company busy, and because of the demand for real estate, Bruno began thinking of getting into the commercial development sector.

"In 1981, we got into constructing the first condominium project in Sault Ste. Marie," he says. "It was a $10 million venture with three towers that were 12 stories high that was to have a shopping mall, doctor's offices, and condominiums for sale."

One of the financing incentives for the condominium project came from a government program called the Multi Unit Residential Building program, or MURB. This program was designed to stimulate housing in the area, and offered a 100% tax deduction on soft costs which would have included development fees, financing fees, management fees, and some legal fees.

"The aim of this program was to create a lot of local investment, which it did," Bruno says. "We had a lot of investors that put money in, such as doctors and lawyers, and they were looking for a tax-sheltered investment."

To move this project forward, Bruno's company had to incur legal fees, engineering fees, surveyors, and other associated costs, and once activity on the condominium unit started one year later, Bruno needed to secure professional services to begin taking care of the legal and accounting issues. When looking to lawyers in town, nobody had any experience with condominiums, but Bruno still needed to select somebody.

"Because of the project, every lawyer wanted to get into offering legal advice in the commercial development area," he says. "The problem was that in Sault Ste. Marie, we had no lawyers that were experienced in doing these kinds of legal matters. Because of that, the lawyer we hired was learning as he went along."

The next step was hiring an accountant to take care of the numbers side of the business. The accountant chosen seemed to think that he knew he was doing, but he did not have any experience with condominiums.

"This accountant's projections were completely way off," Bruno says. "He was assuming 100% condominium occupancy in six months, and all his financial projections were tied to that occupancy. The reality was we only ended up selling 20 to 30 condominium units out of the 120 that were offered."

Although one of the cornerstones of the financing projections prepared by the accountant was based on the MURB program, the accountant failed to find out any details of this program. If such an inquiry was made, then the accountant would have known that the MURB program was being phased out within a six-month timeframe, meaning the tax deductions built into the projections would no longer be available.

Because of the reliance of the project on the MURB tax deductions, the condominium project went from being financially attractive to a project that Bruno should have been running away from. But Bruno was not aware of this, and secured a significant amount of debt by obtaining a loan and line of credit to help finance the project.

"I could not predict that the MURB tax relief program would be pulled by the federal government," he says. "We relied on our accountant to know this information, and the accountant was not aware that the government was going to suspend this program. At the time that the government suspended the program, we were heavy into the project and very highly leveraged. We were granted a six-month extension, but that time didn't matter as the financing was tied directly to the MURB status of the project from initial funding, with CMHC underwriting the final sale of the project. With no cash available to pay off obligations, the bank called in the loan and foreclosed on the project, eventually selling it to a southern Ontario developer for $2 million, about 30% of the value of the work done to date."

To compound this problem, the major employer in Sault Ste. Marie had declared bankruptcy because of the economic downturn in the 1980s. Originally employing 13,500 employees, after coming out of the bankruptcy, it only retained 3,000 employees.

With Bruno personally being liable for the loan, and a shrinking base of potential customers for the condominiums, the future of the condominium project looked bleak. To make matters worse, the Bank of Canada increased their prime rate to almost 20%, which made paying off the loan exorbitant.

"We were being charged 24% at [the bank] for our line of credit," he says. "In 1920, they used to put the Mafia in jail for loan sharking. Our government gives the banks a license to make money off the backs of the entrepreneurs, who take all the risks and guarantee the loans personally. Needless to say, I eventually had to declare personal bankruptcy in 1984, three years after starting the project."

Eventually, Bruno was able to dust his shoulders off and returned to school. Eight years later, he completed his MBA. Today, he works as a senior administrator at a local university and teaches business courses at a US-based university. Ironically, Bruno's incredible experiences were among the reasons why he was selected to teach management students.

The importance of finding the right professional services for the business cannot be understated. Doing so will eliminate many hardships, and in some cases, it may actually help the business on the financial end. Of course, it is definitely advisable to shop around and find the best price, but it should be for the right experience. Shopping around to look for the cheapest price for professional services generally ends up in getting what you pay for.

In addition to having proper professional services who can advise the entrepreneur in the legal and accounting departments, proper advisors are also necessary to help steer the business in the right direction. No matter what stage the business is in, advisors are always recommended, according to Richard Ivey, Dave Renwick and Doug Davis.

Seek Advisors

Boards, no matter how they are constructed, or how conservative they may be, add value more often than not.

– Richard Ivey, Chairman – Ivest Properties Ltd.

Put an advisory board together that consists of business people that the business owner respects and trusts. This way, the business owner is able to bounce ideas off of the advisory board from time to time to see if these ideas make sense.

– Dave Renwick, Business Development Director – KPMG Canada

Even though you cannot afford to pay much, try and get more advisors who think like you and that could help grow the company.

– Douglas C. Davis, Vice-Chairman – Davis Rea Ltd.

Naturally, entrepreneurs will always face business hurdles in the quest for success. However, if they prepare for these hurdles by getting advice from the appropriate resources, success will come faster.

One of the ways of seeking advice is to assemble a small board of advisors to provide valuable input into such business issues as strategy, financing, operations, and so on. These advisors should be people that the entrepreneur is familiar with and can add value to the business. Provided the entrepreneur respects the advisor's time and only asks for advice once every three or six months, for example, assembling such a board should not be an issue.

Entrepreneurs would be wise to shy away from advisors who cannot effectively contribute relevant advice that adds to the success of the business, however. For example, if an entrepreneur is looking to open a restaurant, then the obvious choice for advisors would be other entrepreneurs that have experience in that area. Having an advisor that comes from the automotive industry would not be an appropriate candidate, unless this advisor has specific experience that directly relates to the restaurant business. With a random collection of advisors with disparate backgrounds and experiences, issues often do not get addressed properly or decisions are made at a slow pace when the business needs crisp, clear, and quick advice.

For small businesses that do end up growing, owners should consider graduating from a group of advisors to a formal board of directors. The selection process for formal board members should be the same: they should have relevant experience and knowledge as advisors to the business to move the business forward. Advice from these groups is essential to ensuring that the business continually grows successfully, according to Richard Ivey.

Richard Ivey is currently Chairman of Ivest Properties and has served as both a board member and Chairman of the Board for a large number of businesses. He is also active in organizations such as MaRS, an organization that provides advisory support for start-ups in the science, technology, and social entrepreneurship areas.

The importance of having an independent board of directors, or an excellent set of advisors, cannot be understated. In fact, one of the more difficult experiences Richard had was when purchasing a company in the consumer product space, and not finding the time to set up a board of directors to oversee the company.

"The company was in a turnaround situation," he says. "I found a partner who had deep experience in the consumer product industry, who I had worked with for many years, and complemented my skill sets. The partner would run the company and I would provide the appropriate backing and advice. The company had sales globally, Asian sourcing, licensing arrangements with vendors, and a product development arm."

Existing management had some internal knowledge of the niche product that the company produced, but it was clear that the earlier management team lacked enough knowledge to grow the business. Problems began to surface in areas such as the quality of management, logistical issues, and product development, among others, which were not apparent when the company was bought. By the time Richard was able to change the existing management, the company was in trouble, and after 24 months, the company was shut down.

"My partner and I were consumed with the business, and needed another collective set of eyes to look at the business and keep management on track," he says. "Installing a board would have helped challenge the previous management to address some of the ongoing problems the company faced at an early stage."

Richard also states that boards, no matter how they are constructed, or how conservative they may be, add value more often than not. Although private companies are not mandated to have a board, Richard is adamant that private companies think about having one.

"It is important that board members are not friends, but accomplished business people that are sourced using proper avenues such as search firms," he says.

Richard, with the CEO, took corporate issues to the board members, soliciting their advice. Of course, Richard and the CEO would not know what to expect, but with excellent members on the board, Richard was confident that they would actively challenge management's decisions if needed, holding both Richard and the CEO accountable for their decisions.

"This ensures that all aspects of the business are properly looked at," he explains. "There are some who may not like being held accountable and may be able to operate without a board, but the advantages outweigh the disadvantages."

A fascinating story that Richard shares, atypical of what a Chairman would deal with, was when Richard was Chairman of one particular company riddled with corporate politics, affecting the company's overall performance.

"People would walk into my office, close the door, and start talking about problems with a particular individual," he says. "The following day, that individual comes in and complains about the first individual, and the cycle continues. I was able to constantly feel the tension in the workplace."

Richard could not believe how caustic the work environment was; he was consistently exposed to individual complaints, negative body language, and people rolling eyes in meetings, as examples.

"This cultural problem was allowed to continue as the CEO did not even see the problem, and in a way condoned it," Richard says. "After trying to address the issue with the CEO, I let him go. After bringing on a new CEO, one of his tasks was to take care of this cultural issue. Over time, the CEO was able to identify the senior executives responsible for this cultural malaise and brought in new people that had a desire to run the business, respect their peers, and do the best job possible."

Although Richard's experience with board members comes mostly from larger companies, the essential message that he gives is for business owners to get solid advice. With smaller companies, initially rallying a few advisors may be an excellent first step. Dave Renwick has seen a couple of companies that did not take this route and rapidly collapsed.

Dave Renwick has worked for KPMG in its London, Ontario office since 1999, and has seen a tremendous number of businesses come and go as clients. Many of the businesses with whom KPMG consults are those looking to get to the next level or may be thinking about selling either a percentage or all of the business. Therefore, some of the consulting that KPMG does involves getting the business ready for sale.

Coming from this perspective, Dave says that one of the biggest issues, especially for privately held family businesses, is the emotion tied up in the sale, which tends to prevent the business owners from having an objective opinion of the value of their business.

"The value of their business, in their minds, is always on the high side, as one would expect than what the market is willing to pay for it," Dave says. "This can be from a multiple of cash flow, synergies that a strategic purchaser may gain, etc. It is hard for them to be objective as they can be too close to the business and have the obvious emotional ties."

The entrepreneur may feel that he or she knows the value of the business, but will rarely ask for advice on valuation. If business owners do ask for advice on the valuation, more often than not, they are disappointed with the number as the gap between the true valuation and the emotion-filled one tends to be wide. At some point, someone might agree with the business owner's valuation, but that person is usually not the one writing the cheque, or it is someone who clearly wants to grossly overpay for a business.

"When giving [business owners] advice, we sometimes find if they don't agree with it they will go around finding someone who will be more in line with their own opinions," says Dave.

Dave suggests that a business put together an advisory board consisting of business people that the owner respects. This advisory board ideally should have those with backgrounds in a few different areas, but who can still contribute relevant business advice. This way, the business owner can bounce ideas off the advisory board from time to time to see if their ideas make sense. Of course, KPMG and other firms exist to provide such realistic advice, but balking at recommendations of their trusted business advisors can have some negative consequences to the business.

"We have had six or seven examples of companies that have not taken our advice and are no longer around," says Dave. "These were companies that had sales between $5 million and $60 million. Gone!"

When an exciting opportunity arises and the business finds an interested investor that would accelerate growth by providing cash to the company, Dave says that sometimes greed gets in the way. This greed can tend to inflate the amount that the business owner thinks he or she should get for the investment, and sometimes, the investor walks away. As a result, the business may fail to grow, and the business owner wastes time trying to find another investor and gets distracted from the core business. Eventually, these distractions can result in the business losing market share to the competition.

Bringing on senior talent also functions as a form of advice as this talent can use its experience to steer the company toward higher growth. But in Dave's experience, some business owners do not invest wisely in key senior management positions.

Dave illustrates this with an example of a company that did not see the value of having a senior human resources (HR) manager on board. Without a senior HR manager, the company had weak HR policies and practices and a loosely defined bonus system with few metrics to justify it. Consequently, this company's biggest challenge was, unsurprisingly, attracting and retaining talent!

"On the finance side of things, some companies are looking to cut costs and hire a controller or book keeper when they really need a VP of Finance or CFO. This impacts their ability to generate reliable forecasts and other performance metrics on which they may rely to make business decisions," Dave says.

In the end, Dave says that the best companies – the ones with the most value – are the ones where the owners have been proactive and have made themselves redundant.

"[The business owners] have to work themselves out of a job," he says. "If they were successful in doing this and they got hit by the proverbial beer truck, the value of the company would remain relatively unchanged as the management team would continue to operate the business. There's so much personal goodwill created in the relationships with suppliers, customers, etc. If that goodwill is tied up in one person and an investor comes along potentially looking to buy or invest in the business then they will need that person around for a longer period of time until other key relationships are established. If you are looking to sell all or part of your company, the sooner you make yourself redundant, the better chance you will have of achieving your goal at a reasonable multiple."

When assembling an advisory board, an early stage company should have members with a broad base of experience dealing with early stage companies. Advisors coming from more mature businesses need to have an understanding of the entrepreneurial environment that is much different from the structured environment that they may be used. Doug Davis experienced such a situation early in his successful investment career.

Doug Davis has had a 46 year career in financial services, starting his career in commercial banking, securities analysis and sales, venture capital management, and investment banking. He has spent the last 31 years of his career with Davis Rea and its predecessor companies.

Early in his career, Doug ran a company in the investment counselling business, successfully running a small-cap fund[27] and achieving an impressive compounded annual return of 48% over five years. Because of his excellent track record, he was fortunate to meet a senior person in the investment community who wanted to do business with him.

"On a trip to New York in 1982, I was introduced to the president of PaineWebber," Doug says. "He loved our results and proposed that they launch a small-cap fund for us, which they would market worldwide."

The president felt that his company could raise anywhere from $1 billion to $1.5 billion in capital for investments, but he wanted 5% of the money raised as underwriting fees. In addition, of the 2% of the management fee that Doug Davis was to charge, which equated to $20 million to $30 million annually, he wanted half of that amount. To Doug, this was an easy decision as this would propel his company's growth significantly and give his company considerable credibility by associating with PaineWebber.

"I was ecstatic and called a meeting of our board to present the idea," he says. "Our major shareholder was irate that I would agree to pay PaineWebber more than their normal underwriting fees. He demanded that I renegotiate and take the management fee off the table. They wouldn't budge, and the deal was killed. Because some of our board members were too greedy, they failed to understand that the glass half-full was still a fantastic deal for us. Subsequently, the small-cap market went into a seven-year bear market."

As it happened, within two years of the start of that bear market, the same principle shareholder was upset with the lack of growth, and by this time, Doug had decided to buy him out. In fact, Doug made some major revisions to the board because he felt the members did not understand the entrepreneurial nature of the company.

"My associate and I bought the company from [the principle shareholder] and changed the board which had been too institutional in

27 A small-cap fund is a mutual fund that focuses on investing in a number of companies with each having a market value generally between $250 million and $1 billion.

mindset to one that was more entrepreneurial," he says. "We were quite small and therefore could not afford to pay much for directors, but it was also equally hard to get board members who think like you and that could help grow the company."

Because of the bear market, the general investment sentiment became much more conservative, and Doug had to change his strategy from investing in small-cap stocks to safer, large-cap stocks, and adapt his company to match the conservative investment climate which had developed. Doug's associate left to continue his interest in small-cap investing, with Doug buying his shares, after which he approached the board for support in changing the investment strategy.

Board support was given because Doug had board members who understood his business. This was crucial because if the change in strategy was not approved, Doug had the assets of his customers invested in small-cap stocks that could rapidly deteriorate value in the current bear market. Shifting to large-cap stocks was a much safer bet to protect his customers' assets from losing their value.

Whatever stage the business is at, the advice from the three gentlemen in this chapter is clear: assemble advisors or formal board members to filter the strategy and get appropriate advice on where the challenges may be.

Advisors are not necessarily expensive, and may come free, or for a token amount when the business is in its infancy, with generally more compensation as the business grows. Given the ongoing challenges that a business owner will face, being able to tap into an experienced group will prepare the business for those challenges, ensuring that it grows at a much more efficient pace.

FAIL FAST
SUCCEED FASTER

PART 4

Can You Run a Business?

Greatness is not achieved by never falling but by rising each time we fall.

— Confucius

The business plan has been properly prepared and key resources gathered. The business is ready to open its doors.

Now it comes down to execution.

A business has many moving parts that need to work together, and as captain of the ship, the entrepreneur needs to ensure that all these moving parts work together using the resources brought on board. The entrepreneur will be thrown in many directions and will need to tackle a tremendous number of issues, such as marketing to customers, ensuring that suppliers are being paid, establishing a healthy level of inventory, putting in business processes, properly monitoring the finances, and establishing a culture, to name a few – and the list keeps growing as the business keeps growing.

In the quest to be successful, the business will face a number of challenges, some personal and others relating to the business. Yet somehow, despite the emotional roller coaster that an entrepreneur may go through in addition to the constant ups and downs that the business will go through, the entrepreneur must remain steadfast and press on to continue the success of the business.

The stories in this section touch upon both the personal and business related challenges that the entrepreneur may face while running the business. Some of the interviewees were able to overcome their business challenges, but for those who were not prepared, the business had to shut its doors.

Personal and Professional Values Are Intertwined

Take a step back and really define your core values. What are they and do they align well with my personal and professional lives. If there is a misalignment, then you simply cannot be the best you can be, either at home, at the office, or both.

– Stacey Mowbray, CEO – Second Cup Ltd.

When starting up a business, entrepreneurs often seem to think that professional values that are imparted onto the business are different than personal values that are upheld. The reality is that they are both intertwined. If one was to try and separate the two, one would have to consciously make that effort.

Over time, the entrepreneur becomes so busy that trying to maintain two sets of values becomes difficult, which could affect the business as well as his or her personal life. Others may begin to see different values applied to a common situation, which could cause confusion. Running a business that resonates with both personal and professional values is much more efficient, and less taxing on the entrepreneur.

For Stacey Mowbray, separating these values resulted in her not being a happy person. Combining these two values into one has not only made her personally happy, but it has also made her professionally successful because of the way she imparts values onto those that work for her. At some point, every entrepreneur needs to realize this.

Stacey Mowbray is CEO of Second Cup, Canada's largest specialty coffee franchisor, with over 360 cafés across Canada. Her previous roles include VP Marketing for Pepsi Canada, SVP Marketing and Branding for Cara Operations, and President of Milestones Restaurants for Canada. For Stacey Mowbray, going through the exercise of defining her core values was necessary to ensure that she would overcome a business challenge she had in a previous professional role. She needed to ensure that both her personal and professional values were in alignment, what she calls a "values fit".

"Personal and professional values don't stand out alone. Your values are a bundle because you're a bundle," she says. "Even though we may act slightly differently at work than at home, your behaviour and actions are driven by the same set of values. We should really be the same person. When you are not the same person, it creates stress. If you have to consciously drive a persona just to fit in that is not you, then, ultimately you are going to fail."

When Stacey looks back, the lessons she learned during her career were always about the alignment of the career and her personal values. At one point in her career, she was working hard and seeing success at work but was not a happy person. She had been in a company for quite some time, and over this period the company had changed, and Stacey had changed in where she was at with her life.

"I wanted to continue to excel at my career, I did have a small family at the time, and I did not want to give anything up," she says. "This was the life that I wanted to lead. But I discovered that the company I was at was not a good values fit. And that creates stress in your life, and when stress happens in your life, you cannot be the best that you want to be."

She discovered, through an executive coach, that she needed to understand and define what she was striving for. When Stacey had switched roles and worked for a company where there was a great values fit, despite a heavier workload, she felt less stress and was a happier person both at work and at home.

"What are my values, what are the things that are important to me, and am I in an environment that is conducive to those values? If I am, then I am absolutely going to be the best that I can be," she says. "If I'm not, I either need to change my role, or I need to rethink my values if I can't make that change. Right? Not many people can change their values, so they are more likely to change their role. And some people can't change their role right away. But I think you need to start to have a plan to say that I recognize this, and here's my plan on how I am going to deal with it. And, I think that people can be successful knowing that they are in control and that they have a plan to move to the next stage."

She relates her thinking to an example of a colleague who was working in a high-paced and high-stress environment while, at the same time, her home was being renovated. Despite not having a family at the time, somehow she just could not get the renovation finished; at that point in her life, her work was her priority, and rightfully so. However, she did not pay attention to what values she needed to change on the personal side to align them with those in her professional career.

When this person reflected on her values, she found that calm and serenity helped her recharge. Going through a realignment exercise made her realize that it was necessary to take some time to get the renovation completed. Not having the renovation complete was creating a stressful situation which bled into her workplace, and hence, she could not be at her best at her place of employment.

Keeping with her priorities, she took a couple of weeks off and hired a few people to finish the renovation. In the end, she was able to inject calm and serenity into her life, finish the project, and return to work being the best that she could be, and she did so without changing her overall goals in life. This is a clear example of recognizing her values and how those values fit with her overall life at that point in time.

For Stacey, her "values fit" is apparent when leading the company, Second Cup. On a personal level, her family values stand for care and quality, and they directly translate to how she leads her corporate team because she cares deeply for the people that work for her, the franchise owners that are responsible for promoting the brand, and the guests that visit the cafés. This care and quality is a point of difference with Second Cup's competitors.

The Second Cup cafés are not about maximizing the number of customers per hour simply through speed; it is more about getting to know the guests and creating a quality experience. For Stacey, this is an environment that she can foster, and she can identify with and comfortably move forward with a brand that is more humble than others.

This alignment of goals translates into the team members that she surrounds herself with. For Stacey, running a successful business is about the team, and how this team aligns with the professional and strategic goals of the company.

"Having a great team makes a world of difference," she says. "Having the right person and the right team is incredibly important. The team members do not have to be the same. One needs to figure out what skill sets are required at that point in time, which could also mean that the team that you assembled today may not be the same three years later. One needs to take a step back, and really think about what is required of your team."

Stacey reviews her team on an annual basis, asking herself if her team has skill sets that are congruent with the strategy moving forward. Assessing the team requires consideration of each team member's adaptability and ability to move forward, and she supports them with feedback, mentorship, and an opportunity to develop the right skills. If, after this support, the team member still fails to move forward with the strategy, she makes the decision to let that team member go because, if she retained that person, he or she would eventually become frustrated.

"After doing the right things and supporting them, if you still know that keeping them is not right, you owe it to them and to your company to make the move, and move on," Stacey says. "In most cases, that person moves on and does very well in the next phase of their professional life that is right for their skill sets and where they can be heroes and win."

Being all about supporting the individual has also translated into having quality franchisees, because they are the front line in promoting the Second Cup brand. Other franchises may be driven by a formula or big advertising, whereas Second Cup is driven more by what happens within those four walls. It is about fostering the community, getting to know the guests, and being involved in the café.

The results speak for themselves: Stacey can proudly state that of the 360 cafés, the top 25% were able to grow on average by 15% in the previous year. This reinforces that the successful operation of the café is all about the individual, and this individual is critical to the success of the café, and the success of Second Cup.

The statistics help Stacey alter some of the business processes when trying to source the potential franchise owners that are critical to the success of the café. There are various screeners that Stacey and her team use to ensure that each potential franchisee is able to maximize their experience of owning a Second Cup café. She has also changed some of the royalty schemes to ensure that the corporate office invests in the franchisees during the first couple of years, a time that the franchisees need to build their presence in that particular location.

With these new processes in place, Stacey can bring on franchisees that are savvy on the retail side, engaged in the franchise location, possess great leadership skills that foster a healthy working environment for their staff, continually communicate with the corporate office when required, and take extra steps to make sure customers walk away happy.

When reflecting on how she successfully straddles and aligns her core values, Stacey first talks about her personal values.

"Family is really important to me," she says. "It doesn't mean that I can't be a CEO just because my family is very important to me. Having valuable time with my family is what I cherish the most. I just make sure it is valuable time. I may not be with them the whole day, but it just means that my time with them is valuable."

She then talks about how this personal value relates to her professional role.

"You need to take a step back and really look at those core values. It may not be about family time, but more about meaningfully affecting people," she says. "You know, if I think of my own values, it is about modelling behaviour for my daughters. It is also about mentoring people in the workforce, and it is also about this role because these franchisees are putting their hard-earned money on the line and I really want them to be successful. I can impact them. I am not in this big huge machine. What I do here today is going to be affecting their lives. I take that very, very seriously. It's a value I cherish. It just manifests itself in different ways at home than it does here, at the office."

Knowing that personal and professional values are intertwined, an entrepreneur needs to realize that both sets of values affect the business. These values also impact the resources that are hired. If the values of the entrepreneur are not in line with those working for the company, the resources will likely think about whether there is a fit with the company, and if not, they might leave. If this seems to be a common occurrence, then the entrepreneur should take a look at the values he or she upholds, and make a change.

One set of values could be in ensuring that the business becomes the best at what the entrepreneur wants to deliver: customer service, product quality, service experience, and so on. I am sure that almost every entrepreneur feels this way, and there are various signs hung on walls that try and describe the same feeling through different mission and value statements.

But if an entrepreneur wants to be the best, then why not benchmark the business against the best in the industry? John Rothschild implemented benchmarking and turned a business that was operating like a Wild West show into a successful portfolio of eating and drinking establishments.

Benchmark Your Business

*Financial discipline was the key to reining in a
chain of restaurants that operated like the Wild West.
You have to be careful to not have too much discipline
that stifles creativity. We took the best of everything, and
benchmarked every new location against these metrics.*

– John Rothschild, CEO – Prime Restaurants Inc.

Benchmarking is a concept where a product or service is compared to a certain standard. The product or service is then made or delivered as close to that standard as possible. When an entrepreneur thinks about bringing a product or service to the market, it is important that the product or service is the best that it can be, given its application and its price point. If not, potential customers have other choices, and they will gravitate to the other choices as, in their mind, the competitors have a better offering.

John Rothschild is a member of the board of directors, and CEO of Prime Restaurants Inc. which franchises, owns and operates casual dining restaurant brands and premium Irish pubs in Canada. The founders of Prime, pioneers since 1979 in the Canadian casual dining industry, opened the first Casey's restaurant in 1980 in Sudbury, Ontario. Today, Prime's portfolio includes East Side Mario's, Casey's, a family of authentic Irish pubs operating under the trade-marks Fionn MacCool's, D'Arcy McGee's, Paddy Flaherty's, Tir nan Óg and Belgian-style brasseries operating under the trade-mark Bier Markt.

John has been a senior officer and member of the boards of directors of Prime's predecessors since 1988. From 1979 until 1993, John worked for Cemp Investments Ltd. (later Claridge Inc.), rising to become Vice-President of Investments, and then President of one of that company's subsidiaries specializing in investing in small to medium sized businesses.

For Prime Restaurants, the previous management ran it with no clear discipline or standard. This resulted in the operations coming close to bankruptcy, and a perfect opportunity to rescue the company by simply benchmarking. To bring Prime Restaurants back "from zero to hero", John Rothschild tamed the Wild West by benchmarking.

John's career has been one of monumental change by microscopic movement. Leaving an investment banking background, he got an opportunity to take over a troubled operating company, Prime Restaurants, which he has been with for close to 25 years.

When John took over this company, he had to change the haphazard way it was being run. By implementing some much-needed financial discipline, John brought great success to the company. But John cautions about putting in too much financial discipline.

"Like all things, if you do them in excess, you end up on the wrong side, such as creativity," he says. "It is much like knowing when to hold onto the reins and when to pull back on the reins, much like when to listen to the wing nuts and when to listen to the accountants. It's a constant balance. That, to me, is what leadership is, which is the ebb and flow of working with teams and people, managing them, moving them in the same direction."

When John started with Prime Restaurants, the phrase "strategic planning" was one that nobody had heard of before or ever applied. It is now applied regularly. John was able to turn it around quite quickly, thoroughly enjoying his role there. He organized a management-led buyout of other early shareholders to become the company's major shareholder, took the company public, then privatized it, and finally ended up with the well-respected Fairfax Financial as his partner.

"It's been an amazing ride of ups and downs and all-arounds," he says.

Because John was not from the food industry, he did not have the relevant experience to draw from. To gain knowledge, he tapped into colleagues respected for their food industry experience. He would call up his idols, invite them for dinner, and ask them questions. He would inquire about issues such as franchising versus corporate stores, fresh fries or frozen fries, and many others. This is the way John learned the language of the restaurant business.

To implement financial controls, John wanted to introduce the concept of benchmarking to the team. He wanted to benchmark every new restaurant location against the best location and the best franchisee that was currently in the inventory of restaurants.

John went to his team and asked everyone, "What is the definition of a great location? How would you identify a great location? What makes a great franchisee?"

Surprisingly, nobody could answer these questions. John was not satisfied, so he told the team that he would begin to do some benchmarking. He would take two of the top franchisees, a couple of mediocre ones, and a couple of the poorest franchisees and, through personality testing, benchmark the characteristics of an ideal franchisee.

He performed the same exercise with locations. He selected a couple of excellent locations, a couple of mediocre locations and a couple of bad locations, and tried to understand the differences. From a benchmarking perspective, the characteristics of the excellent locations were identified as the key ingredients for future locations.

Once he was able to establish benchmarking on virtually every aspect in the business, the ambiguities in location and franchisee characteristics were taken out of the equation. This benchmarking continues today.

"Benchmarking was critical," John explains. "Nobody had ever thought that you could benchmark and identify what made a good franchisee. At least it reduced the risk. It is all about risk reduction. Mistakes don't get made. That was it. That was pretty much how the Wild West got tamed."

When a new location comes up for consideration, every member of the senior management team must sign off on the new location to signify that that team member had understood and approved of that location. If the location does not prove to be a good one, there is no finger-pointing; the whole team gets together to resolve the issue.

There are two pieces of advice that John gives his son, which are relevant to how he operates and runs a business. The first is that when you are listening, you are learning. John spends a tremendous amount of time listening to the people around him. The second piece of advice is to never make an important decision hastily. Take at least 24 to 48 hours to make your mind up.

"I also tell my guys that if you want to get an MBA on a weekend, they should go rent *The Godfather*," he says. "I don't preach killing people, but I do preach organization and delegation. It's nothing personal, just business."

John started many ventures under the Prime Restaurants flag, some successful and some not so successful, making the harsh decision to kill a concept if it did not fit, and would move on. One such harsh decision came for a restaurant concept called the Red Devil, a unique barbeque concept. Because the company needed its own culinary and training department for this concept to be successful, the overhead costs began to rise. John's magic number of restaurants required to be a successful concept was 50.

As a result of the higher overheads, he was able to get to eight restaurants, suitable enough to manage a small to medium sized company, but not Prime Restaurants. John had to make the hard, but necessary, decision to kill the Red Devil concept and move on. All the old restaurant locations were transformed to those more in line with existing concepts under the Prime Restaurants portfolio. Although this decision did not make John a popular person, from a business perspective, the decision made sense.

In the end, John says that he can run anything, as long as he loves what he is doing. He is absolutely enamoured with Prime Restaurants and takes pleasure in leading his team.

"I'm having a ball," he says. "Every day I feel like I'm still putting my feet in starting blocks in this crazy race we're involved in. Every day I set a goal, then reach it, and then set another goal, and keep on going. We do lots of listening and lots of planning. It's like a rhythm around here. If I wasn't here, all of that stuff would happen. It is now part of the DNA of the company."

John reiterates that having financial discipline is a strength, but it could also be a weakness.

"I'm in the entertainment business as much as I'm in the food business," he says. "Too much financial discipline will totally wring the soul or the heart out of the business."

Surprisingly, entrepreneurs will take notice of who the competitors are, but they will not tease out the strengths and weaknesses of competitors' products and services that may be similar to theirs. Benchmarking against the competitors' strengths and vastly improving over their weaknesses should give a huge advantage. As long as these strengths and improvements are relayed to the customer, the entrepreneur should find some traction in the marketplace.

Benchmarking is extremely important in being the best that you can be. Companies often hang mission statements or vision statements that incorporate "being the best" at "something", but the execution is just not there. John Rothschild not only states it, but executes it on a daily basis. That is why he is able to succeed where others have failed.

Once a business gets going, it is important that the entrepreneur keep tabs on the various parts of the business. This is not as important when the business is just starting, but, as it grows, the entrepreneur will simply not have the time to be directly involved in every aspect of the business.

To make sure that everything is going according to plan, various controls should be instituted to provide some feedback to the entrepreneur. If things begin to go sideways, then the controls will alert the entrepreneur ahead of time.

An important area to monitor and establish controls is corporate finances. We have already seen that not having financial controls was a contributor to the business failing in Section 1 where Sean Miller shares his story on how he and his brother were running blind financially, resulting in the business failing. With no financial controls in place, Rick Spencer's company was another fallen statistic, and David Ciccarelli's company was about to become one.

Establish Financial Controls Early

By not putting the right financial controls in place, we allowed a situation where the numbers could be manipulated. By the time we caught this, it was too late, and we had to fold the company.

– Rick Spencer, Former President – Spencer Steel Ltd.

When we started, our financial controls were absolutely horrendous, which allowed the fraudster to take advantage of us. We were literally 30 days away from losing the company.

– David Ciccarelli, Co-Founder and CEO – voices.com

If an entrepreneur is running a successful business, then revenues, cash flow, and profits should be healthy provided costs are controlled. To ensure that an entrepreneur is able to catch any part of the business that is showing signs of trouble, controls should be put in place in every potential business area. These controls should provide much-needed feedback so the entrepreneur can act accordingly to catch any slipups that might be starting to occur.

Because cash is an absolute necessity for the business to run, it is essential that controls are put on finances early. Even though the entrepreneur may trust others to ensure that the finances are taken care of, financial controls are still a priority. If things start to slide in the financial area, and it is not caught in time, the business could be lost for good, such as Rick Spencer's company, or the business could be at death's door, such as David Ciccarelli's company.

Rick Spencer was 15 years old when he joined the family steel business, started by his father in 1962. After 36 years, Rick took over the business in 1991 and grew the company from $4 million in annual revenues to a peak of $30 million at one point, eventually settling to $20 million.

Given the company's excellent track record, it had a strong relationship with the bank and with the banker who oversaw the company's banking needs. Knowing that there would be annual swings in the company's business, the banker usually loosened some of the tight restrictions on the sizable loans the company had taken out, given the healthy financial statements and strong track record the company had over the years.

However, in 2003, the banker Rick had dealt with for many years passed away. A new banking contact was assigned, but he did not understand the steel industry, nor did he have any relationship with the company. To the banker, Rick's company was just another company on paper. When Rick needed some relaxing of the restrictions on the loan covenants with the bank, there was some hesitation on the banker's part to do so and he asked for a second opinion from his senior colleagues.

The decision from the bank did not go in Rick's favour, and he was left with a voicemail stating that his company had only 10 days to pay off all the loans. This stressful news also came at a time when Rick was scrambling to find someone to take over the company's day-to-day accounting. Rick managed to find a controller to fill the position on short notice, giving him some help through this trying period with the banks by aiding the negotiations for an extension on the bank's request.

"At the same time this banking issue was happening, I hired a new controller who was very eager to contribute," Rick says. "Together, we visited the bank to try and see if the bank could extend the deadline to pay the loans. With some aggressive negotiations, we were able to extend the deadline for two months, and the controller was able to establish a relationship with another bank, which kept the business alive. Soon, we were able to turn around, and make good on the loan covenants while solidifying a new banking relationship."

The relationship with the controller was going smoothly, and Rick trusted him to continue with the accounting while Rick concentrated on the growth of the company. In 2010, Rick found out that his controller had been convicted of fraud, stealing $30,000 from a non-profit group.

Rick confronted the controller, who seemed genuinely remorseful for his actions. Against the advice of his colleagues, Rick decided to keep the controller because he had helped out when the company was in trouble, and gave him the benefit of the doubt.

As time passed, the controller began having issues working with many of the staff, criticizing them about the accounting process, their jobs, their projects, cost overruns, and other issues. This became a constant topic of conversation between Rick and the controller, yet he continued to badger the employees.

Finally, in 2011, Rick decided to let him go, and called the controller into his office to break the news. During the exit interview, the controller tried to convince Rick that he alone could help the company move forward, and that Rick should work with him to make that happen. Despite these pleas, Rick did not relent. He escorted the controller out of the building and immediately hired a new controller in his place.

"The very next morning the bank calls me to let me know that my loan was at risk as the company did not have high enough receivables on the balance sheet to cover the loan," Rick says. "But that just did not make sense."

Rick was surprised because, at the time, the company was earning approximately $20 million in revenues, and, based on the results presented by the controller he had just fired, Rick thought his company was financially sound. Nevertheless, Rick had to scramble to find more money to respect the bank's wishes. After finding a financial backer, Rick began negotiations with an entity to obtain $2 million in debt to keep the company alive.

Relieved that he had averted yet another problem with the bank, Rick returned to his office, where the newly hired controller approached him with a perplexed look on his face and explained that he had found problems with the inventory on the balance sheet.

The controller stated, "Rick, your inventory, your Work-in-Process[28], it's really screwed up. It's really out. Like, it's out by $4.4 million."

Rick was confused. "Maybe you don't understand our system. That's got to be it," he replied.

---

28 Work-in-Process is an inventory term that provides a value for a company's partially finished goods that are waiting to be completed for eventual sale. These items are either just being fabricated, or are waiting for further processing.

Rick asked his auditor to review the financial records; the auditor concluded that the controller was right. With this money "missing", it became clear that the previous controller, who Rick had trusted, had fudged the financial numbers to appease the loan covenants put in place by the bank.

At this point, Rick sensed that the end of the company was near, and saw the process of events that would unfold: with the breaking of the covenant, the bank would bring the loan under review, and upon completion of their review, the bank would have to pull the loan from Rick's company, and ask Rick to begin paying back the loan immediately.

With no other financing avenues left for Rick's company, that spelled the end of the family business.

Rick listened to his high ethical standards and let the bank and the financing entity know what was happening.

"I had to go to the bank to tell them what was going on. I also approached the financier that was close to inking the deal on the $2 million to let them know what was going on. Of course, everybody ran for the hills. Immediately, it went to special loans. Two weeks later, that was it. It was over. The bank was out. That quick," he says, snapping his fingers.

Rick points out that this was his mistake; he should have been aware of what was happening financially, despite having resources in place to provide financial numbers. There should have been financial controls put in place to ensure that the numbers being entered into the accounting system were correct. Had the numbers not been entered correctly, Rick would have been able to ask certain questions. If a satisfactory answer was not given, he would have been able to investigate the financial anomalies further, and would have caught the "magical" movement of inventory much earlier.

"The biggest lesson that I had learned from this failure was that if there's something that is confusing or you don't understand, dig into it and find out why you don't understand it," he says. "You have GOT to know. You have GOT to know. You can't just sit back. I had no idea that it was that important and that it could possibly be manipulated in that way."

Rick's main piece of advice to entrepreneurs is to put the proper controls in place to monitor complex transactions.

"There are no secrets to things going bad. You find out what is broken and you fix it. If I had the controls in place back in 2003, I would not be in the situation that I am in today," he says.

In addition to having the controls, Rick also suggests that a company spend the money to have an outside firm take a look at the company to make sure everything is okay. Rick says that at the time, he would have probably balked at the price tag of $5,000 to bring an outside firm in. But, with the advantage of hindsight, he would never make that mistake again and suggests that other companies do the same.

For Rick, putting financial controls in place would have enabled him to sniff out some of the "magic financial management" that the controller had performed, which brought down his company. For David Ciccarelli, financial controls would have been able to catch a potential fraudster, but because these controls were not in place, the company came incredibly close to seeing the end of its days.

David Ciccarelli is Co-Founder and CEO of voices.com, the industry-leading website that connects businesses with professional voice talents. Its clients include radio and television stations, advertising agencies, and businesses of all sizes, including Fortune 500 companies. The company has over 75,000 talents that speak over 100 languages that anybody can hire right through the company website.

David and his wife, Stephanie, started this company with a higher purpose of helping others.

"We are blessed to be a blessing for others," he says. "By taking that approach, we view ourselves as merely a channel to helping our voice talent find work. This changes the perception of why we are doing what we are doing. A lot of companies know what they do. 'We sell XYZ'. But why are you doing this? When you build a culture around people understanding why you're doing what you're doing, they come to work with a reason and a purpose. We spent a lot of time on that."

Before voices.com, David had a background in audio engineering and had a passion to start some kind of business. He got the opportunity to start a mobile studio.

"I went to school for audio recording and knew that I wanted to start a business," he says. "In 2000, the first Apple laptop came out and gave me the ability to have a mobile recording studio where I could go on-site to record digital recordings. I wrote a business plan, put together the financing with my dad, bought all the equipment, and started a recording studio in London."

Soon after, an article appeared in the London Free Press about the business, which is how he met his wife, Stephanie, who co-owns voices.com.

"Stephanie, my wife-to-be, was in university at the time," David says. "She was getting a music degree and was a vocal major, and was going to weddings and other such events. She approached me to do a CD as a marketing tool. After working together very well, I ended up marrying her, and we ran the recording studio business together."

After the newspaper article, David and Stephanie saw a big uptick in business and were asked to do recordings for phone systems, radio commercials, and other such requests. They bought the website domain name www.interactivevoices.com, and once it went live, David and Stephanie received a tremendous number of requests from people looking to advertise their voice talent. This was David's "ah-ha" moment where he began to think about building a global community that would bring all of these players together through a web platform. David and Stephanie sold the recording studio and began concentrating on building that web platform.

From a brand perspective, this website name was not very attractive, so David began the search for an appropriate website name, eventually purchasing voices.com for a large sum of money, the company's first large capital investment.

Operating from the kitchen table, voices.com was born in David and Stephanie's condominium.

"We had a toll-free line piped into the condo and people were calling us at all hours of the night, which was not good for our newborn baby," David says. "The phone would ring and we would look at each other and ask 'whose turn is it to take the baby?' Whoever it was would grab the baby and run down the hall and the other one would answer the call in the most calm voice, 'Thank you for calling voices.com. You've reached David. How can I help you?' People would think that they were calling a giant call centre. I would wipe the sleep out of my eyes and take a sip of water to get the grogginess out."

The company graduated one year later from that condominium to a room at a research park, and eventually moved into a sizable office location in downtown London today. In terms of technology, there was a similar path to graduation, starting with the first customer relationship management system going from a notebook to a whiteboard to an Excel spreadsheet and finally to salesforce.com today. Given the substantial growth of the company, other areas of his business, such as the payment system, needed a solid technical solution to ensure a smooth process to generate revenues.

However, David and Stephanie missed implementing financial controls around the payment system. A lack of these controls meant the potential for fraud. Unfortunately, this potential turned into a reality that almost brought the curtains down on the company.

"The credit card fraud story is really interesting because, at this point, we had been doing business for, you know, five to six years, and we did our first $1 million in revenue, which is a pretty big milestone," David says. "We had two credit cards systems, one of which was PayPal, which is what we had always used from Day One, and which was very straightforward. You insert a snippet of code on your website, the person goes to buy, then gets redirected to PayPal, they complete the transaction, and it says 'return to voices.com'. They clicked a button to return to voices.com."

What David was looking for was a credit card solution that kept the customer on the voices.com website for the whole transaction. David did a comprehensive evaluation of all the credit card processing service providers that acted as intermediaries between the bank, the website, and the credit card companies. Each service provider had an exclusive agreement with a particular Canadian bank. Because David and Stephanie dealt with one particular bank for their corporate accounts, they were forced to use one particular credit card processor.

David approached the credit card processor and filled out an application with some help from a representative of that company.

Representative: How much business are you going to do the next 12 months?

David: I don't know. We are a growing business with a new product line. I don't know, maybe $3,000 a month, $36,000 a year. We might do $100,000.

Representative: If you just don't know, then put down zero.

David: Okay, easy enough, zero it is.

Representative: The other question I have to ask is what's the average ticket size? What's the average transaction size of a purchase?

David: Well, again, some talent could be hired for $100, somebody might be hired for $500, maybe $1,000. I don't know.

Representative: Okay, put zero.

David: Okay, zero dollars.

"In hindsight, you look at this application: zero dollar revenue projection and they don't intend on selling anything. So, the application goes through and it gets green stamped all the way through, and we're good and we're set up that day," David says.

The application was approved in 2005, and with no annual checks by the service provider, three years went by without a problem. There were no frauds, no disputes, and no returns, which resulted in no issues whatsoever for the service provider.

"In the summer of 2008, going into 2009, there were some general rumblings of a financial crisis brewing," David says. "During that summer, I was on vacation at a wedding, and we actually had somebody use our website using a fraudulent credit card to hire a voice talent."

The company's payment system used an escrow service where a typical voices.com client would pay for a voice talent online, with the money from that payment being held in an escrow account separate from all the main corporate accounts. The voice talent being hired would then get an email notification that a payment had been made for services. The talent would then provide the service, deliver it to the client, and the client would then authorize voices.com to release the payment to the voice talent.

With a fraudulent credit card, a person could continually hire several talents, with no financial controls in place to prevent this from happening.

"The amounts started small," says David. "First it was $100, then it was $200, then $500, then $1,100 and then it's $2,200. And then [the fraudster] goes 'I probably pushed my luck,' stops, creates another account, and then creates the same pattern again."

These kinds of suspicious transactions would normally be reviewed by David as a particular client would rarely make two purchases for talent. Generally, someone looking for voice talent would make a single purchase, hiring one talent. With the pattern of financial transactions that went on, it was impossible that a client would hire four people at a time for work.

"My suspicion is that he went through the whole process four or five times, and it tallied up to over $50,000 to $60,000 in fraudulent payments," David says. "At this time, the credit card owners don't even realize that these charges had gone through, so it takes little bit of time for all the information to go to Visa and MasterCard, who then go back to [the credit card processor] to tell them that there is something wrong with this particular vendor and to go to voices.com to get the money back. They're called chargebacks."

The credit card processor gave David a call, and with 26 chargebacks, put his account under review. The following conversation ensued.

David: Well, no problem, we cleaned up the situation. It seems to have stopped. We've identified and suspended those accounts. I think we're in the clear.

CC Processor: No. We completed our investigation and our review and we no longer want to do business with you.

This was a big deal for David because his company had over 2,600 encrypted customer credit cards on the credit card processor's system, that were automatically being billed every month.

"You can't export them. You can export who they are, but then you need to make 2,600 telephone calls explaining that you need the new credit card numbers," David says.

The conversation continued.

David: Okay, do you need some more security from me? Like, what you need? That's not good because you're just basically shutting us down. We'll be out of business.

CC Processor: Well, we have the authorization to shut you down right now, with zero warning. After we had done our risk profile review, you are 17 times outside the normal threshold of what's acceptable. We shouldn't have been doing business with you before.

David: Why is that?

CC Processor: Because you said that you are doing zero dollars of business and yet you're doing $1 million a year now.

David: But you guys told me to put that down!

At this point, David had to contemplate what to do.

"The solution was to close down the business because there were no more ways to possibly cover the bills that continued to roll in when I knew that in 30 to 60 days, we might be able to get a handful of customers into the new credit card system, but that would be a huge challenge. That was all that we could possibly do," he says.

David had to buy some time, and immediately negotiated a 30-day window of time with the credit card processor during which he agreed to switch his credit card processing to another company. He also had to shut down any ongoing credit card payments because, although the charge would go through, David would never see the money, as the credit card processor would be holding it. All payments had to be routed through PayPal so the resulting cash could go toward payroll.

David began phoning the other credit card processing companies, who were elated at the amount of business that voices.com was doing, and wondered why David was switching from another company. David let them know that he was just interested in trying out another service. Because David had no track record with the other credit card processing companies, they all wanted a $50,000 deposit because he was a risk to them as he had no business dealings with them. Of course, David did not have that kind of money floating around, and what little money that was trickling into the business was helping to support payroll.

Eventually, David found a credit card processor in the United States that was merging with a Canadian bank that did not require a deposit. Extremely happy, David filled all the paperwork out and implemented a technical solution onto his website to begin taking in credit card payments. He was just about to go live when he got a call from the company asking for a $50,000 deposit, putting him back at Square One.

David tried to reason with the company, saying that this was not requested when doing the application. The credit card processor told him that he required a $30,000 deposit for Visa and a $20,000 deposit for MasterCard.

With his back to a wall, he secured a line of credit for the $30,000, and knowing that his credit card payment split was generally 75% on Visa and 25% on MasterCard, he paid the $30,000 deposit for Visa, allowing clients to now use their Visa cards to make payments.

He then batched a large number of Visa payments from clients whose payments to the company were halted due to the problem with the previous credit card processor. Putting through this large batch of payments allowed David to amass $20,000 to pay the deposit for MasterCard, and he was now free and clear.

"Looking back, I really didn't think that fraud was a possibility," he says. "Our financial controls were horrendous and we've since drastically tightened them up. A lot of this stuff – there's just no way that it will happen now because we have so many instant alerts and so many early warning systems for that type of behaviour that the payment just wouldn't go through, and the talent wouldn't start the job. I think we have an eight-point check on every single transaction that goes through the site."

The former credit card processor told David that they would hold on to the payments for up to 30 days and then continue processing renewal payments for another 30 days. At its height, they had almost $300,000 that was owed to voices.com, which David would now see 30 days later as part of the agreement.

Then, another financial shock hit David. The original credit card processor notified him that, from a legal perspective, it was allowed to hold onto his company's money for up to 180 days after it had terminated the business relationship.

"I find this out, and I had to say to myself, are you kidding me? I believe when I ran the numbers once, we were $500,000 in the hole after all this was done because we had to pay for programmers and consultants to navigate through this whole thing," he says.

David pleaded with the credit card processing company to release whatever funds it could as the company desperately needed the money. Eventually, the company agreed to release 10% of the funds per month.

"It was like a consolation prize," he says. "It took us another year to dig ourselves out of that."

Given his experience, David has some words of advice for entrepreneurs.

"Entrepreneurship is not for the faint of heart, that's for sure. You just don't see this stuff coming. If you can't deal with the stress, then you might as well not try because you think that everything is going to be a great idea and when it is going extremely well, things flare up that you just can't anticipate."

Putting in financial controls is generally not at the top of an entrepreneur's mind when trying to establish and run a business. But when the finances allow you to start the business and grow it, putting controls in place on any process that affects the finances should be a high priority. The entrepreneur should think of the worst possible outcome for a particular process and how that would affect the business's finances, and establish controls to eliminate that outcome. Not putting in these financial controls may result in a sudden change in financial direction, quickly going from north to south as illustrated in the two case studies above.

With the satisfaction that financial controls are in place, a business can then continue on. To see whether a product or service is able to provide the proper outcomes for a customer, an entrepreneur may approach a particular client as a test case. This is excellent as a proof of concept tool, but the entrepreneur should begin to spread its wings to capture other customers at the same time. This spreads the risk as, if something happens to the one customer, there are others that will bring in revenue streams. But if one is locked into one customer, then the risk has all its eggs in one basket. This can paralyze the business severely as it did for Sean Higgins and Kerry McLellan.

Don't Focus Your Resources in One Area

We made the mistake of concentrating our resources to represent one vendor. It hedged its bets by finding other representatives, and we should have hedged our bets by finding other vendors to represent.

– Sean Higgins, CTO – The Herjavec Group

Having one company as the sole customer increased the risk in this strategy and in retrospect the risk should have been shared among working with several lead companies.

– Dr. Kerry McLellan, Founder, President & CEO – Kinek Technologies Inc.

When starting out, an entrepreneur may want to test products or services on one customer to establish a proof of concept or approach a particular vendor to represent its products to customers. In either case, the entrepreneur is able to properly align his or her resources to maximize sales for other customers and also provide a much-needed stream of revenues.

The danger in this scenario is that there is a risk in just having one customer or vendor. Without a clear and tight relationship, a souring of that relationship or a sudden back door move could cripple a company financially resulting in the entrepreneur scrambling to find a new source of revenue.

For The Herjavec Group and Kinek Technologies, this was certainly the case.

Sean Higgins is Chief Technical Officer (CTO) of The Herjavec Group, founded in 2003 by Sean, Robert Herjavec, and George Frempong. The Herjavec Group is one of the fastest growing companies in the Canadian market, specializing in integrating IT solutions. The Herjavec Group exceeded $100 million in sales in 2012, and has achieved a growth rate faster than other technology giants such as Microsoft and Oracle.

The Herjavec Group started as a value-added reseller (VAR), finding success by selling a single vendor's anti-spam technology. This particular vendor's technology became popular, and The Herjavec Group was their number one VAR in North America.

"Everything was going very well, and the company was ramping up, spending a lot of time, effort and resources to help push this particular vendor's technology," says Sean. "Then suddenly, the vendor decided to hedge its bets by signing up other vendors to push the same technology."

Now, The Herjavec Group was not the exclusive avenue to access this popular anti-spam technology. Instead of having companies knock on The Herjavec Group's door, they could go to a more familiar vendor who had also signed up as a VAR.

Unfortunately, this caused the company to lose revenue from year three to year four as the company was not prepared for the competition with other VARs. The Herjavec Group learned that a portfolio of products should be carried at any one time to ensure that this does not happen again.

Sure enough, the year after this incident, The Herjavec Group were VARs for three or four different products, and revenues began to climb. The company continued growing, successfully acquiring companies and adding to its portfolio of services offered, and today counts itself among the Canadian technology juggernauts.

The Herjavec Group had all their eggs in one basket, becoming a value-added reseller for one particular vendor, and was lucky enough to spread its risk by representing other products as it learned its lesson. The same lesson was learned by Dr. Kerry McLellan of Kinek Technologies.

Luckily for him, a valuable lesson was learned early and he was able to pivot his software and turn it into a successful business today.

Dr. Kerry McLellan is Founder, President & CEO of Kinek Technologies. He also serves as executive liaison with Kinek's directors and advisors, executive level stakeholders, and investors. Prior to Kinek, Kerry was Chief Operating Officer of 724 Solutions. During his two-year tenure, 724 Solutions grew from fewer than 20 employees to more than 500, with a market capitalization of $12.8 billion at its peak. The IPO of 724 was one of the most successful in Canadian history.

After developing software to help drive operational efficiencies, Kerry's company, Kinek, applied its software to an initial customer, the Royal Mail Group, Britain's famous postal service. The efficiencies gained would have allowed the Royal Mail Group to better compete with companies such as Federal Express and DHL in the rapidly growing parcel business. Unfortunately, the unions at the Royal Mail Group were not in favour of these efficiencies, believing that jobs would be lost. They did not see the long term implications – efficiencies and subsequent increased competitiveness would have protected employment and potentially increased jobs. Focusing on the short-term implications, the union rallied against this change and other austerity measures and went on strike. This almost destroyed Kinek's business.

Timing for Kerry and the employees could not have been worse. Christmas was around the corner and spirits were up. Kerry had to take a deep breath and go through the unfortunate experience of letting 50 people go.

After this experience, Kerry kept the company going but took a step back, only running a skeleton crew. He needed to take the time to think through his mistakes. Kerry was running other companies at the time, and immersed his time in them. He determined that going to another postal outlet would have been a bad decision because he was not keen on dealing with another company with unionized employees, and he did not want to concentrate all his resources on one more company again.

In 2007, Kerry began to consider reshaping Kinek's business model.

He looked at how smaller community stores struggled to carry a wide variety of products because they did not have the sales volume to drive prices down or the space to diversify their product lines. In addition, the last mile cost[29] of delivering to residential addresses accounted for 60% of the delivery cost. This situation could be viewed as the threat of online commerce and big box shopping to local merchants and the creation of significant cost inefficiencies in e-commerce.

Kinek gave smaller retailers the ability to participate in the e-commerce value chain by signing up to be a shipping/receiving point, or Kinekpoint, for online purchases. Customers would shop online, choose the most convenient Kinekpoint, and would be notified by SMS, push, or email that their product had been securely delivered to their chosen Kinekpoint.

By being a Kinekpoint, the community store could offer a wider selection of products at online prices and serve as the secure delivery point. Kerry changed the business model from a traditional software licensing agreement by adopting cloud-based software as a service model, giving away the software for free to the stores and charging them on a transaction basis. Each retailer charges the customer $3.00 (or slightly more for large packages) for receiving and holding the delivery, retains $2.00 and sends $1.00 to Kinek. The Kinek service has been a hit, and the number of outlets in North America has grown from launch date in 2009 to over 1,200 Kinekpoints in three years, growing at the rate of 4% per week today.

From this situation, Kerry learned to not dedicate all of his company's resources to just one trial partnering customer, where not all stakeholders were aligned in achieving fundamental change. Although having a lead customer is a traditional model in the software industry, the presence of disaffected unions increased the risk in this strategy and in retrospect the risk should have been shared by working with several lead companies.

The Herjavec Group and Kinek's stories demonstrate how concentrating resources for one entity can be detrimental to business. Some

---

29 The "last mile" cost refers to the cost in transporting goods from a major distribution location, such as a freight terminal or a port, to the final address.

companies may decide to test a particular product or service with an initial company, which is an excellent way to begin. However, without an exclusive long-term contractual agreement in place, the company should have a plan to broaden its customer base once the product or service has been proven, bringing on additional resources to support this plan.

With increased resources and customers, it is necessary to ensure that all the resources understand the strategic vision and how they are an important part of that vision. Customers also need to link the business's products and services with the vision to ensure that they make purchases from a company that they understand.

Managing this requires constant communication both internally and externally. A lack of communication could cause customers to make their purchases elsewhere and employees to be disengaged, or worse, disenchanted, with management.

The latter situation was one that Noah Tepperman had to face, resulting in a strike by the employees. He quickly learned his lesson on communication and was able to apply that lesson externally to customers, turning an angry customer into a customer for life.

Communicate Both Inside and Outside Your Firm

Communication inside and outside the firm is absolutely crucial. Lack of communication with the employees led to one the largest labour strikes our company has faced. By paying attention to and communicating with customers, I was able to turn around a situation that could have resulted in negative comments about the company. All of this eventually hurts our brand perception, which we rely on for our survival.

– Noah Tepperman, Partner – Tepperman's Furniture

To ensure that all stakeholders understand what a company stands for and where it is headed, communicating within the business and to external stakeholders, particularly customers, is critical. This is fairly simple for an entrepreneur when the business is in start-up mode because there are fewer stakeholders to address. But, as a business grows, others resources are added and more customers are buying. The entrepreneur finds that time to communicate becomes limited as he or she, along with other management, take on full-time roles in a more structured environment. This effectively reduces the number of opportunities to continually communicate.

Yet the sharing of information on the business's strategic goals cannot fall by the wayside despite the growth. This type of information helps tie the business units together so that each one understands the roles of the other business units, and they all work in concert to support the overall strategic goal.

Communicating this to the employees ensures that they are aware of the role they play in making that strategy happen and to see how the fruits of their labour help with the growth and success of the business.

Communicating the strategy to customers keeps them engaged with the company and its products and services. It also shows that management truly cares about their opinions, ideally establishing a more personal connection, making a customer think twice before moving to a competitor for purchases.

For Noah Tepperman, current partner at Tepperman's Furniture, the lack of communication between management and employees became a problem, and engaging customers through online communication tools, such as social media, helped ward off a potential hit to the brand.

Tepperman's Furniture, a store that primarily sells furniture, appliances, mattresses, and electronics, was founded in 1925 by Nate Tepperman, Noah Tepperman's grandfather. Nate started his business in an obscure part of Windsor, Ontario, but foresaw that this area of Windsor would at some point be a major attraction for customers. Nate was right, and that one store has now grown to four stores in Southwestern Ontario.

Because Tepperman's Furniture was small initially, Nate insisted that he and his management team communicate with the employees early on. However, with the company growing, Nate got busy with increased responsibilities and trusted another individual to help with the communication. But this individual failed to perform his duties. Communication between management and employees became lax and problems ensued, most troublingly an increasing distance between management and the unionized staff.

Noah came on board in 2000, and a year later, he faced the largest labour stoppage in Tepperman's entire history. Noah blames this labour stoppage solely on the lack of communication.

"People had to be in a position to hear what others were saying and wanting to listen to it," he says. "It was not really the negotiation that was the first problem. It was all the underlying communications and the relationship that suffered fragmentation over a period of a couple of years that culminated with the strike."

To compound this problem, a member of the union's bargaining community sitting at the bargaining table was negotiating in bad faith. He had his own agenda and did not really represent the union members as a group. He had agreed to recommend a negotiated deal, but when he stepped away from the table to present the deal to the members, he essentially did the opposite, an extremely rare situation in bargaining with unions in general.

"The underlying issue wasn't just that you had this one person operating with bad intentions and bad faith," Noah says. "The relationship, going into it overall, wasn't as strong and open as it should have been. So it set the opportunity for someone to take control of the train so to speak."

Noah states that the communication between management and the frontline not only has to be open, but also energetic. Management has to be proactive and take responsibility for communication and cannot wait and assume that the frontline workers will initiate communication with management. This could be hard and tiring for management given their busy schedule, but it must be done. Because the management team is responsible for this communication, it cannot blame anybody else; it is management's role to ensure that all areas of the business are under control for the business to move forward.

Although Noah grew up in the business, he says that much of what is done in retail is trial and error. When he looks at failure, he believes it comes more from failing to identify the customer's needs in terms of style or functionality, than a company that designs or builds a product. He would not know what these needs were if he, or members of his extensive staff, were not able to communicate with the customers, as his business success is tied directly to ensuring that customers' furniture, appliance, or electronic needs are met.

Some companies get stuck in having key individuals imprint their sense of taste to guide the inventory available to customers. When Noah was being trained at Tepperman's, he faced this hard lesson. While living in New York for eight or nine years before coming back to join the business, Noah developed a more contemporary taste, but he soon found that his tastes did not matter. It was more a question of knowing what his customers wanted. He also knows that his company is not going to be right all the time.

The importance of "getting it right" has been magnified with the rapidly increasing use of online tools as a vehicle for customers to voice their opinions. As any good retailer should know, these vehicles are more used for complaining than praising, so Noah makes these tools a part of his communication strategy – a big leg up on his competitors who are just starting to find out what social media even is. Because of his savvy, Noah can pay particular attention to addressing customer communication through these channels. The more he is present for that communication, the better.

"I got a nice holiday greeting today from someone over Twitter," he says. "This is a guy from Windsor who is a lawyer. And the first time I even heard of him was shortly after I had signed up for Twitter and he was talking about something that had gone wrong at Tepperman's. He was using very strong language. And I sent a response back saying, 'What's going on that I can help you with? Here's my number, give me a call. I'm at my desk.' He was floored. I think some people think that I am a figment of somebody's imagination. They hear me on the radio and they think I'm an actor. First of all, he was surprised that Noah Tepperman actually existed, second, that he was on Twitter, third that he was paying attention, fourth that he responded within 15 minutes of the tweet going out."

This customer had experienced a situation where a problem he had was not resolved to his satisfaction. Just by being there at the right time, Noah identified the problem and corrected it immediately. Although the same steps would have been taken if the customer had phoned into the store, the whole transaction was done via Twitter. Since that time, that particular customer has been the strongest online advocate for Tepperman's, retweeting Noah's tweets, sharing feedback, giving positive recognition, tweeting about coming back into the store, tweeting about the purchases he made when he made them, and so on.

"I had another experience recently from someone else who submitted some information through social media," he says. "We did everything like we would've done if she had phoned in, but we got to take care of her and she was so appreciative. People are using social media like they are using the telephone, or emailing or even driving to the store. It gives customers an avenue to vent, and they don't expect you to be there. So there is the opportunity for the 'wow' factor."

Using these online communication tools, Noah focuses his efforts on brand communication to tell others that the company values their relationship with their customer. For potential customers who are younger, this demonstrates that Tepperman's communicates the same way that they do. Noah hopes that, "When they become people who need to make a purchase, maybe they will think of Tepperman's."

As much as the vehicles for communication have evolved since then, the importance of communication with employees certainly hit Noah hard when he came on board. Walking into one of the toughest situations between management and employees was not a walk in the park. Fortunately for Noah, he was able to take a step back and recognize that the problems were more about communication rather than the finer points in the contract negotiations.

Certainly, communication with customers, either in person, on the phone, or via social media is crucial to show that Tepperman's Furniture values that relationship. Not many businesses take the time to put effort into this type of communication, and in some cases, send out regular, mundane email blasts that quickly lose value after the first couple of messages.

Making customers feel that they are listened to will ensure that the company is at least in their decision set, which becomes much more important when there are a high number of competitors. If you are too busy to communicate, it should be understandable when your customers look for a connection with your competitors. Often, companies will not realize the implications of poor communication until customers have fled, leaving management scratching its head wondering why sales have flat-lined and then begin descending.

Using an older way of communicating with customers such as mail and possibly phone campaigns may have worked in the past, but it may not be as effective moving forward with social media as a tool. One can also make the same argument more broadly to the past experiences of an entrepreneur that may not necessarily be relevant to future business opportunities.

Some entrepreneurs mistakenly assume because they were employed by a firm in a particular industry, that somehow, this experience would enhance the chances of a new business venture. Of course, having that industry knowledge is great, but it should not be used as a proxy for success.

Shane O'Leary faced such a situation and had to scramble to put resources together to move a venture forward.

Your Past Experience May Be Irrelevant

When going from a larger company to a smaller one, you need to have an entrepreneurial spirit. If not, you may assume that the new venture will automatically come with these structures and processes, and there will come a time when you actually realize that you have to start from scratch. At this point, it may be too late for the venture.

– Shane O'Leary, COO – Gran Tierra Energy

Entrepreneurs generally start businesses because they see an opportunity in a field in which they have experience. Jumping on this opportunity, entrepreneurs will rely on their past knowledge and skills to start the entrepreneurial venture.

Many entrepreneurs coming from larger companies make the common mistake of assuming luxuries such as structures, processes, and even capital are already in place. These entrepreneurs start the venture, and soon find that the assumptions they made were clearly wrong.

These entrepreneurs now face a series of questions on how to even start building new structures and processes given the limited capital that they may have. Even asking questions on how to begin putting these in place may take valuable time and capital, which the entrepreneur may not have.

To make the transition from the corporate world to the entrepreneurial one, there needs to be a shift in thinking that can help adjust from being pampered in a corporate setting to making decisions on how to save money. For example, a decision can be made to have a home office rather than immediately moving into an office space given that there are little to no revenues, a situation illustrated in the next chapter that resulted in the business collapsing. Without such thinking, the business may not even get off the ground as the entrepreneur finds himself or herself outside a corporate comfort zone and possibly incurring unnecessary costs.

Such a challenge was faced by Shane O'Leary as he moved from a large company to a much smaller one. Luckily for him, his entrepreneurial thinking drove him through that challenge.

Shane O'Leary is Chief Operating Officer (COO) for Gran Tierra Energy, an exploration and development company focused in South America with operations in Colombia, Peru, Argentina, and Brazil. Previously, Shane joined First Calgary Petroleum Ltd. in 2006 as COO and was appointed to the board of directors in 2007. In April 2008, he was appointed President and CEO and led an effort to explore strategic alternatives which resulted in the sale of the company to the Italian energy giant, ENI, for $1.3 billion, in September 2008. Prior to his position with First Calgary Petroleum, Shane served as VP and Business Unit Leader, Brazil, for EnCana, where he led the Brazil team in the appraisal and evaluation of EnCana's offshore reserves as well as the acquisition of new acreage.

Much of Shane's management career has been with companies that were fairly large in size, but an opportunity to help a junior oil and gas company, First Calgary Petroleum, came up in 2006. This company had a number of large gas discoveries in Algeria and Eastern Sahara.

Shane was hired to look after the development of the gas fields because of his deep experience in the gas industry in that part of the world. This development included putting together the proper distribution network, which required the construction of pipelines, infrastructure that was hundreds of miles away, and the building of a cryogenic gas plant. This plan required close to $2 billion, cash which the company simply did not have, in addition to scarce resources – one of the first business challenges Shane encountered.

When Shane was tapped to lead larger firms, not only did he have the cash required to put these projects together, but he was also able to draw upon a vast amount of technical and engineering resources if required. Because First Calgary Petroleum was a smaller company, it had a restricted cash flow and faced a cash crunch, so the company's management team had to decide between selling some of their assets to raise money, or cautiously move ahead aggressively to start developing the gas discoveries.

Lack of working capital also limited the amount of technical and engineering resources available. For example, if a reservoir was not performing to expectations, at a large company, the problem could easily be assigned to several technical teams of geologists, geophysicists, completions engineers, drilling engineers, etc. to assess what the problems were and what could be done to fix them.

Shane says that, "When moving to a small company, what strikes you immediately is that the resources that were available at a large company to tackle problems are no longer there for you."

Unfortunately, some industry executives make the assumption that they can help run junior companies with limited resources, but soon hit a wall. Shane has seen this type of problem time and time again.

"Some executives that have transitioned from large companies to junior companies have failed miserably because they can't function without the support systems they once had," says Shane. "In other words, they were great at harnessing the resources available to them at a large company and that is what made them successful. Put them in a situation where they don't have those resources and they are paralyzed."

Shane comments on what it takes for executives to successfully make that transition.

"To make the transition from a big company to a small company, you must have a certain entrepreneurial spirit that may have been somewhat dormant at a big company, but kicks in when you make the transition and helps with the adjustment," he says. "People thinking of making the transition from a big to small company should be honest with themselves if they will be able to function without the big support groups they once had. You have no idea about the support systems that are present in the bigger companies until you don't have any."

This same problem had hit Shane, and hit him hard. He had to find a way to build the company, and its resources, with a limited flow of capital so that he could be in a good position to put in the planned distribution network.

"Everything, you have to re-create yourself," he says. "That includes staff in all areas such as accounting, technical, and administration. I never had a sense of how difficult it was to re-create the basic support functions in a small company that you take for granted in a big company. It's really a case of cost and attracting people to small, higher risk ventures. It's too expensive to have technical 'Centres of Excellence' in smaller companies because there are not enough projects to keep people fully busy even though their expertise is needed from time to time."

Luckily for First Calgary Petroleum, Shane was able to build up the staff with a full engineering complement, reservoir engineers, and facilities engineers. He hired staff in other areas and built the company from nothing to a sizable operation.

With the international operations in place, Shane also had to worry about hiring people in Algeria and staffing the corporate Canadian office in Calgary, as well as opening an office in London, England to maintain a corporate presence in the same time zone as Algeria.

Shane was also pulled in a different direction when the major shareholders were putting together a proxy battle[30], bringing a whole new slate of directors on board. In 2008, the shareholders had won the case and asked Shane to become the President and CEO of the company.

Shane was wary about operating the company in the not-so-rosy financial markets during the recessionary period. Using his entrepreneurial mindset, he took the unique and difficult step of running a parallel process: continuing to operate the company while at the same time preparing the company for sale because he was unsure if the company would survive the recessionary period given the banks' risk-averse reactions to the credit instruments they had approved for many companies, including First Calgary Petroleum.

"I've got a sense that, you know, this credit from the bank side might

---

30 Proxy battles occur when shareholders rally together and, as a majority, vote to make a change to the current management and/or board of directors of a company. Proxy battles are generally started by a major shareholder, as a natural voting majority would exist, and are often due to a collective opposition to an under-performing strategy or direction current management has taken. The result of First Calgary Petroleum's proxy battle can be read at http://www.resourceinvestor.com/2008/04/14/first-calgary-petroleums-ceo-anderson-gone-waterfo.

not work out," he says. "And if it doesn't, you know, we are screwed, we are going to go to zero."

He approached the board of directors with this idea, and initially they disagreed because they wanted to grow the company and not sell it. Eventually, the board relented, and agreed with his strategy. After putting this in place, Shane noticed that there was a huge stress on the staff because they were not sure which way the company was going.

A large Italian conglomerate, ENI, had offered to buy the company at a 55% premium to the shareholders and an 8% interest on the convertible bond. Shane needed both shareholders and bondholders to make the sale happen, but the bondholders were not happy with their share.

"It was a crucial time because the bondholders were telling me that they will reject the deal, yet I was saying that ENI was not changing its offer and the credit markets are going to hell so that option was looking good," he says.

After the financial markets collapsed, Lehman Brothers had gone bankrupt, and the credit markets came to a grinding halt. Given this situation, the bondholders became eager to approve the sale of the company.

The lesson for those starting businesses is to be cautious when thinking that previous experience working in a larger company, although in the same industry, will be directly transferable to the skills required when building a business. The supporting processes and business structures that existed before are no longer present, which means that these all need to be created from the outset.

If an entrepreneur does not have an entrepreneurial spirit and cannot build these supporting mechanisms and structures at the outset, then the business will eventually flounder. In this case, the entrepreneur should prepare for a hard fall.

Building supporting mechanisms and structures from the ground up requires a smart use of capital. Some entrepreneurs may erroneously think that it is important to be comfortable in an office setting before looking for customers. The cash in the bank should be sparingly used to support the growth of the business, incurring expenses as the business grows. Spending the money on irrelevant expenses ahead of running the business is like putting the cart before the horse, which is exactly what Tristan Smith did.

Don't Put the Cart Before the Horse

I put the cart before the horse. I started the business with everything I needed: brand new truck, desk, chair, and printer. The only thing missing was customers. I just couldn't dig myself out of the $100,000 hole I created.

– Tristan Smith, Former Owner – TS HVAC Solutions Ltd.

Every entrepreneur revels in the moments spent sitting in a chair and thinking about the eventual success of a business. The entrepreneur imagines a long line of customers just waiting to buy the business's products or service, and imagines what the office may look like from a customer's point of view. The daydream breaks and the entrepreneur thinks hard, again, about customer perception, and how the office needs to look to spur sales.

With this vision in mind, the entrepreneur hurries to perfect everything about the business before the first customer buys the product or service. Credit cards are maxed out, money borrowed, and savings dipped into as the entrepreneur starts purchasing office furniture so that when the customer walks in, there is a 'wow' factor.

With a slow start, and few revenues coming in the door, given the exorbitant purchases already made, the business starts with a bad profit equation. The profit equation in this case is quite simple: costs > profits = loss.

If the projected revenues fail to materialize, losses will grow until the entrepreneur can no longer finance the business. In that case, either more money needs to be put into the business just to stay afloat, or, as in Tristan Smith's case, the business closes its doors.

Tristan Smith was part of one of three teams working for a company that sold and serviced both industrial and residential heating ventilation and air-conditioning units (HVAC units). The company had been operating in the community for over 25 years, and had an excellent reputation and a continuous backlog of orders. Tristan had joined the company five years earlier as a junior team member.

He was paired with a senior HVAC technician who had worked for the company for over 15 years, from whom Tristan gained substantial knowledge and experience, allowing him to excel in his job. Because of this, he was often asked to work overtime to work the backlog down.

"Because of the backlog of orders, I worked long hours during the week, about 60 to 80 hours in fact," he says. "But my downtime was in the late evenings when I spent time with my girlfriend, friends, and family. Funny enough, I would sometimes fix their air-conditioning and heating units just because I knew them so well. The payment was very simple: a case of beer. After fixing number of issues for a couple of friends, they actually suggested that I begin my own company because I just knew how to fix these things. I seemed to be a natural. I had never really considered this before but when they mentioned it to my girlfriend and I several times, that's when I got thinking more seriously about it."

Tristan did some math in his head. With the company he worked for, he averaged about five appointments a day with an average customer bill of $200 for the residential appointments and a much higher amount for the commercial accounts. That would result in a pay day of $1000 a day. If he worked seven days a week, Tristan calculated that he would make about $350,000 a year, keeping two weeks of holidays in mind.

"I talked this over with [my girlfriend], and she was so supportive of the idea," he says. "For about a year now, we were calculating how much money we could save for a wedding as we were getting married next year. This business would blow the doors off the bank account and we would be able to pay for the whole wedding in cash. She just told me to be careful not to burn out, but I was already working 60 to 80 hours a week with the other company, making decent money, but I could be making more with my own company."

Tristan and his girlfriend began to investigate how to open up a business, including registering a business number, looking at incorporating a company, and deciding what equipment Tristan would need to buy to get the business up and running. Tristan had a set of tools to begin with, but he needed to dip into his savings to purchase some specialized tools.

"I registered the business as an incorporated company, and called the company TS HVAC Solutions Limited," he says. "I then put together a plan of how I was going to operate the business. I knew the HVAC trade inside and out, and I was pretty good with customers, so I thought that I could go out and talk to people, and they would become my customers. Two weeks later, I resigned from the company. The very first thing I thought about was that I was going to need a decent truck to carry my tools and equipment. So I went to a car dealership, and bought a brand-new [truck]. It set me back about $65,000, but I knew that I could pay this off very quickly because of the money I would pull in."

Tristan signed the lease papers for the truck, turned the keys in the ignition, and gave it a good rumble. His first destination was his girlfriend's place of employment.

"She was in the back with some customers, but I showed some of her coworkers the truck, and they were very shocked and happy for us," he says. "Then, she came to the front and was surprised I was there. I got her to close her eyes, walked her to the truck, and opened her eyes. She started jumping up and down as this was a truck I was eyeing for a long, long time and we weren't going to buy this until after the wedding. Of course, the first question she asked was if we were able to afford this, but I reminded her of our calculations that we did for the business, which would mean that we would be able to pay this truck off in no time."

Next, Tristan thought that if he could get a steady stream of clients, he would need to showcase a number of different products they could buy, much like what his previous company did. That meant he needed to secure an office space. There were a couple of strip malls located downtown that had "For Lease" signs in the window, and Tristan called the respective landlords to get an estimate of the lease payments.

"There was one that I really liked, but it was going to cost me about $2,000 per month for the whole space, which was a lot," he says. "What I suggested was that I rent half of it for now and maybe the other half after six months, once I get more customers. The landlord agreed, but let me know that he would need to rent the other half right away if he found a suitable tenant, which made sense. The other office space I looked into needed a lot of work inside, and I just didn't have that kind of time as I needed to get the business up and running. So I settled on the first one, and signed a five-year lease with a personal guarantee."

That evening, Tristan and his girlfriend began phoning their friends and family to let them know of the good news, and told them that they were counting on them and their extended social circle to help Tristan get off the ground. Within the first week, Tristan received three calls for service, and had two other calls for estimates on residential HVAC unit replacements. With customers starting to call in, Tristan needed to get the office ready in case customers decided to visit him.

"That weekend, I went to Staples to look at buying a new laptop, a desk, a chair, a printer, paper, and I think a few other things, just to get me started," he says. "I had a couple of friends help me assemble the desk and the chair and arrange the office. My girlfriend put up some posters, and now I was in business. And with three calls that I got last week, things started looking good."

Through one of Tristan's friends, he had heard about a marketing company that provided advertising solutions by mailing out postcards. By signing up for the service, people would be made aware that TS HVAC Solutions Ltd. would be able to fill their HVAC needs. Tristan contacted the company, and pretty soon, he signed up.

"I was sure that these postcards would have me really busy when they came out, and then I could start paying my credit cards off and also the truck. Then, I could expand into that second part of my unit," he says.

Knowing that the postcards were going out the next week, he had to be prepared for an onslaught of calls. Tristan returned to the office to work on some invoicing forms and pricing sheets. He also called one of the HVAC dealers that he had met while working for the previous company and called to see if he could get a preferential rate on their equipment.

"The HVAC dealer told me that he could possibly get me a residential air conditioning unit to display in my office for free, as long as I would sell his particular product," he says. "Of course, I agreed, and let him know that I was expecting a number of customer calls the following week."

The next week came, and sure enough, there were several inquiries, all from residential customers, into what services Tristan offered. One of the gimmicks that the marketing company suggested Tristan use was to have an HVAC evaluation done for free, which would get Tristan into the door where he would be able to make upsell suggestions. Tristan's calendar filled up quickly for free assessments, blocking off the next four weeks. The next day, he started making the rounds.

About 50% of visits were for people who wanted to get Tristan's advice, but were not interested in purchasing anything. The other 50% were interested in an HVAC tune-up, which Tristan would do for $39.95.

Some inquiries ended in a discussion about upgrading the existing HVAC units, which Tristan would install at a cost upwards of $1,500.

"Two people were kind of interested in upgrading their HVAC units, which is excellent because there was a lot of profit for me," he says. "But they wanted to see if I had any financing arrangements, and of course, I never thought about this. I told them that I would have to get back to them.

Tristan returned to the office, desperate to find a finance company he could establish a relationship with. He did find one, but the financing rate was prohibitively high because Tristan's company, being new, carried high risk. Regardless, he signed up and began pitching financing to potential customers, but they all shied away because of the high rate. Because he was not able to sell any major units, his main source of revenue came from tune-ups, which did not bring in enough money to pay the bills.

"After two months of just doing tune-ups, I needed some cash badly," he says. "So I phoned my old boss to see if I could work maybe part-time. Thank goodness that he let me do that because I needed that money very badly. I kept trying to sell major units but nobody was willing to pay cash up front and the finance company wouldn't budge on the interest rate. After a few months, I reached the limit on my credit cards and I was barely able to make both the lease payment on the truck as well as rent."

Even taking shifts at his old job did not ease the strain, so Tristan had to make the hard decision to let the business go; he simply could not generate enough cash to pay the bills. He had no money left. Tristan approached his girlfriend and broke the news.

"I never saw her cry so hard," he says. "It seemed like our wedding plans went up in smoke because we could no longer afford to get married. We didn't even have enough credit to get married because I did not have any at the time. Everything was maxed out. There was only one thing I could do, and that was to go back working full-time."

Tristan was able to get his old job back and found a buyer for the truck. However, he was still on the hook for the interest on the truck payments, and the landlord sued him in court for the balance of the rental contract. An agreement was struck with the landlord to pay one-third of the total rental payments, to be paid over time, with the caveat that the landlord would keep the office equipment.

"I went berserk trying to ensure that some phantom customer would be impressed when visiting my office," Tristan says. "I never thought about concentrating on doing sales first and then buying all this equipment later. Was the office necessary? Probably not. Was the new truck necessary? I still think it was, but maybe at a later time. I was also stupid in assuming that I could immediately have what my old company had after 25 years in business. Maybe, if I took it one step at a time, I may still have a business today. But that will never happen again."

Entrepreneurs looking to get a business off the ground need to take a slow and steady approach to business. With few sales coming in, there should be little purchasing done to run the company as lean as possible. Once revenues start to climb, the business can slowly start incurring additional operational costs. In some cases, large purchases may need to be made as they are vital to moving the business forward. But the entrepreneur needs to be certain that these purchases are 'musts', without which the business will slow or even stall.

The entrepreneur must be extremely conservative when spending money. Doing so will generate a tremendous amount of respect from those who may be tapped later on to invest in your business, as told by Som Seif.

Be Conservative in Your Spending

A consistent mistake entrepreneurs make is that once they have money in hand, they seem to get a bit lazy in maintaining some control over how they spend. They run out of money and then begin looking for more, trying to convince others that with an injection of money, it will help them grow faster. Nothing is further from the truth. Be very conservative in how you spend and operate the business. This will establish fiscal discipline, and eventually this will earn you respect from investors who may be watching. Take it one step at a time.

– Som Seif, Former CEO – Claymore Investments Inc.,
CEO – Purpose Investments Inc.

After raising money from personal finances, friends and family or even investors, the entrepreneur opens the business's doors and begins the exciting path of convincing customers to buy the business's products and services. With a disciplined approach, each dollar spent should be stretched as far as it can to ensure that the business gains revenues without breaking the bank. This requires a conservative approach to spending money, which is tough to do.

Some entrepreneurs may see a big bank balance and begin a spending spree, rationalizing unnecessary expenditures on items that are not important. After the spending spree the financial projections that looked excellent in the business plan are not met, and the bank account falls short of the cash balance projected a few months earlier.

Now the entrepreneur struggles to find more cash, and possibly gives up some equity in the company so that it can be saved, and tries to convince investors that the company is a "winner". A smart investor would be able to see the financial strain on the business due to irresponsible spending. This could be a danger signal which may result in the investor walking away.

This is a reputation that an entrepreneur does not want to have. In fact, by exercising discipline when spending money, not only would the entrepreneur demonstrate an ability to run the company without sacrificing equity, but if the business needs investors to take advantage of an opportunity, the potential investors will respect the entrepreneur who is disciplined in the management of cash. This kind of enhanced reputation was something that Som Seif was rewarded with as he gained market share in the Canadian investment industry, all because he grew his company conservatively.

Som Seif founded Claymore Investments Inc. in January of 2005, and built it into a company with $6.5 billion in assets under management, becoming Canada's second-largest provider of exchange-traded funds over a six-year period, before being sold to Blackrock Global Investors Inc. in 2012.

When reflecting on starting a business, Som mentions that being an entrepreneur is not a science, and it does not require any special intelligence. Only those willing to get over the initial challenges and hurdles of running a business become entrepreneurs.

Coming off of an illustrious career in the investment banking industry, Som saw a unique opportunity to offer consumers the chance to invest in exchange traded funds, or ETFs, which were introduced to Canada in the mid-1990s, and became popular 10 years later, compared to mutual funds, which became popular in the 1980s.

As an investment vehicle, ETFs behaved essentially the same way as mutual funds, holding a basket of stocks that investors could partially own for a much lower investment of capital. The difference is that mutual funds have a team of professionals with access to substantial capital who decide which basket of stocks to hold, whereas ETFs would have a basket of stocks already picked, generally conservative in nature, and investors could then buy ETFs from the stock market, much like stocks[31].

---

31 A comparison of mutual funds and ETFs can be seen at http://www.bnn.ca/Blogs/2010/10/25/Mutual-Funds-Vs-ETFs.aspx

Som knew that ETFs were an attractive business opportunity; he diligently tried to understand where the future of the investment industry was headed, and saw lower-fee investing as one of the bigger investment trends on the horizon. But he faced an extremely stiff competitor.

"At the time I was contemplating my entry into the ETF market, there was only one company that offered ETFs to the Canadian investment market, Blackrock Global Investors, but this global giant had six or seven years of experience and had 100% of the Canadian market," he says.

Through hard work and sheer dedication, Som created great brand awareness with Claymore Investments Inc. Although the barrier to entry was low, allowing several other competitors the opportunity to enter the ETF market, Claymore had a solid value proposition and was respected in the marketplace. Som focused more on his company and its growth rather than the competition.

"You need to realize that you lose a little bit to the competition, but you really need to focus on where the growth is in the industry and be a player in that growth," he says. "The competition, as frustrating as it may be, legitimizes the story of lower-fee investing. This only helps the industry grow. The importance is in getting through the competitive noise so that when individuals are thinking about getting into lower-fee investing using an ETF, they think of Claymore Investments."

Focusing on branding, Claymore grew its market share dramatically and soon led in sales in the ETF market because it maintained its core philosophy and fundamentals, despite new entrants. Some of the other new entrants decided to carry riskier ETF investments such as derivative strategies, where there is high reward if things go right, but a tremendous risk if things go wrong. The recent implosion of the economy was in part due to such risky investment strategies.

"I wanted to bring products that ultimately had value in the marketplace and sure, we won't win every asset and we won't win every dollar, but we make sure that the dollars that we do get are dollars we care about," he says. "I'll be honest with you, we had this one product with a great intention of selling it. It was our natural gas product. It was the one product that made me not sleep at night because it was the black sheep in our lineup. Everything we built was about low risk, building low-cost, better solutions for the long-term investor, but at the same time, we had this one product. And we talked, and talked, and talked about this one product to the point where I just wanted to get rid of it because it didn't make sense for us. We built our business around something else."

For Claymore, getting into these different asset classes required spending more money on marketing, branding, and resources. But Som knew what he wanted Claymore to be, and he wanted to be careful and conservative to ensure that he established a brand that Canadian investors could trust and rely on. Spending dollars willfully to chase risky products was not a smart way to spend money. Som is a big believer in spending money conservatively to grow the brand in line with the company's values.

"When you are starting a business, you should make do with what you have," he says. "It is common to hear an entrepreneur saying that if there was just another million dollars, then he or she would be able to grow much quicker. The reality is that you need to keep moving your business forward with the resources you currently have. For many great leaders and business people, capital ultimately gives them discipline. For most businesses – especially start-up businesses – a lack of capital also gives them discipline."

Som knows this first-hand. He started Claymore with a limited amount of capital in the early years, and decided to spend his capital on products that provided good value and an excellent long-term investment for his customers, such as his reluctance to have a gas ETF as part of his lineup. This financial discipline gave him executional and operational discipline, which ultimately helped Claymore become more profitable and valuable down the road. Som has seen the exact opposite situation happen with his peers after raising lots of capital early on.

"Many were much more wasteful of the capital," he says. "Over time, they may grow decent businesses, but they don't have the same discipline in the way that they spend and think about money, and how that capital can be utilized."

Of course, building the business plan should include both aggressive and conservative scenarios for growth with matching financials. Aggressive scenarios provide an excellent target to reach but one should operate with the conservative scenario in mind. By acting conservatively, Som was comfortably able to meet or exceed his expectations and garner credibility within the marketplace. If expectations are not met, and the business has investors, before long the investors will start asking some hard questions.

"Unless you have projections that are very attractive, and you meet or exceed them, you're going to have a financial partner that is much more invasive and may lose trust in your abilities," Som says. "This is where the leader needs to really manage expectations very early on, and be realistic with the business growth when there are really no certainties."

A fiscally conservative attitude should allow the business a chance to generate a healthy stream of ongoing profits, providing a nice return for the entrepreneur and investors and providing the means to pay down any debt. This significantly increases the business's credibility in the marketplace, which is paramount to the future financing needs of the company. Som illustrates this with the story of one of his friends who, while working in a capital-intensive business, had successfully raised a significant amount capital when he needed it.

"My friend told me that in the previous 10 years of running his business, every time he borrowed capital or used capital, he paid it back quickly," he says. "He followed through on what he told people, and gained credibility. This leads to other people telling themselves that if they were to give this individual capital, they have the comfort of knowing that he does not abuse it and does not play around."

Conservative behaviour means that, from an operational perspective, the entrepreneur should do more with fewer resources. But one wise decision is to secure more capital than you need when the business is operating well, serving as a financial backup to be used when times are tough, such as an economic downturn. In the next chapter, Paul Hill alludes to having this extra capital set aside, called a "lock box", for those tough times.

When going to the markets for money, Som recommends that the conservative mindset be used again. If the business needs to ask for money to propel growth, the entrepreneur should ask for less capital than what he or she would love to have. Having the personal discipline to run a business with less capital for the operations will garner tremendous respect, and would ultimately result in an easier time raising money the next time.

Som notes that, in spite of a conservative mindset, not all businesses will avoid failure. Still, he believes in the importance of learning from failures.

"Good leaders know that there will be success and failures," Som says. "The successes will usually be great successes, but they will also be very open-minded about the losers and the failures, and are able to manage around them."

Establishing a financially conservative mindset right from the beginning obviously has its rewards, as alluded to by Som. This will help the entrepreneur with his or her confidence in knowing that the business is growing in a financially responsible way.

Entrepreneurs should also begin to start thinking about establishing a financial safety net early in case unforeseen events begin to affect the business negatively. The banks are never your friends when you actually need the money. So why not accumulate a safety net when the business is going well and banks are clamouring to offer you a line of credit?

Paul Hill advises that a business should always have a financial safety net, and must be disciplined not to touch it so that, when the business begins to hit financial rough spots, backup financing is available immediately.

Always Have a Financial Safety Net

My experience has taught me that one should look at raising capital when the economic times are good, because, when they are bad, and you really need the financing to make your obligations, nobody will be opening their financial pockets to help you. If not, you could lose your business entirely.

– Paul Hill, Chairman, President & CEO – The Hill Companies

Many businesses make the mistake of not having enough capital to move forward. In some cases, aggressive revenue projections made on a spreadsheet do not match reality, and the company finds that it needs to access more capital to pay its monthly obligations such as salaries, rent, utilities, and so on. Of course, there are many different guidelines floating around such as having twice as much capital as you think you need, but regardless of the multiplying factor, it is wiser to have more money in case projections fall short or you run into bad economic times.

Normally, companies look for money when they start to feel financially strained. This is exactly the wrong time to look for money. Lenders will analyze financial statements, and rest assured they will also see the financial strain. This may have them running away, or, if they do decide to finance you, they will either give you a lower amount than you need or attach aggressive repayment terms, which is definitely not in a company's best financial interest, although it may have little choice at this point.

As an astute business owner, Paul Hill has extensive experience dealing with financial ups and downs both within his companies and across economic periods. Having extra money available has helped his companies get through the tough periods.

After graduating from Georgetown University in Washington, DC and the Richard Ivey School of Business MBA program, and gaining significant experience in the investment banking industry for approximately eight years, Paul J. Hill is the third generation in the Hill family to lead The Hill Companies. His leadership and strategic direction serves as a catalyst to diversify The Hill Companies and the employment base of the province of Saskatchewan. He was the driving force in structuring the 1991 transaction that led to obtaining the controlling interest in Crown Life and relocating its head office from Toronto to Regina.

He subsequently became Chairman of The Hill Companies; it now operates in the areas of real estate, insurance, broadcasting, oil and gas, manufacturing and technology. Paul's extensive network within the North American business community facilitates his ability to aggressively seek out unique business opportunities.

His extensive career, business experience, and network have given him a deep understanding of the challenges that businesses go through to be successful. Although the businesses under his direct portfolio of companies have never undergone any business failures, he certainly has had his share of business challenges.

"If you are a traditional business, you have to expect failures and need to plan for every consequence to ensure that you minimize the risks that you will face," Paul advises. "You have to try and minimize your risk and exposure to that risk. You still cannot predict all the events because things such as market shifts, financial markets, and economic activity are not in your control."

Paul knows that failure should not be thought of as a bad thing. During a visit to Silicon Valley in Palo Alto, California, he heard from young entrepreneurs constantly experimenting with technology ideas, many of which fail and only a few of which are successful.

"The ratio may be 1000 failures to one success," he says. "That is why it is their motto to fail as fast as possible to minimize the loss when an idea does not work, and to fail as many times as possible at an early stage in order to learn, each time, what does not work, while embarking on another experiment to see if it does work."

In the late 1970s, out of concern for the mismanagement of the Canadian federal fiscal situation, Paul decided to enter the US real estate business in order to get a footprint outside of Canada. The 1980s proved to be good years for him while in the US, but between 1987 and 1991, the real estate business collapsed, setting off a worldwide recession. In the process, hundreds of US companies and financial institutions went bankrupt during the Savings and Loan scandal, and the US government set up the Resolution Trust to acquire and re-sell the assets of these financial institutions.

In Canada, the real estate collapse did not occur until the early 1990s, culminating with the collapse of Olympia & York, a large Canadian real estate company operating in Canada, the United States, and the United Kingdom. Several Canadian banks had financial exposure to this company, and when it collapsed, most banks stopped lending to real estate businesses in Canada. Under restricted lending practices, real estate values in Canada began to decline, which furthered a substantial slowdown in the real estate industry.

This slowdown affected Paul's Canadian real estate holdings. Paul's company co-owned a major Canadian office building in a joint venture with a foreign company. The joint venture partner had been bought by an Australian company, which was financed by a Canadian bank. During the collapse of the Canadian real estate industry, this building, originally valued at $75 million, experienced a severe decline in market value to $28 million, while still having a mortgage of $48 million. Although Paul's company was well capitalized to carry its financial obligations, the other companies went bankrupt. The creditors then came after Paul's companies, which proved a challenging time for him.

During challenging times, Paul strongly advises that a firm establish a surplus fund of cash, termed a "lock box" to get them through the tough times.

"The next time the downturn happens, you need to ask how do you get through that period? You will have a certain burn rate[32] and you need to at least match that. It's easy to talk about it, but there are also a lot of demands for your capital. You need to have some discipline and

32 The amount of cash a business goes through during a certain time period.

ensure that you have extra money above and beyond those necessary demands for your capital," he says.

Paul's extensive background in the investment banking industry taught him that money in the public markets is not always available to companies when they need it, especially when the economy goes sideways. Therefore it is wise to raise money through the public markets during good economic times. Of course, there is a cost to doing this as the company may dilute its existing shareholders, and it may not be able to get an immediate return to offset the dilution with the money that the company has raised. But the advantage is that raising money will position the company well strategically to acquire assets at a lower price when others are forced to divest their assets.

Paul has the same financial philosophy with raising money using lending institutions.

"I learned that it was important for survival to have good and healthy relationships with several banks so that when one bank may not be available for certain financing, chances are another one will be," he says. "I also learned that it is always important to keep a certain amount of liquidity separate from your operating businesses and that is where the phrase 'lock box' comes in."

Having a lock box would result in a trade-off – one would have to incur some sort of cost and some financial inefficiency in having that financing in place versus the alternative of paying down bank debt. However, if one paid down the bank debt in good times, and the economic environment turned negative, it is unlikely that the bank would lend money back to the company because banks are reluctant to increase credit lines or lend more money in a recessionary environment. In such an environment, the extra liquidity kept aside in the lock box provides a financial safety net to get through this period, ensuring that the company can meet its financial obligations and survive.

For Paul, having a lock box in place for his portfolio of companies helped him get through the market collapse in October of 2008. Prior to the collapse, certain financial commitments from pension funds and banks were made to his companies to help finance their projects. After the collapse, the pension funds pulled their financing and the banks tightened their reins on their financial commitments. This put a big strain on the capital available for the company's projects. Tapping into the lock box, Paul's companies were able to make their financial obligations and also used the capital as a financing vehicle for projects during the collapse, which would normally have been provided by a bank.

"This helped us get through a difficult period when many others could not survive as a result of their banks withdrawing credit," Paul says.

Paul had also been involved in three companies where having a lock box in place could have saved them.

One company that produced solar panels, in which Paul was a minority shareholder, had a healthy number of government contracts in both Ontario and California, and was gearing up to produce solar panels between late 2008 and early 2009, and needed financing to begin production. Given the weak economic conditions during that time, the company had a hard time tapping the banks for money given the risk-averse lending practices. In spite of the fact that they had secured contracts with governments, they were not able to raise the money and had to sell those contracts to third parties while at the same time liquidating their other assets. Had a lock box been in place, the company would have survived this period, and would have been able to produce the solar panels for the contracts.

In another case, Paul was involved as a minority shareholder in a public company in the oil and gas sector with operations in the North Sea. The company had a healthy stock price of $16.00 at the time, and had arranged financing primarily with the Royal Bank of Scotland. During the recessionary period, this bank experienced its own financial troubles and was unable to extend the credit and financial arrangements given to the company. Despite having excellent assets and good cash flow, the oil and gas company could not find another financial institution to replace their existing banking arrangements because banks around the world had stopped lending and taking on new accounts.

"In this circumstance, if the oil and gas company had a combination of lending relationships, it would have been able to have some money put away in a lock box, and it may have been able to work through this difficult period," Paul says. "Unfortunately, this was not the case. The company stock dropped to zero, and the company was forced to go into bankruptcy and liquidate all their assets."

Yet another company Paul was involved with, this time as a major shareholder and board member, was in the forestry industry, specifically the lumber and plywood business. The company operated on the west coast of the United States and had plants there and in the South and had a solid relationship with its banker. The company found it easy to deal with this banker as he had also resided on the West Coast – although he worked for a bank in New York – and he understood the company, the nature of the plywood business and the seasonality and cyclicality to its products. Unfortunately this banker, who was in his 40s, was hiking with his daughter in the mountains when he slipped and fell to his death.

When he died, the company's account shifted to New York, where no one understood the business. Despite the company being healthy financially and making all of its financial obligations, the bank decided to restrict its lines of credit and forced the company to pay down all of its debt by using its incoming revenues. This left the company strapped for working capital to pay for its operations and any other financial credit obligations. The company had no choice but to enter into bankruptcy and reorganize.

Paul points out that this latter example illustrates yet another lesson in business. No matter which bank you are dealing with, you should make sure you develop a good relationship with the head office decision-makers. They are usually available to their clients, and that personal relationship can be critical in a circumstance such as the one in which the forestry company found itself.

As one can see, not having access to capital during the tougher times can result in some pretty challenging circumstances for companies. The lesson is simple: when the ducks are quacking, make sure you feed them. Get the money when you do not need it, because it can save your company's life.

Having a financial safety net is an obvious strategy to employ, and can be difficult to implement if one is cautious about being in debt. For those looking to have as little debt as possible, Som Seif's advice in the previous chapter on operating the business conservatively should be taken.

What some entrepreneurs want to have is the financial safety of a dedicated stream of cash coming in while trying to operate a business. With this thinking, an entrepreneur clings to a full-time or part-time employment opportunity while believing that somehow the business will take off on its own, and when it does, the entrepreneur will dive into the business head-on on a full time basis.

Running a successful business needs full-time commitment, plain and simple.

If an entrepreneur is running a small business on the side and is truly happy with the small revenue stream and part-time commitment, this can be considered a successful business. But the entrepreneur must realize that the business will stay at that level. Any plans to grow it requires more time in the business.

For those who think that they have a winning business idea, the commitment must be there from Day One. If you are not committed to the business, you are effectively telling your customers, employees, bankers, investors, and whoever else is listening or watching that you do not believe in the business enough to be committed to it on a full-time basis. If you simply cannot start the business because of a lack of capital, then wait until you have the capital.

If an entrepreneur is not committed full-time right from the start, there is an incredibly high chance that the business will stall, as in Bill Green's case, or the business will collapse, as experienced by Jonah Lupton and Peter Langdon.

Being Committed

You absolutely have to have a full-time commitment from Day One if you hope to have a successful product in the market. Anything less and you open yourself up to failing fast.

– Jonah Lupton, Serial Entrepreneur and Investor

Going into business takes a lot of time and effort and one must be cognizant of ensuring that you are not going into business to try and create a job for yourself. The biggest challenge is having a great idea and not doing anything with it. Ideas are not part-time jobs.

– Bill Green, Entrepreneur

Oh yes, I was committed to the restaurant. And because it was not doing so well, I thought I had to be MORE committed. I thought the business needed me to be there more, but what I really should have done is close the business. It was just never going to work right from the start.

– Peter Langdon, Former Restaurant Owner

If entrepreneurs want to make their business successful, they must fully commit to it to ensure the business runs smoothly. There are rare lifestyle businesses that afford entrepreneurs the ability to work fewer hours, but there is often a trade-off in revenues and potential growth. If higher revenues and company growth is not in the cards, then all is well.

But for entrepreneurs looking to make it big in business, commitment is the only way to make it grow, assuming there is a market for the associated products and services. Some entrepreneurs feel they can carry a part-time job to supplement their income, but this lack of focus could cost the business opportunities to gain additional customers, find cost savings, increase the efficiency of operations, and so on.

Having commitment is commendable, but make sure that you are putting everything into the business for the right reasons. If the entrepreneur is running a business part-time, and the business stalls, then the reason for the stall may be obvious. However, no level of commitment will guarantee success for a flawed business; a further stalling of revenues even after the entrepreneur commits to the business on a full-time basis would make this evident.

For investors, it is imperative to see the management team fully committed right from the start. It would be foolish for entrepreneurs to try to convince potential investors that they could successfully operate a business on a part-time basis, as clearly, this shows a lack of commitment. Although this may seem intuitive, some entrepreneurs seem to think that this is a reasonable situation. For Jonah Lupton, he has seen both ends of the commitment scale when listening to pitches from companies looking to him as an investor.

Jonah Lupton is a serial entrepreneur and has been an angel investor to a number of start-up companies. He has been successful in picking the right ones to invest in, and because of his track record, he is a much sought-after advisor.

As an advisor, Jonah knows first-hand that when entrepreneurs start a business, they simply cannot do so on a part-time basis. All the energy and spirit around an idea must be channeled on a full-time basis to ensure that the proper attention and resources are put into the project.

"Many start-up team members believe they can do it part-time while having full-time jobs, and have found that often these people are looking for introductions to those with money to hire more resources, but do not want to put in the time or effort themselves," he says.

Jonah made an investment in one such company with a business plan in place, but within 16 to 18 months, there was fighting amongst the team about equity, there were additional legal fees in getting the product ready, and progress stalled. Most of the original team members had full-time jobs already. The continued arguments and distractions turned into a lack of commitment, and eventually, their full-time jobs pulled them away from even working on the project on a part-time basis. This left the project unfinished, and the company shut down and Jonah lost his investment.

Swinging all the way to the other end of the commitment scale, Jonah served as an advisor to a four-person team that was developing a certain product. When watching the team's members, he saw the level of commitment each team member had, and helped them raise their seed round through his network of investors.

"These four guys, all in their 30s, left their families behind to move into a cramped apartment in Cambridge, Massachusetts, and worked 20 hours a day to make sure that their product was ready to go to market," says Jonah. "This was an extraordinary level of commitment, but in the technology product space, this is the level of commitment needed to be successful."

The decision to make such commitments is never easy, especially with limited funds to start the business. Under financial constraints, entrepreneurs often convince themselves that they can be gainfully employed either part-time or full-time, while opening and operating a separate business. Doing so introduces a huge trade-off: the time that one could use to establish and run the business is spent being gainfully employed elsewhere.

This severely curtails the ability for the business to get off the ground. If the business is a good idea, a lack of commitment may result in that business idea stalling, or worse, falling flat. Such was the case with Bill Green, who joined forces with a colleague to help develop a Swiss Army-style device intended to help hockey players fix loose skates and helmets, considered a safety issue.

"The tool addresses a problem where, in the change room, skates come loose or a helmet has come loose," says Bill. "This becomes a safety issue and if the referee sees someone with that [loose] equipment, the kid will not play the game."

A minor issue, which only needed a quick fix, could force a player to sit out the rest the hockey game, ruining that player's game and forcing the team to juggle lines to fill the void. Bill's tool would allow a hockey player to make a quick fix in the dressing room, and once the fix was approved by the referees, that individual would be allowed to return to the game.

Bill and his partner knew they had a unique product, and because there was a real need, once hockey players adopted it, sales would take off. They were certain that the success of the product would allow them to retain their full-time employment.

Bill's partner was not as embedded in minor hockey as Bill and his family. It was only natural that Bill's role would be in the marketing and sales area. Knowing that he was a voracious networker, Bill was confident that he would be able to talk to all the coaches, parents, and players to introduce this tool. Bill also used some social media tools to help spread the word about the tool.

Unfortunately, the tool was limited to the junior hockey leagues where teenagers typically play recreationally.

"This is a great gift item and would typically be sold as gifts for coaches and also kids who were playing in the [recreational] leagues," says Bill. "It is not something that can be sold to competitive hockey in the teenage years as this tool is not cool enough, or you have an equipment manager that will help you."

With limited capital and time, the tool moved from idea to product, and the first batch was given as charitable gifts to youth hockey and various fundraisers. With some excellent feedback, Bill continued to tap into his network affiliated with youth hockey to sell the tool. But Bill quickly discovered that trying to bring this product to market required much more time and effort. Sales did not meet expectations, and the business achieved a break-even state. Bill also realized that the product itself needed some improvements.

"We had rose-coloured glasses on and we thought we were unique," he says. "I thought this would take off like wildfire. We thought that once it was adopted, it would take off. We are currently on version 2.5, and we are disappointed with the overall results. We are at the stage where we need to think about changing it to version 3.0. We are at break-even now, but how much more work and time and money do we want to put into another version? When do you let go? And if we go to version 3.0, what about version 2.5? Do we cannibalize[33] our product? If so, we would have to write down a lot of inventory."

Bill and his partner failed to correctly estimate how much time and effort they required to make this product into a viable business, and they realized that more time and money would be necessary to move the business forward. But, given their financial situations, neither was keen to leave their full-time jobs, although they knew that their tool provided tremendous value.

At the time of writing this book, Bill and his partner were still contemplating how to move forward. A silver lining to this experience was that both Bill and his partner were completely satisfied with the break-even position because they both loved being in the hockey industry, giving back, and working with each other. The path from this point is uncertain and the partners will take whatever time they need to decide, but for now they are at an inflection point and still feeling positive.

Although Bill and his partner realized that things were not going as smoothly as they wanted, for some others, having commitment in the face of a bad business idea could spell trouble. Such was the case for Peter Langdon.

Peter Langdon had been employed as a chef in a number of restaurants in the Vancouver area and was famous for his smoked meat sandwich. In fact, many of the local residents would flock to the restaurant for his sandwich. With this popularity, he began to have grand visions

---

33 Cannibalism is a strategy used by a company that introduces a new product or service with hopes that its sales will better those of another similar product(s) or service(s) it sells. In essence, a company competes with itself. The company may do this to increase market share, increase profit margins by introducing an "enhanced" product or attract a different type of customer base.

of owning his own restaurant. After 10 years of cutting, chopping, preparing, and serving food to customers, he began discussing this idea with his friends and family, who encouraged him to do so, and assured him that they would be regular patrons.

Making the decision to open the restaurant excited Peter. He sat down with his colleagues to map out a menu, looked at pricing based on the restaurants he worked at, and roughly sketched the interior of a restaurant with a seating plan.

While visiting a shopping mall, Peter noticed a small space where a former restaurant had been, and copied down the phone number listed underneath the "For Lease" sign. He met with the landlord a few days later, and asked why the previous restaurant had gone under. The land-lord explained that a number of restaurants closed their doors simply because they did not offer anything unique on the menu. For Peter, this was not a problem – he had a unique smoked meat sandwich that was going to drive the mall patrons to his restaurant.

Peter also noticed that there were empty retail spaces for 15 other businesses in that mall, but the landlord convinced him that this was a good thing because those visiting the mall would not have many choices of where to spend their money. This sounded reasonable to Peter, and he asked for a tour of his space.

During the tour, Peter found the space perfect with just a few tables in the front and existing kitchen equipment already in place. With a few interior touch-ups such as wallpaper and new tables and chairs, he would be off to the races.

"I originally thought that I was lucky finding this location," he recalls. "It had a previous restaurant that went out of business, but it had both equipment and the small size I was looking for. I would not have to spend too much money on equipment and my rent was pretty cheap. I did not see a lot of people in the mall, but I was sure that the ones that were coming would want to try one of my special smoked meat sandwiches. And of course, they are going to tell their friends, and business will do really well."

Peter was able to scrape together some savings and convinced one of his friends to give him a $50,000 loan payable in one year, made improvements to the restaurant, and opened his doors on August 1, 2010.

Many of the patrons were there for the outlet mall, with a few going to the barbershop, the tailor, the lottery ticket kiosk, or were just hanging around. Of course, initially business was slow, and Peter had some flyers printed to pass out to the mall patrons. Some of the mall patrons were at the mall as early as 9:00am and often watched Peter enter the restaurant at 10:00am, only to open it an hour later for lunch and close at 6:00pm as the rest of the mall closed at that time. Some suggested that Peter open for breakfast because there were a number of people in the mall right at 9:00am, when the mall opened.

Sales were healthy for the first six months, with the business making a tiny profit each month. But soon after that, despite the rave reviews of his smoked meat sandwich, the number of customers started to wane and the business dipped into the red by the end of the year.

After this first year, it came time to pay his friend back for the loan, but the business had no cash in the bank, and no assets to its name. His friend stopped by to ask about the loan, and Peter explained the financial situation and said that he needed more time and more money.

"I told my friend that the business was not doing so well and it was really my fault," he says. "I know I was not as committed as I could be. I know there were suggestions to open up for breakfast, but I was famous for my smoked meat sandwich and not bacon and eggs. But if I was committed to opening a restaurant, then I should be able to open up for breakfast. I could also convince the landlord to keep the doors open so I could be open for supper. That was free money for me because I was never open for supper. So I told my friend that I would open up for breakfast and supper, which would be instant money for me because I was shut during those times."

The friend decided to give Peter another $25,000, but the full $75,000 would need to be paid in one year, and there would be no extensions or exceptions. With Peter's financial estimates, the money that he would make from breakfast and supper would easily pay for that loan, and once that loan was wiped out, Peter would be able to put money in his own pocket.

Peter opened for breakfast, and was shocked to find out that most of the patrons came in to only buy coffee. And with no stores open in the evening, only the odd person would order supper from him. Six months later, Peter had to shut his doors and make a hard phone call to his friend.

"I was wrong about the commitment," he says. "What I should've seen is that my business was failing. Just because I opened longer hours did not mean that people would come to the restaurant. But I hoped that they would. I should've realized that early on. The previous restaurants closing down, the low number of tenants and the reason why people shopped at the mall should've all been clues, but I made a mistake. And I've also lost a very close friend."

In Peter's case, the restaurant never had a chance of success from the start. Being more committed to the business by extending the restaurant's hours did not translate into an increase in diners. This restaurant business was flawed right from the beginning.

So, when looking at commitment, if one wants to open up a business, you definitely need to jump in with both feet to be successful. But if you jump in and you do not know where you are going to land, you may be jumping into a hole that you are not prepared for, and that will sink the business. Yes, be committed, but be committed to a business that is viable.

With both feet in, and the excitement around moving a business forward, it is important that the entrepreneur understands that emotions need to be controlled when making business decisions. Of course, emotions will be involved in any decision at some level, but once a particular decision has been made, it is important to not let emotion change that particular decision, as recollected by Janet Winkler, or let the emotion cloud judgment, as recollected by Justin Aniballi.

Emotional Decision-Making

There may be emotion involved in getting to a particular decision, but once it is made, you need to stick to it. We allowed emotional excitement to affect a decision on a new product, and it cost us a lot.

– Janet Winkler, President – in-sync group

It was an emotional decision more so than an investment decision. I threw in my own capital to help buy time for a company in distress, a company in which I had no ownership. I lost my capital, but never again will I lose my emotional control when making business decisions.

– Justin Aniballi, Vice President, Worldwide Sales – Veloxsites

The appropriateness of allowing emotions to help shape business decisions often spurs a debate. Some believe that all business decisions must be devoid of emotions, whereas others believe that a good dose of emotions in business decision-making makes for better decisions.

It is virtually impossible to make business decisions on logic alone; an element of emotion always plays in one's mind. The art of making the right decision is to find a balance of emotion and logic. Too much logic can stifle creativity and innovation, while too much emotion carries the risk of tying the idea back to the business. For Janet Winkler, having too much of an emotional influence on a decision resulted in a lackluster financial return on a project.

Janet Winkler is President of in-sync group, a company that provides corporate insights, marketing and brand consulting, and organizational transformation. Janet started the company in 1989, growing it into a multimillion dollar business primarily serving clients in the healthcare industry.

Over the years, Janet has perfected the balance of logic versus emotion in her decision-making abilities. After considering all factors, when Janet makes a particularly important business decision, she has learned to be disciplined in not allowing emotions to sway her.

"An important aspect of running a business is to ensure that one consistently has discipline in decision-making," she says. "Any injection of emotion into this mix can quickly put a company on dangerous ground."

However, on one occasion, many years ago, Janet did allow emotion to creep in and influence a particular "go/no-go" decision regarding a new product her company was launching. She would have remained steadfast, but because of the excitement of a potential client, moving the decision point cost the company money.

In-sync group's new product measured the productivity of a company's sales force, and it was initially marketed to the pharmaceutical industry.

"The product would optimize the client's sales force and maximize business results," she says. "As this was a new product, we would have had to incur some initial ongoing costs until the clients began to provide a revenue stream."

With ongoing costs, Janet had to decide whether to continue marketing the product if revenues did not materialize.

"This meant that there was a clear and distinct decision point at which time the product would be shelved as it would not have made financial sense to continue, given the incremental sales, marketing, and administrative costs that would ensue with no revenues to balance these costs, and provide a healthy return on investment," she says.

Although there was a strong business case for using this product, with healthy predicted returns on a client's investment, an unforeseen problem was that, in pharmaceutical companies, the sales force did not want to be measured.

"The only metric that mattered to the companies was measuring how many scripts the sales force generated," Janet says. "We also found that the sales force in pharmaceutical companies had a lot of power, and they resisted having top management use this product. Because of this, the sales cycle became longer, and the decision point to shelve the product was approaching fast. At the eleventh hour, one of the largest pharmaceutical brands in the world took notice of the product and expressed an interest in using it. The feeling was that once this company used the product, it presented an interesting tipping point for the company. This added some emotional excitement to the team."

Because of this excitement, the clear and distinct decision point to shelve the product had come, and then it was gone.

"At this point, although logic dictated that the product be discontinued, the biggest mistake we made was in waiting for the 'big one' as the team knew that it was only a matter of time that revenues for the product were being collected," Janet explains. "The question was – when? We continually marketed the product for a few more months, continually hoping that the client would buy the product. Eventually the client did buy it, but the wait to get the business was way too long. The process of winning the business was very painful and it got caught in a series of administrative processes within the company, which reduced the overall profitability and business case for the product. After all that waiting, the eventual result was a disappointing loss of a significant amount of money."

Janet feels the failure came from not having the discipline to recognize that the decision marker was reached, which would have shut the product down. The marker came and went. The level of optimism at the prospect of landing a big client if the product was still being marketed for a short period of time led Janet's company past the point of no return – an emotional decision which did not carry any logic. That mistake was a costly one not only in terms of money, but also in terms of lost time and unnecessary tying up of resources that could have been working on other projects.

"Looking back, there were a number of other lessons that I learned from this experience," Janet says. "Certainly, at the time, we thought that we had a great product, but due diligence was not done to really understand what the emotional issue was with the product. The product made sense logically, but the balance of power in the pharmaceutical companies was heavily weighted towards the sales force, which was not taken into account."

During her HBA days, Janet remembers an accounting professor saying that you should not put good money after bad, and this was such a situation.

"The business owner must have the stomach to say that, even though $1 million was spent, one should shut the project down, and not get into thinking of waiting for another month and only spending $100,000 more, and so on," she says. "It is often much longer and more costly to keep going, even if you think you have the best idea in the world. There often are stories about businesses that did wait just a couple more months and then the business took off, but these are exceptions. It is similar to going to Vegas and putting a coin in a slot machine."

In Janet's case, emotions created a situation where a particular decision point was ignored, resulting in a significant loss to the company and a valuable lesson learned. For Justin Aniballi, emotion-filled actions resulted in Justin throwing personal finances into a dire corporate situation, exposing him financially, which he would never do again.

Justin Aniballi currently holds the title of Vice-President, Worldwide Sales for Veloxsites. Justin has had a successful 20-year career leading organizations in sales, operations, and finance in Canada and the US. He also holds an MBA degree.

Justin held his first senior executive position back in 2005, when he was asked to lead a company by the legal counsel representing four entrepreneurs who had recently acquired a small company in Ottawa.

"The entrepreneurs fell into legal troubles before they even took possession of their new company. They had actually left their positions at a large telecommunications company to purchase this smaller company," Justin says. "The problem was that the smaller company was in the same product segment as the division where the entrepreneurs had previously worked. This essentially broke their non-compete clauses[34] in their employment contracts with the large telecommunications company. The company took them to court, and won."

As part of the settlement, the legal counsel for the four entrepreneurs had to remove them from the company, hire an independent resource to run the company for a period of one year, and also had to identify and hire an independent director who would act as the sole board member and advisor for the company.

"I happened to be in the legal counsel's professional network and I was approached with the opportunity of coming on board with a one-year contract, with the possibility of an extension to a two-year contract, and I accepted the role," says Justin. "At the same time an advisor was also brought on, and he was an individual from a boutique private investment firm. I reported to this advisor, although he gave me free rein to operate the company."

Originally, the four entrepreneurs bought the company from a large US distributor with a promissory note that was to be paid back in monthly installments. When Justin joined, he reviewed the financials of the company and noticed that it was operating at a break-even level. At this break-even level, the company could not afford the monthly payments on the promissory note.

Justin needed to delay the monthly payments so that he could find ways to bring in cash. He tapped the advisor's shoulder and got him to negotiate an extension with the US distributor.

"We had to work some magic with trade credit and it was a daily challenge," he says. "This inflow of cash would go to paying off the promissory note and buying the company time. This was a house of cards ready to fall."

After one year, the four entrepreneurs were allowed to come back in but elected not to; rather, they were pleased with how Justin ran the company and offered him a one-year extension based on performance. After the one-year extension had passed with the senior debt holder, the advisor asked for an extension on a monthly basis so Justin could

---

34 A non-compete clause in an employment contract is usually added to prevent an employee from selling products and/or services similar to the employer either during employment or for a period of time after termination. The obvious reason for the clause is to prevent a competitive situation. Employees would have had access to an employer's information of a sensitive nature: client lists, future products, trade secrets, research and development details, and so on. The clause prevents current and past employees from leveraging this information to possibly gain a competitive advantage.

continue to work his "cash management magic", but he still found it difficult to keep the company afloat while meeting its financial obligations to the US distributor.

Nine months into the second year of Justin's contract, the US distributor had had enough. It parachuted two individuals into the company to act as receivers to help take back the company, effective immediately.

Justin believed in the company and its potential, and, with a sense of urgency, decided to orchestrate a management buyout. Justin then approached the company to state his offer.

"I went to the receivers and said, 'Listen, if you take this company back, you are only going to make $.20 on the dollar. I can offer you $.40 on the dollar'. The problem was that the senior debt holder wanted $.80 on the dollar."

With Justin's ability to generate significant sales in a short period of time, the company secured millions of dollars in government contracts, but payment generally came at the end of a contract. Justin felt confident that the company would survive because additional projects in production would generate revenue that would sustain the company. The receivers did not feel the same way and gave the company one week to operate before freezing the bank accounts.

"The company had its back to the wall and there was no capital coming in from the original owners, the director or any other investor," Justin says. "The company was essentially at the end of its rope and everything would've been lost: jobs would have been lost, suppliers would have been unpaid, and revenues would be uncollectible. I had two choices: I could either walk away, or put my own capital in to help float the company."

Justin made the emotional decision to put money into the company, using personal funds, to help pay for one week of payroll and buy time. In addition, a prospective investor also invested funds to cover one week of payroll, as a show of commitment.

"I knew that the reason I made the investment was to be creative in finding a solution to delay the eventuality. This would buy me time to find some investors and possibly bring in some revenues. But all these reasons were fueled by emotion and I did lose objectivity," he says.

Despite the extra two weeks, and a last-ditch effort to bring in another investor, which did not work, the company was taken back by the US distributor, bank accounts were frozen, employees and management fired, and the assets were prepared for sale. It was over.

One month after the company was dissolved, Justin reflected on his actions.

"In hindsight, I would never recommend my actions to anyone. At the time, it felt a little heroic, but there was more naiveté attached to it than heroism," he says.

Justin had assumed the mantle of CEO and therefore had a personal, emotional stake in its success. He was unable to separate that from his professional stake in the company. Ultimately, he was simply an employee. He happened to be CEO, but remained an employee and not an owner.

"As an employee, my obligation is essentially just to do my job, and does not include making personal loans to the company or the owners," he says. "The lesson learned is that as a senior leader in a company, especially a private one that is in distress, the intent is to work to save your people, but limit your personal exposure."

Despite this experience, Justin enjoyed the opportunity to lead the company with a solid team of skilled professionals surrounding him. He maintains contact with his senior management team to this day. Justin's advice to entrepreneurs – take care of both your people and your revenue.

"If you get the revenue right, which takes a lot of time and effort and focus, and if you hire the right people, and that requires both skill and luck, everything else looks after itself," he says. "Usually, the one differentiator I see in almost every successful company is that it hires really good people and gives them the freedom to simply create."

Emotional decision-making usually leads to impulsive decisions with little logic involved. This can easily take a business down the wrong path. If this is not realized soon enough, the ability to turn around, go back and begin traversing the correct path will be lost, as will the business.

Once an entrepreneur begins to find success, he or she may begin to sit back a little and think about what has been built so far. These moments are needed for the entrepreneur to revel in the effort and sacrifice that has been put in to get the business to this point. But this should be short-lived; the entrepreneur needs to get back in the saddle again to continue to push the business forward.

Otherwise, the entrepreneur could get lazy and substitute his or her efforts with another resource. The business found success on the back of the entrepreneur's efforts, and bringing in a substitute is just not the same. Getting lazy could mean getting in trouble, as it did for Kelsey Ramsden.

Getting Lazy

I got lazy thinking that there was an Easy Street,
supposedly thinking I would save some management time.
Not only was there MORE management time involved, but
I lost money in the process. Not once, but twice.

– Kelsey Ramsden, Founder – Kelseyramsden.ca and Sparkplay, Former
Founder – Belvedere Place Development and Tallus Ridge Development

After spending a tremendous amount of energy building a business, one of the easiest traps to get into when running the business is getting lazy. The entrepreneur has spent precious time, effort, and resources getting a business off the ground, and is constantly trying to increase the revenues while controlling costs. There may come a time when a situation presents itself that would help relieve pressure from the entrepreneur to get the business to the next level.

Because entrepreneurs wear many hats during the start-up phase of a business, finding extra time could be a windfall. Taking advantage of a situation that gives an entrepreneur a chance to focus on other areas of the business may make sense, but one must carefully choose which situation to get into.

Ideally, entrepreneurs should add resources or capabilities to those areas in which their skills are lacking, as Irene Chang Britt realized in Section 1. Adding skills to areas that the entrepreneur excels at may be redundant, with two people doing the same job. This may be okay if the entrepreneur is looking to move into another business area vital to ensuring the business moves forward, but it is a tricky situation.

To make the decision to go ahead with such a hire, entrepreneurs need to ask a hard and honest question: Are they really adding extra resources or capabilities to move the business forward, or are they merely adding them out of laziness?

Kelsey Ramsden was able to look back and realize that she brought on a partner to handle the operational aspect of construction projects, something she was good at. This seemed like a great addition at the time, but things did not turn out well.

Kelsey Ramsden is Founder of www.kelseyramsden.ca, a business services firm, and SparkPlay, a children's subscription company. In 2005, she founded Belvedere Place Development, a construction firm, and Tallus Ridge Development, a residential project management company, both located in Kelowna, British Columbia, reaching revenues of $15 million. In 2013, Profit Magazine named her Canada's Top Female Entrepreneur.

Yet Kelsey readily acknowledges her failures. "I have been a colossal failure," she says. "Failure is my greatest success. Success happens through a series of failures that are recognized and acted upon. It's that simple. If you've had no failure, in my opinion, you probably are actually not succeeding properly. If you are not pushing the boundary of failure, and are not asking 'how can we get bigger, better, faster, different', then there is someone else out there that is smarter than you, faster than you, bigger than you or better financed. It is simply a fact. You need to have a unique skill set and know what that 'X' factor is. Most people don't know what that 'X' factor is right out of the gate."

Despite her business success, surprisingly, Kelsey would often fail in many of the courses she took in both high school and college, not because she could not pass, but because she applied herself only to the extent that she needed to get the job done.

"I would never pay $100 for a $60 ticket," she says. "I would put just enough effort to get a $60 ticket. That has always been my mentality. I'm not going to over-dedicate myself to something that is not going to pay me more than a certain amount."

This meant she would add tremendous value to those areas that she excels at, and leave the rest to others. She needed to define what those areas were.

Kelsey started out in the management consulting area, but soon found that she did not enjoy working for people, being dictated to, or following process. These were all key ingredients in maintaining employment. She would obviously do this if she had to, to the best of her ability, and add value.

However, she was most satisfied starting a business in a field where she was able to deliver something tangible, using the knowledge that she already had. So she tapped into her large network of contacts in British Columbia to start her construction business.

With her business under way, Kelsey quickly learned to rid herself of any emotional decision-making. In one instance, she stayed up all night to prepare a major bid for a construction project. This was Kelsey's first real contract worth a sizable amount of money, and she reminded herself that she could not fail at this project for fear of serious consequences. She won the bid and began moving construction equipment into the site, but she ran into a problem right away.

Before anything could happen, Kelsey had to source a major piece of construction equipment to the site to start the work. Once transported to the site, this equipment needed to get into the site through a set of gates. Unfortunately, the machine was too wide, and the construction project stalled right away, leaving a large construction crew standing around.

Upon reflection, Kelsey just did not think about a tiny detail like measuring the width of a piece of machinery, but instead focused her attention on the bidding process. She forgot to measure the tire-to-tire size to make sure that this major piece of machinery could fit through the gates. For her, this was a trivial part of the project compared to everything else she had to worry about. But this insignificant detail turned out to be a huge financial and operational problem.

"What I thought about was that there were going to be 30 construction guys standing around at 7:00am watching a girl on her first real proper job," she recalls. "And there is this stupid thing that is going to sit out in front and is going to be on the street and everybody's going to see it. Oh my God! That was really the first time that I thought, 'Okay, well, what's the worst that could happen.' That became a mantra. The worst thing that could happen is that I get a smaller machine. Really. Anybody else's opinion actually did not matter. This is when I really started to get brass tacks about things. Cut out the emotion, cut it all out. That really made my decision-making skills very quick and concise."

Within a few weeks of that incident, Kelsey was sitting in her lawyer's office writing out a cheque for $1 million for her company expenses and she continued to make critical and insightful decisions for her business, "Not so much because of the fear of failure but more for the rush of risk and the rush of opportunity. For me, this rush of opportunity is a signal that anything is possible."

To finance the project, Kelsey went to a bond company that would lend her the funds based on her strong credit worthiness. Kelsey would then pay the financing off at the end of the project, which is when she was paid. The project would start, and Kelsey would begin working along-side the construction crews, shovel, steel-toed work boots and hard hat in hand, a part of the project she loved. She was able to complete the project successfully, generating some excellent profits.

Soon, another project came her way, which Kelsey bid on and won, and this is when she got lazy.

She had found an individual with experience running construction projects, and thought if she could finance the project, he could run the operations, and they would each split the profits. Kelsey took on some risk because this individual had past credit problems and so could not secure a financial bond for the project, and needed a financial partner. In Kelsey's mind, this relationship would require less of her time to manage operations with someone else doing it for her while she backstopped the project financially. She entered into a joint venture agreement with this individual, and for a brief moment, Kelsey began thinking that this was "Easy Street". But that street never ended up being easy.

The risk Kelsey took on this individual had huge financial ramifi-cations. This individual did not live up to his expectations, creating a circumstance where the bond company was close to pulling the project financing from Kelsey's company. With no money to help complete the project, she would be unable to finish the project and collect the revenue from the client. With the financing collapsing immediately, so would her company. That would have signaled the end for her.

"This situation became very personal for me," she says. "When you have worked so hard for something, and you lose it, that is difficult. I initially made the failure about HIM. But really, in the end it was my own decision. This is my failure. This is my lazy, greedy, terrible decision that I have to live with. If I wasn't lazy, I would've still wanted that job, but I would've hired someone and paid them to do that job, which was going to be more management. Ultimately, that job with that individual running it took more management than if I had my own guy at the site. Absolutely. Hands down. It was the opposite of what I wanted. And that was terrible."

This laziness also brought Kelsey some legal issues that she is currently still dealing with; seven years later, she is still in court over this individual. Other circumstances from the project also led to a lawsuit from a Canadian province.

Going to arbitration for that lawsuit, Kelsey sat alone behind the desk staring at five lawyers representing the Province. The arbitration went on for three days, and Kelsey got no sleep for the entire duration. She took several breaks during the arbitration to walk out of the room and let herself know that she had gotten herself into this mess and would need to get herself out of it.

Surprisingly, the bond company, which was set to lose money if Kelsey won the arbitration, actually supported Kelsey and hoped she would win. She did win, and earned considerable respect from the bond company. They had witnessed Kelsey's abilities in one of the worst situations she could ever be in. The arbitrators for the government came with one binder, whereas Kelsey came with seven binders that contained every piece of information about the construction project organized in several ways. If the lawyers required information about the project, she had an answer for them almost immediately. This preparation, despite what Kelsey faced, impressed upon the bond company how hard Kelsey was willing to work.

This profound faith in Kelsey resulted in the bond company overextending the amount of financing they would typically provide her. For example, if Kelsey was able to show $1 million as securable assets to the bonding company, it would previously have guaranteed $600,000 of that money. After the arbitration hearing, for that same collateral of $1 million Kelsey provided, the bond company would guarantee $2 million.

This whole ordeal taught Kelsey she was personally able to push through her failures and get to the other side.

In addition to stripping emotions out of decisions, Kelsey successfully tapped into her intuition to get out of a situation that she did not have a good feeling about. In April, 2008, just before the big recession, Kelsey got involved in land development that solely concentrated on developing the land where houses could be built.

She was getting offers to buy property from people who she suspected could not afford it. For example, she had a colleague who was a teacher, and whose spouse was a plumber, who were approved for a $700,000 mortgage. She knew that there was something not right with that financial picture.

"Wait a minute. There are all these people I know who don't know the first thing about investing, real estate, markets, and they are all saying that they are going to buy a house, flip it, and build the money back up," she says. "At that point, I knew it was time to get out. And I remember at that time, everyone was saying that I was crazy because the markets were so great. But, I don't know, there was something. There was a feeling about it that I knew that something was not right. And I had to do something about that feeling."

Acting on her intuition, Kelsey secured a large amount of financing to protect her businesses. Although she had to pay significant fees to do so, she had the comfort of financial security to back her should "something" happen, the same advice given by Paul Hill in a previous chapter. This appeased her feeling of unease, and luckily for her, she was right.

Six months later, in October 2008, the recession hit Canada hard, and many businesses lost a lot of money, with many failing. With Kelsey's crucial insight, the financing she had arranged allowed her to survive the next two years. She acknowledges that without that financing, her businesses would have failed.

Although Kelsey survived, once again, her laziness reared its ugly head.

With her financing in place, she was well on her way to surviving the recession when she got tired.

"I was not making the tough decisions because I was tired. I had poured my heart and soul into that business and I was not working as hard as I could. By just staying alive I was successful compared to my peers, but I knew I was not the best person for the job, and so I fired myself."

At that point, she approached the construction company's board of advisors and told them that she was letting herself go. She knew that she built the company, had some good ideas that resulted in it making money, but she was failing, which she found hard to admit.

She was too emotionally attached to this project, and it started to define her.

"We had a lot of cash and we were the most successful land development company in that area," she says. "We were constantly in the news, and the local government would tour our project to show an example of a best project. Despite all the stuff from the outside that looked fabulous, I was failing as a leader of that business at that point. That was hard to reconcile. I think that is really hard for a lot of entrepreneurs to admit."

She knew that if she stayed in that role, she would be able to do what was expected of her, but this was not who she was. As an entrepreneur, she needed to do more than what others expected to consistently add value. Because this was no longer the case, she knew she needed to replace herself.

She found the right person to move the business forward, and this individual turned the company around based on the fundamentals that Kelsey had put in place. By allowing a key resource a chance to take over, he was able to throw his full capabilities into the company, significantly increasing the company's bottom line.

Surprisingly, Kelsey's failures have led to companies supporting her, so much so that they often give her business rather than awarding a project to a company with a perfect track record. When Kelsey was bidding on construction projects in the oil and gas sector a few years later, for example, what set her company apart was that it had come back from failures, whereas other companies had a perfect track record.

"This is interesting as you would think that companies would choose the other guys as they were just sailing," she says. "But what they wanted to know is that when a construction job goes sideways, which they often do, what the private client values is a contractor that sticks with the job. We're going to keep going and we're going to find a solution. All that failure got us a bunch of work which we otherwise would not have had. It's a funny thing to think that our success is a direct result of our failure. It actually opens up opportunities and people value your failure. That had never occurred to me that this would be possible."

Laziness has bitten Kelsey twice, but with the experience she has gained, she is much more careful to properly define why she brings on resources to help her out, and if there really is a benefit, weighing all of the options.

It is essential that every entrepreneur perform this same evaluation, properly weighing these options, and being honest with the pros and cons. It is easy to become lazy and have others do some of the work for you. But, it is not their passion or efforts that built the company from the ground up. The entrepreneur must ensure that the decisions made add value to the organization. Not doing so may result in lost opportunities, or, as in Kelsey's case, money down the drain, not to mention her ongoing legal hassles.

The key issue for Kelsey is that she was able to bounce back from adverse situations, turning the seeming failures into successes. One cannot lose hope. It is important not to dwell on failure. After all, business challenges and failures are a part of business. Focusing on it will not allow you to move on. Use the lessons you have learned from your own failures as a springboard to success.

Failure, in the previous case, was a result of Kelsey becoming lazy. Failure could also result from an entrepreneur, a partner, or even investors becoming greedy after seeing the bank balance increase or realizing the incredible potential. Christine Siegel faced greed from others twice in her career, and both times, greed turned a potentially strong business opportunity into a failure statistic.

Being Greedy

You have the technology, you have the code, you have the product, you have the brand name, you have contracts, and then you have nothing, all because of greed.

– Christine Siegel, President & CEO, Natural Health Product Company

With the continued success of a company, there are incredible rewards for all stakeholders: the owner, the employees, and any shareholders. With increasing revenues, everyone wins. However, when greed gets in the way, logical decision-making and ensuring that everyone wins both get tossed out the door.

Clouded judgement soon leads to selfish requests, and a possible breakdown in communication, trust, and teamwork. With this breakdown, the company, which was firing on all cylinders, begins to lose its success, stagnating, or in some cases, imploding, much like what happened for Christine Siegel, not once, but twice.

Christine Siegel is a business development and operations professional with over 15 years of experience working for start-up companies in the international business, healthcare and pharmaceutical industries. She completed her MBA degree and worked at a business where she received extensive exposure to the technology transfer activities at US research institutions.

Christine began working with a particular firm where the founders were developing a patented minimally invasive technique, a breakthrough technological process that used neuro-modulation technology.

313

This process would help patients with certain medical conditions relieve themselves of a persistent bothersome muscular reaction.

The firm was in the process of continuing on with testing and working to perfect the technological process and go through the proper approval processes to launch it in both Canada and the US. Christine was brought on board to help establish the network of relationships to bolster support for the scientific claims as well as to help build the technology with the objective of successful commercialization.

The company wasted no time throwing Christine into the fire. On her third day on the job, she had to begin negotiations for key license agreements regarding the neuro-modulation technology, meaning she needed to know some aspects of neurosurgery: she had to be a quick study! Her studying paid off and Christine negotiated a licensing deal that was favourable for the company, a rare feat.

Over the next three and a half years, Christine organized a number of collaborations with key neurosurgeons, scientists, and biomedical engineers from both the US and Canada, and the company won a US-based award for the most promising neuro-technology company of the year.

She also felt that this time was personally rewarding for her because she was developing her skills and gaining some deep knowledge in technology transfer and technology commercialization.

But after this honeymoon period, things began to stagnate for the company, despite the rosy outlook. Christine blames the founder solely for this stagnation. She noticed that he always had a "me, me, me" attitude, and did not want to give up any aspect of the business. He was constantly trying to save money and would not allow the regulatory or other resources critical for successful commercialization to be brought on board when he should have been thinking with a vision toward commercialization.

The founder knew that if he asked for outside capital, he would need to give up some part of the company in return. However, he failed to realize that this capital was required to take the company along its potentially successful path with a bright financial future with profound scientific application around the world. This short-term mentality starved the company in two key areas.

The first area was in the crucial research and development (R&D)

work that needed to be performed. The founder was obsessed with using research grants, which would inject small amounts of money and restrict research to a narrow part of the required R&D work. This curtailed the proper R&D process flow that should have been going on, making the process sporadic and choppy. But, from the founder's perspective, he was able to save money for the next phase of technology, and so on, eventually being able to possibly fund the whole R&D process, although it may take longer. The main goal for him was that he did not have to give up any part of the company.

"The sporadic development is exactly the process you are trapped in while only following the granting agencies' programs," Christine says. "But from a business perspective, this made no sense. From a business perspective, the founder should have seen the research and development continue from start to finish, making it attractive for a larger company to come in and help commercialize the product, and the exit strategy is what the founder should have thought about."

The second area affected was in access to much-needed resources. Due to his cost-conscious nature, the founder wanted the team to continue their efforts with as little expenditure as possible. This lack of financial support prevented the team from bringing on new critical resources who could properly help put together the major components of the technology that would have resulted in speedier time to commercialization. Once again, there was a clear lack of vision from the founder.

After the team began banging their heads on wall after wall trying to find out how to make something from nothing, the founder was confronted with these issues, and suggestions to have the founder step aside and have a CEO with some industry experience come on board to help commercialize the product were made. Christine needed a CEO with the ability to open doors to begin negotiations with larger companies that may be interested in commercializing the product. Despite the requests for an experienced CEO with the right expertise and the founder's agreement with this approach, the founder delayed.

Eventually, the founder relented, and surprisingly found an individual with some industry experience who was also ready to provide some capital funding to help relieve the financial pressure. A new problem arose as the founder requested that the team misrepresent some company information to this individual to make the financial terms more favourable to the company, yet another greedy manoeuver. Christine and the team all faced a difficult moral personal challenge, introducing unnecessary drama.

At this point Christine felt tremendous failure.

"I was so committed to the company and the founder that I was forgetting about my personal needs and my personal takes on what needs to be done right," she recalls. "I was forgetting about some of the underlying requests that I had made. I think the founder was beginning to misuse this to his advantage. I felt this was a failure after all that commitment that we put into the company, after everything that we have given to the company and the founder personally, giving up a lot of family time during the start, saving money, and so on. This was a success from a learning point of view, but things were so disorganized; now there is a moral conflict, and now I feel that I don't belong here."

Christine made the decision to leave.

The founder decided that instead of re-building the company, he would try to sell his patents, as clearly the money had run out, and the talent that would have helped the company grow was gone. In addition to this, he created considerable ill-will with respected scientists and peers, and lost credibility through his own actions. He was now saddled with a watered-down reputation with no support from the community. Any efforts to try and revive these efforts would have been futile.

For at least 18 months, Christine had felt an intuition that she should have left the company. In addition, once she left, she needed six months of personal downtime just to get over the emotional trauma that she had just been through.

This experience taught Christine to be more forward and demanding. She should have asked for more aspects of the position to be put in writing and should have been more forceful when asking for certain key team members to be added to move the business forward. If these things did not happen, then she would have made the decision to simply walk away.

After some time off, Christine was asked to join a software development company. This company had developed a software solution that made it much easier for medical records to adhere to US privacy compliance requirements. This software had global applicability due to the surge in stringent requirements because of privacy concerns.

The company was looking to raise some money from an existing shareholder who, at the time, owned 50% of the shares. Because of the conditions attached to that financing, the shareholder who owned the other 50% was not satisfied with the proposed terms, resulting in a deadlock. Christine was brought in to represent the interests of the scientific team.

Christine helped build the new financial and business plan to the satisfaction of all stakeholders, and after some back and forth discussions, she helped strike an agreement with the shareholder's representative. With the president's blessing, the company was able to raise over $1 million despite operating in a recessionary period.

The financing had an immediate impact. It took just two years to have the company become a major emerging entity in medical record privacy compliance, gaining significant traction in the United States and with international organizations such as FIFA. The company's prowess was in the privacy area, with the team getting the opportunity to meet the Chairman of the US Federal Trade Commission. The company was approached by a large company that was ready to inject a significant amount of capital into the company, and only a signature was required.

Success was imminent, and all those involved would be rewarded handsomely through increased share value and an exponential increase in revenues for the company. But once again, Christine faced a situation where greed got in the way of the success.

The shareholder, an extremely prominent businessperson in the local financial community, did not want anyone else to share in the success. He was looking to restructure the percentage allocation of company shares such that the operational team, who was an absolute key component for building up the company from inception, would be deprived of their shares, giving the shareholder a majority stake in the company.

The president of the company obviously did not support this request, and the company could not move ahead until this request was dealt with, causing yet another deadlock, this one lasting for at least two years.

The bizarre part of this company's story is that all the shareholders were already facing a significant increase in wealth from the many revenue opportunities that were already lined up, promising to bring in hundreds of millions of dollars. With the deadlock, the revenue opportunities dried up, and the company fell apart.

After the investment of time and resources in getting the company to this successful moment, greed brought the house down, the company failed quickly and catastrophically, with the imminent success disappearing into thin air.

For Christine, "Whenever it comes to greed and egos, this is the most difficult part to deal with because people do not want to listen to logic and reasonable thinking, or consider other people's interests. They just get stuck in their notions that things have to be done this way for their personal interest. They disregard the other shareholders' interests."

The shareholder's greed prevented him from seeing the bigger picture and the long term success. Instead of having a small piece of a large pie, he wanted the whole pie. The problem was that the pie never made it into the oven to bake. No pie meant there was no opportunity for success, and everybody lost.

Both of these experiences have resulted in Christine really looking at defining her value system.

"I was able to define my self-identity: where you belong, how you want to do business, and who you want to do business with," she says. "You learn to spot different people from different angles and assess them differently. You learn to assess who is a talker and who is a doer. Who does the [fake] stuff and who does the real stuff. This whole situation has taught me to spot people who I want to avoid even though they may be talking nicely or they may be talking well and might make sense. You see them through different lenses."

Upon reflection, Christine realized that she became attached to what she was doing with the companies she was immersed in. She provided a personal level of commitment that went above and beyond what would be considered necessary, creating room for abuse and manipulation. This also resulted in her nurturing her colleagues along, which would preclude her from making the best decisions for herself personally.

She feels the need to teach herself to move to a higher level of thinking, and make a concrete decision.

"Making that kind of decision eventually results in the right way of thinking, and helps me get over that emotional hump," she says. "The emotion should be targeted towards a passion in moving the process forward for the company. And it is that passion that people really pick up. And it is through passion that great teams and companies get built."

The emotional roller coaster Christine had to face was seen during the interview. Although greed resulted in two lost business opportunities, Christine found the brighter side of both situations and came out with a strong sense of self-identity.

In the unfortunate situation where a business finds itself weakening at the seams when facing business challenges, an entrepreneur will try hard to rally the company's resources to overcome those challenges. If the challenges take the business to the edge of failure, resources within the company may begin to think twice about sticking around. But with a strong culture, resources can band together to add an extra dose of corporate adrenaline to get the business through the tough times, which Geoff Smith realized after his business faced possible failure on a number of occasions.

Establish a Strong Culture Early

My company went through crisis, upon crisis, upon crisis, yet the only positive thread through that period was that none of my key employees left. Without the strong culture that the employees established, I am not sure that the company would have survived.

— Geoff Smith, President & CEO — EllisDon

Corporate culture is defined as a blend of the values, beliefs, taboos, symbols, rituals, and myths all companies develop over time, according to Entrepreneur.com[35]. When a business begins to amass a number of employees, through both personal and professional interactions, these aspects of corporate culture begin to develop. Over time, these solidify and become a base of reference in terms of culture fit. Of course, there are many ways to reinforce the corporate culture through team building exercises, company social events, and so on.

The importance of corporate culture cannot be underestimated. In a 2005 Waterstone Human Capital study[36], in-depth interviews with senior managers at 107 Canadian companies revealed that 82% of them said that corporate culture impacts corporate financial performance and another 82% said that corporate culture helped with recruiting.

Given these statistics, when a business looks to add resources, apart from the obvious match with relevant experience required for the position, management should also examine whether this resource fits with the current corporate culture. Doing so will encourage a positive work environment, and possibly a social one as well, in addition to the benefits

35 http://www.entrepreneur.com/encyclopedia/corporate-culture
36 http://www.pearsoned.ca/highered/divisions/blogs/management_inthe_news_hitt_s/archives/00000002.html

that flow through to the business, as the percentages in the 2005 study allude to. A misalignment between a resource and the existing corporate culture creates a danger that this resource will become professionally and socially isolated, affecting that person's productivity, and possibly leading to an exit from the company.

A strong sense of culture also acts like glue, bonding employees together with obvious results such as enhanced teamwork and increased productivity. The ultimate outcome is a vastly improved workplace environment for employees. When the going gets rough for a particular business, this glue keeps the employees together and indirectly helps a company survive. Just ask Geoff Smith of EllisDon.

Geoff has been involved in the construction industry for over 25 years, and began full-time with EllisDon in 1982, which was founded by his father, Don Smith. Apart from two years of law practice after graduation, Geoff's career has otherwise been spent in various management positions at EllisDon, where he gained valuable hands-on experience in field operations, business development, and corporate affairs in preparation for his current responsibilities as President and CEO.

Geoff did not realize until much later that the management practices he and his father had established regarding treatment of the employees had instilled a strong sense of culture within their organization – so strong that, no matter what business challenges came their way, including a recession, a management shakeup, extremely restricted cash flow issues, and looming bankruptcy, the employees made the conscious decision to remain loyal to the company.

A few years after Geoff joined EllisDon full-time, he faced his first two major business challenges. First, the business faced a major recession, and second was a management shakeup due to a failure in the process of succession planning.

"We should have seen the recession coming," says Geoff. "It certainly had hit us pretty suddenly at the end of 1989 and through the '90s. We should've been prepared much better. We should've made the tougher decisions much earlier because we put ourselves in harm's way. I underestimated the depth and the length of the recession. It's all about making hard decisions earlier. I didn't do it, and we didn't do it as a company."

Geoff recollects the signs of the looming recession.

"Oh yeah, we had a lot of knowledge," he says. "[The banks] kept jacking interest rates up. They finally jacked it up to 15 % prime rate, hard to believe now, 14.75%. And [construction] projects just started getting canceled. It wasn't like you had to be a genius to see it. It was hitting me every morning like a hammer."

For Geoff, his failure came from not making the appropriate hard decisions at the right time, given the recessionary times.

"The failure was in not really coming to grips with the enormity of the problem because you are inclined to be optimistic and say, 'Well I know it's bad but it'll get better, so I'll just go along'. Really, what you got to do is to make significant structural changes and you need to make them immediately," he says. "We made them eventually, but we should have made them about 18 months before. We had to make overhead cuts, we had to shut a couple of divisions down, that kind of stuff. These are very hard decisions. We just didn't make them early enough."

The second business challenge came during the recession as well. Internally, the company struggled with succession planning issues. With Geoff's father turning 70, the succession issue clearly needed to be front and centre.

"My father, being a true entrepreneur at heart, did not want to let go of his position, yet constantly talked about leaving in two years, which became another two years, and then another two years," Geoff says. "At the same time, I was pushing too hard to take over because of my ambitious nature. There was an outside board of directors in place, but my father had appointed business associates that he had good relation-ships with to fill the board seats. This made it difficult to challenge him, resulting in them taking on more of an advisory role. This resulted in the top being completely dysfunctional with a void in leadership, all at the time of a recession."

It was natural that Geoff, as President and COO, would be the chosen successor, but with no formal succession plan in place and Geoff's father getting involved in other ventures, taking his attention away from the company, Geoff found it difficult to move the company forward and resigned in the summer of 1995, at the age of 40, to pursue other interests. This had a tremendous impact on the employees.

"The employees were all very aware of the dysfunction at the top and it had a hugely negative impact on the company in terms of morale and distraction," Geoff says. "I was surprised, looking back on it, on how few people we lost. We basically lost really nobody, especially the key people in Canada. We got lucky as the beneficiaries of their loyalty."

Because the recession and succession planning issues hit at the same time, the company almost went bankrupt. However, Geoff learned a key lesson through this period.

"Soon after [my leaving], my father put one of the vice-presidents in charge, which actually made the situation worse as this individual was not being very honest," he says. "He tried to finance a buyer for the company, which then fell through. After a year, the company is now in real trouble and my dad now wants to sell [his shares] in the fall of 1996. So with the help of a family friend, my sisters and brothers and I borrowed money from the bank, went personally on the line and bought my dad out. That is how we did the succession a year later. He was ready to go."

With Geoff now sitting at the helm of the company, he was hit with a number of business hurdles. Between 1997 and 1999, the company faced a cash flow crisis, and a number of projects in the US were losing money. All of Geoff's effort during this time went to keeping the company afloat.

Just after 1999, Geoff knew that the company was finally beginning to pull through the difficult period, and had an opportunity to reflect.

"At the end of the two years, when it was clear that we were going to survive and we were getting going again, that's when I really realized, and I had a chance to reflect, that none of the key guys had left, not just during the turmoil but between those two years," he says. "A lot of those guys, not only COULD have left, but they were being wooed away by our competitors, and none of the key guys DID leave."

Given this realization, Jeff decided to ask them why they did not leave.

"And I asked them all, actually. And basically, the response that I got was that, 'Well, it wasn't that it was because, at that point, we were particularly loyal to you or your dad because we were pretty discouraged with you and your dad, but we decided that the company was a good company and we liked working with one another, and we could save the company, and so we decided to stick together and do that', which I found amazing when you think about it," he says. "They didn't say, 'Yeah, we did it for you'. They said they did it because 'It was the right thing to do, and we knew we could do it.'

Flabbergasted, Geoff adds, "And it wasn't even like they told me that until after, when I went back and asked them. That's when it really hammered home to me that we had a good group of people, and that really informed my philosophy of giving these people all sorts of freedom and authority because they are so good at what they do, and that's the way we run our company now."

Despite going through the trials and tribulations that EllisDon experienced, Geoff and his father ensured that the people working for them were treated fairly. Geoff's father instilled a flatter decision-making structure early on by pushing the decision-making down to ensure that the employees had some flexibility with accountability. Geoff continued this by pushing the decision-making even further down to the front lines to run an extremely flat organization.

"I go out to every jobsite and every area, which I had been doing for years, and don't do very much anymore, and say to people 'You do your job. You have the freedom to do your job. Our policies and systems are there to help you do your job and if they don't, tell me and I'll get rid of them. You are accountable to your job,'" he says.

Geoff continues this flat decision-making style of management, and remains inflexible around these values and the way he runs the company. He also insists that he run the company like an open book.

"We run [the company] very openly. Everybody gets all the statements, everybody knows where all the numbers are, everybody knows what the business plan is, everybody knows everything," he says. "That's been the success of the company. In my learning curve, that all comes out of the crisis that we went through in the early '90s with this recession, and the succession struggles, and in the late '90s after my dad retired with the cash flow crisis, and getting through all our other problems."

With the type of management style Geoff and his father implemented, the culture that developed over the years had become so strong that the employees decided to help the company out by remaining with the company. In this case, one could say that the culture at EllisDon was a crucial factor that helped save the company in times of need. Of course, most companies strive to have a close corporate culture, and some companies insist that incoming employees be able to "fit in".

The important thing for entrepreneurs to note is that when starting a business and bringing on initial resources, instilling a corporate culture requires a sense of respect and a feeling of importance for all those joining the company. When the business grows, formal mechanisms to support the corporate culture such as social clubs and teambuilding exercises can become regular occurrences. It is important that the employees feel that management values their work and their opinions. Ultimately, the relationship must be synergistic in nature. For Geoff, this corporate culture meant everything to his company surviving.

It is well-known that an entrepreneur must make sacrifices early to get the business off the ground. But once that success has been reached, the entrepreneur might be able to slow down. If the entrepreneur is solely focused on growing the company as fast as possible while maximizing both revenues and profits, then personal sacrifices need to be made. But for those entrepreneurs that do value some personal time, it is important to establish a healthy work/life balance while sacrificing profits. It all comes down to what is important to the entrepreneur, a question that Michael Aniballi was able to answer quickly as a single father.

Establish a Healthy Work-Life Balance

If having a work-life balance is important, a trade-off needs to be made. But an entrepreneur needs to define what is most important. For me, it was my personal life that was important as a single father. That meant that I chose a venture that allowed me to have a work-life balance.

– Michael Aniballi, Digital Technology Consultant – R3D

A big issue for many entrepreneurs is trying to establish a work-life balance. When going into a venture, entrepreneurs need to understand that the majority of their time will be spent getting the venture off the ground and they will play multiple roles in areas such as sales, marketing, business development, operations, and so on. For some, this could mean working close to 80 hours a week. For others, they may spend less time on the business and more time with the family, for example.

If the priority is to have time for family, this time needs to be built in when starting a venture because time spent away from family cannot be brought back. However, if the goal of the venture is to make it successful from Day One, in most cases, a trade-off may need to be made. One needs to make the decision to choose between time with family and time on the venture. Of course there are exceptions, but entrepreneurs must understand that this may curtail growth, which may turn the venture into a lifestyle business. The entrepreneur needs to be honest about what kind of growth he or she wants for the venture and spend time accordingly. For Michael Aniballi, establishing this work-life balance was crucial as a single father.

Michael Aniballi started his career in financial services, life insurance, and risk management, working with London Life, and then spent another five years as a mortgage sales manager with TD Bank. After graduating from an Executive MBA program, he leveraged his previous sales experience to find a role at Rare Medium in New York. From there, he held a number of senior management roles at Publicis and Wunderman Canada, and served as Managing Director at JWT Ltd. He currently holds the role of Digital Technology Consultant at R3D, an international IT consulting firm.

In addition to his corporate responsibilities, Michael has grown an investment portfolio of real estate assets. Because a work-life balance was important for him, he developed a process to manage his real estate assets with a hands-off approach. This allowed him to spend time with his family, enjoy a successful corporate career, and have an entrepreneurial venture on the side.

"One of the biggest challenges faced by those running businesses is in managing the work-life balance. Many see this as a zero sum game," he says. "However, many of the values and decisions made in personal lives also bleed into professional lives. I had to learn this balance extremely fast."

Michael faced a challenge of juggling his time with the workload from the Executive MBA program, his corporate responsibilities, and his duties as a single father with a three year old daughter.

"I needed to balance my job, and my schooling, while ensuring that my daughter's life was full," he says. "Juggling time and managing tasks was something I had to perfect very quickly, a skill set required for a busy corporate life. I had to break every large task into smaller, more manageable ones."

Michael learned about breaking tasks into smaller ones during his MBA program.

"At the beginning of each MBA semester, we would be assigned projects for completion by end of the school year," he says. "I would review the assignment in detail and begin outlining my response, and I would review my draft approach with the professor on a regular basis after class. As most students were months away from starting their assignments, I usually had the full attention of the professor who was more than happy to provide me with guidance. Once I had a confirmed blocking chart[37] by having a professor sign off on this structure or offer his feedback on my approach for the assignment, the project was basically finished with some blanks left to fill in. It was a simple matter of researching, then writing each section."

From this point, Michael would break the assignment down into weekly commitments so that each section took no longer than a week to prepare.

On a professional level, his first task was to implement the processes to complete the smaller tasks. The goal was to ensure that he upheld customer satisfaction and properly served his clients while ensuring that his personal life worked at his own pace. This pace required that he always had the time to be there for his daughter, which included feeding, shopping, drop-off and pick-up at school, being home when she was sick, and all the other duties necessary to raise a child.

Because Michael can tackle many smaller tasks at a time, he is also able to pay attention to his entrepreneurial venture managing real estate from afar. He has established contracts with local subcontractors so that, should any issues from tenants arise, he sends an email response back to the tenant and a subcontractor handles the problem. Michael also pays the subcontractor immediately, ensuring that his relationship with the subcontractor stays healthy. By breaking up the process of solving tenant issues into smaller tasks, Michael has effectively satisfied his tenants and maintained a stable real estate venture while having a fulfilling family life and corporate career.

"When I was younger, and a single father, I had my priorities set, and knew that everything I did to make my daughter happy was worth the effort," he says. "I get my inspiration at moments when my daughter looks up at me and knows that she is the safest person in the world because I am her safety blanket. That was all that mattered to me, not the big things in life like others wanted."

---

37 Block chart – a "structure" with essentially a beginning, middle and end. Where assignments are concerned it means a topic, a premise (thesis), three statements or arguments followed by research and support, and then finally a restatement and summary of the thesis.

Because the balancing act is constantly in flux, there are occasions where Michael does get pulled away from his family. But he quickly makes the appropriate adjustments.

"With my daughter now in university and the arrival of twins in April 2013, the only mistake in parenting that tends to cause me to be introspective is when I do not spend as much time with my children as possible. Almost everything I do in work is designed to afford me the time and flexibility to spend quality time with my family," he says. "I control how fast and efficient I am at work and, as I mentioned before, I dedicate my efforts on producing results that allow me to maximize my success in the least amount of time. When my daughter was younger, this allowed me the ability to leave the office early and pick her up from school, or drop her off in the morning, or even leave the office mid-day for plays, recitals, skating and so on."

These priorities are absolute essentials when raising a family. To make these personal priorities work, priorities must also be assigned on the professional side to allow the balance that Michael requires.

"When I spend time at home, I also try to create an environment that does not require a lot of time to maintain and has minimal distractions. My office at work usually only has a desk, a computer and a white board," he says. "I find this helps me focus on the important tasks, namely the people I work with. At home I try to function the same way, with minimal distractions and more time to either relax in solitude, or enjoy time with family, but with very little to distract my attention."

In some ways, the intangible requirements that Michael has on the personal side seem to bleed into his professional life, where tangible items just do not matter anymore.

Michael is quick to point out that people should spend time thinking about what they really need to have in life. Michael decided not to pursue the extras such as expensive cars and large houses, for which he was chided by some of his peers. Those are only tangible items; Michael's relationship with his daughter and newborn twins is much more valuable to him. His primary goal is to secure a safety net for him and his family, so he bought tangible, yet realistic assets. He puts his words front and centre and role models for his family.

"I travel for business often and for pleasure once or twice a year, preferably to Europe or a road trip through the US" he says. "While it is safe to say I am not guided by owning a big house in a named neighborhood within Toronto, or owning the latest sports car, I find that my family finds we have 'enough' of the things which distinguish us from those who 'do not have enough' and this provides a sense of security and comfort for them. As well, because we own a portfolio of homes in London, Ontario, my family is aware that we 'could' buy a home if we want to, but that we 'choose' not to. This again provides a sense of comfort for the family and I believe sets a positive role model for them when determining what security and comfort really mean. Any of the properties we own in London are significantly larger than a standard Toronto home so 'knowing' we could own a big home in Toronto yet choose to invest elsewhere sets the tone for the family that we make calculated financial decisions based on following our own financial plan, and not that of the herd."

Michael also talks about how defining what one wants out of life serves as a discussion around being a role model for his children.

"Because we own a portfolio of homes in London, Ontario, my family is aware that we 'could' buy a home if we want to, but that we 'choose' not to. This again provides a sense of comfort for the kids and I believe sets a positive role model for them when determining what security and comfort really mean. Any of the properties we own in London are significantly larger than the homes our friends own in Toronto so 'knowing' we could own a big home in Toronto yet choose to invest elsewhere sets the tone for the family that we make calculated decisions based on following our own financial plan, and not that of the herd."

The "herd" that Michael refers to is a herd mentality that describes how people tend to follow their peers in purchases, behaviours or trends. The danger in doing this is that there are some who join the herd, yet cannot afford it, or spend an inordinate amount of time ensuring that they are a part of the group, which could take time and resources away from other, more enjoyable areas of life.

Michael grew up in the 1970s and lived through the downturn in the late 1990s, when he personally lost millions of dollars on paper during the tech boom and bust, and the advertising business he was involved with had a large number of layoffs in the early 2000s. He adopted a Japanese mentality, which means saving lots, and living within your means.

Even after the 1990s crisis, he saw that many others began to accumulate unnecessary assets, especially real estate. A herd mentality began, and assets were being accumulated at an alarming rate, and Michael questions why we as a culture feel entitled to certain things that are not necessarily affordable. He believes that leverage buys you a glimpse of prosperity you have not earned.

"Given the financial disasters we have seen such as Nortel, RIM, and the real estate situation in the US, people seem to have very short memories and should be a bit more cautious," he says.

Following a herd mentality often sidetracks entrepreneurs and confuses their priorities. If an entrepreneur has established an excellent work-life balance, then it is assumed that everything around the entrepreneur works in unison. But when influences from others begin to take significant time away from the "life" part, which is often the case, a multitude of not-so-desirable issues may arise, such as increased stress, less family time, and an unfulfilled feeling because there is always a race to keep up with the herd, which seemingly does not stop running.

In Michael's case, it is clear that there needs to be an alignment between personal and professional life. On the personal side, there is no room for failure given Michael's family situation, so Michael's professional life becomes defined. If there is no balance between the two, then there is a good risk of failure in both areas.

Although Michael's family situation is unique, the ongoing discussion around work-life balance is not. For entrepreneurs, finding this balance between their personal and professional lives is crucial because it sets the tone for any potential trade-offs that must be made, given the entrepreneurial goals that are being set.

When being pulled in a number of directions, entrepreneurs may begin to establish business processes in piecemeal fashion, providing some Band-aid solutions as problems in the process begin to come to the surface. What should be done early on is to map out the process fully so any potential problem areas in the process could be identified and rectified. For Wayne McLeish, one such step in a process almost killed the company.

Map Out Business Processes in Detail

*In a particular software process, we made an assumption
that it would run smoothly, and did not monitor the billing
part of the software. So, for four months, we got paid half
of what we should have. This almost killed the company.*

– Wayne McLeish, Former President & CEO – DRN Commerce

Implementing or reviewing business processes within a company should involve taking the time to map them out on paper with stakeholders within the company who will be affected by the processes. In the case of a process with a larger number of steps, it can be mapped out on several large pieces of paper taped on a number of walls in a room or on a large whiteboard.

The next phase is to look at each individual step of that process, what the inputs are from the previous step, and what that particular process step does, which may include things such as production time, amount of labour, materials used, or services provided. Finally, look at what the outputs are for the next step.

Going through such an exercise gives all decision-makers an opportunity to examine the process, comment on the inefficiencies, and improve each step by removing inefficiencies. Doing this for every step in the process will result in a greatly enhanced outcome, with a smooth and efficient transition from one process step to the next.

One particular danger when doing this exercise is to make assumptions in any of the steps. For example, a particular process may require 15 hours of labour, but if the process step involves only one resource that can only work for eight hours, then one can easily miss the additional costs involved in either adding an extra resource or calculating any overtime costs, understating the true cost of that step. Another example may be assuming a process step can begin right away, taking in material from a previous step, when in fact that material is delayed by one day. This would result in an error in the total time that process would ultimately take, which then inflates the total process time.

Sometimes, within a process, there may be dependencies on resources that need to add or update information before the step can advance. Going ahead under the assumption that these resources will do their part, when in fact they may not, creates a danger that the process step will continue without checking whether critical information has been captured, carrying this inefficiency forward. Although this may seem minor in nature, the effects of this missing information may be magnified as the process continues on to the other steps. Such a situation occurred for Wayne McLeish, which almost resulted in his company closing its doors for good.

Wayne McLeish was CEO of DRN commerce, a company that created a large private Internet-based file-sharing network specifically designed for banks. The software was mainly used by the banks' lawyers working on distressed real estate assets.

Wayne mentions that he has always had an interest in entrepreneurship, starting new businesses right from when he was young. At a young age, he had a newspaper route, and in his high school years, he started a company for Junior Achievement. After graduating law school, he successfully ran his own law practice for three years during the 1980s, which was a particularly strenuous time for businesses because of the economy.

After running his own law practice, Wayne joined a much larger law firm to take advantage of becoming a partner, which provided a nice increase on the financial side. Wayne was least happy when working with the larger firm because although he did not have control, he enjoyed running an entire department. But dealing with the overall politics was much tougher for him.

Because of Wayne's entrepreneurial thinking and affinity for technology, he saw internal administrative headaches in tracking the status of files, so he designed software that could be used internally at his law firm to manage these internal processes.

The entrepreneurial obsession to correct inefficiencies hit Wayne again when doing legal work for banks on defaulted loans and mortgages. Although he found the work fulfilling, the administration of that work was not.

"The banks would call you up and ask what's happening on a file, spending a lot of time going back and forth with updates," he says. "In some cases, I would send a spreadsheet or report with the status of every file, numbering in the hundreds. Two problems cropped up, one being that I was constantly buried in paper and the second was that the very next day, any documents or spreadsheets which were worked on the previous day were out of date. Not only were there instructions and information going back and forth by telephone, but the instructions were also being sent through a courier service between all the parties involved, which also ended up extending the length of time to get approvals on taking the next step in the legal process."

Wayne thought that there was a better way to manage these communications between the bank and their external law firms. He began designing a large virtual private network that would allow him, and other lawyers, the ability to update any information on a particular file in real time. This would create an incredible set of efficiencies as banks would now be able to go online to see the updated changes, tremendously reducing the previous administrative headaches.

Wayne learned early that entrepreneurship could have a significant impact on his standard of living. While running his law practice after graduating from law school, he and his wife lived off of his wife's salary of $165 a week. It was a difficult time, but he found that keeping expenses down allowed them to get through the hardest times and quickly get to the point where they were making money.

"Thanks to my wife, we were very frugal. I was driving a 1967 Chevelle that was rusting out that I never wanted to be seen in," he recalls. "But, I knew I had to do it as I always knew I had those entrepreneurial roots. We quickly made it to break-even and started making some money. I remember in my first year, I sat down with two lawyers who wanted to merge their law practice with me. We compared notes and I had billed more on my own than they had billed together just in the first year of our business. My wife and I decided to stay on our own. The lawyers who wanted to merge with me were drawing salaries that were way out of line with the billings they were generating. They ended up going bankrupt and I was grateful that I listened to my wife's advice to stay on my own."

One of the first people Wayne brought on board with DRN Commerce was a colleague he had known for 10 years, and who helped co-design the software that Wayne was using internally at the previous law firm. Wayne appointed him as Chief Technical Officer (CTO). This CTO was also a lawyer in addition to being a programmer, so he understood the legal environment very well.

Wayne convinced him to join the new company, giving him equity for his programming efforts. The CTO worked on a contract basis, but worked closely with Wayne for the next six to nine months, coming to town for two days every week in an effort to complete the software quickly.

Looking at the time and budget that he had to get this software up and ready, Wayne was nervously reminded about how few resources he had when he approached the CTO of another company developing similar software intended for the lending side of the banking business.

"I had a conversation with the CTO [of this other company] to find out how their software development was going," he says. "He was laying out that they had spent a year on their project, found out that they were using the wrong tools, and abandoned that. They were starting a new two-year project where they had a $2 million budget. In the meantime, I was sitting there with my Chief Technology Officer, and thought about how we had a $250,000 budget and nine months to get the software developed, or we were going to run out of money. But, regardless, we decided that we would start. Coming out of that meeting, I wrote his first $10,000 a month cheque, and off we went."

Luckily, within that time frame, a prototype was developed, and Wayne secured letters of intent from a number of banks to become customers. Everything went well with the software implementations, and Wayne was elated at the thought of cheques coming through the door and into the bank account, and waited, and wondered, and waited, and kept waiting. As he continued to anxiously wait, the bank account kept getting smaller and smaller as bills had to be paid.

After four months of much less cash coming in than he expected, Wayne was now nervous about the money coming in. He knew that there was going to be a delay in the billing process as lawyers worked the new files they received. However, he expected any day that the money would start pouring in. At that point the company was VERY cash strapped, with no money for payroll and the whole company surviving on credit cards.

The problem was with the billing process. It was sending about half the billing out than it should have to the lawyers, who were responsible for paying for the software service, although the banks were the actual customers. In the billing process, once a lawyer completed a particular task, the lawyer was to put a checkmark in a box that would not only notify the system that the lawyer had completed a task, but it would also trigger the software to send a bill out.

"The problem was that lawyers were completing their respective tasks, but they were not putting a checkmark in the box," says Wayne. "When designing the billing process, it was assumed that this was a part of the process that the lawyers would go complete the process. Ultimately, what this meant was that, for four months, the software was being used by many lawyers, essentially for free."

Wayne speculates that one of the reasons why this box may not have been checked was because if a lawyer was late on files, checking this box would provide the banks with a time stamp, and uncomfortable questions might start to be asked. Whatever the reason, everyone made an assumption that the box would be checked, bills would go out, and cash would begin streaming in.

"This meant that there were a lot of files being worked on by a healthy number of lawyers, and this should have translated into a number of invoices going out," says Wayne. "This should have resulted in cash coming through the door."

With no indication that things had gone wrong, the company's back was against a wall, and with cash shortfalls each month, Wayne faced the real possibility of closing the company down for good.

And then, out of the blue, Wayne got a phone call that saved the company from financial starvation.

"All of a sudden I get a phone call from a lawyer in Halifax," he says. "And this lawyer said, 'Wayne, I probably shouldn't be making this phone call, but you have been good to me, and I want to be fair. I have been on your system for six months. I've got about 150 files on your system, and you have sent me one bill for *$17.00!* Something is going wrong.'"

Wayne's heart sank, and with adrenaline pumping through his veins, he gathered his team together to investigate the root cause of the problem. When looking at the billing process, the team immediately discovered that this one box was not being checked off for a good number of months on a large number of the lawyers' files.

There was no simple fix. The software could not be taken offline and recoded. Desperate to get cash in the door, Wayne had to figure out what to do next. Finally, with his creative thinking cap on, he decided to change the billing practice from a fee-per-task model, similar to a percentage of billings, to a monthly fee for every file that a lawyer had open on the system.

Just making this change resulted in the billings tripling on a monthly basis, and at that point the company became profitable. But having a huge uptick in revenues did not necessarily result in actual cash coming into the bank account as the lawyers, once billed, had payment terms of 60 days, giving them two full months to send a cheque. With little cash in the bank, the company did not have the ability to wait the 60 days it would take for the accounts receivable to get paid. Wayne was stressed; he needed cold hard cash to hit the bank account.

Wayne came up with a creative answer. He sent out a notification to the lawyers that offered a 10% discount to the lawyers if they paid their accounts within 20 days, rather than waiting for 60 days. Sure enough, $180,000 immediately streamed into the company's bank account, allowing Wayne to breathe a huge sigh of relief.

"That basically saved our bacon," he says. "That was probably the biggest mistake we made along the way. Who knows what would've happened if that guy from Halifax hadn't called me. I might have completely lost my business. At some point in time, we needed to have somebody, if not me, look under the hood and say, 'Why aren't we getting these revenues?' That was a failure on our part. This cost us dearly because we couldn't go back. We didn't feel that, politically, we could go back and charge these people retroactively on the files that they hadn't been giving us money for. So, we lost about half a year's revenue, which at that initial stage is unbelievably crucial."

Making the decision to be fair and not ask the lawyers to pay for the retroactive use of the software was smart from a customer relationship perspective. The banks had extremely tight long-term relationships with the lawyers, and it was important for Wayne not to upset that relationship. In fact, it was Wayne's sense of fairness to everybody involved that allowed him to take the losses on the chin and move on.

With a cash infusion, the company was able to move ahead and Wayne could afford more resources, and he surrounded himself with good people with strengths in areas such as finance and technology.

With this stressful period behind him, Wayne was thinking back to the times when he and his team were able to meet seemingly impossible goals. There was a time when Wayne began approaching potential customers with a prototype, which worked, but was not web-based.

"When I met with one of the banks, the individual in charge said to me that if I could get the software converted into a web-based environment, then the bank would sign up and use it," he says. "Years later, that same banker told me that he never thought that I'd get the conversion to the web done, and that's why he was confident in saying that the bank would come on board. But then when I got the software ported over to the web, and it only took me three months to do it, he felt compelled to, sort of, not back off what he said. So it worked out."

The company hummed along with Wayne still operating the day-to-day operations and making the important decisions, yet always being collaborative.

"My CTO would say to me, 'Wayne, you tell me what YOU want to build, and then I'm going tell you WHAT we're going to build,'" he says. "It was kind of a joke, but it was because he knew so much more about the technology than I did and I trusted him in terms of design. There are a few things in the design that were mine, and stayed mine, but there are a lot of things that he knew a lot better than I did about what could be done and what was kind of far-fetched. He made sure that we kept it inside a certain box and that we didn't get into things that would require a complete redesign of the software."

The company was constantly growing as it retained an increasing number of clients, but it consistently struggled because of weak cash flows.

"Cash flow was an issue from the very beginning," Wayne says.

"In our first year, I think we lost $350,000. In our second year, we lost $925,000. Luckily, we had a $1 million investment offer from a strategic investor. We were fortunate in that, even though we were a company that was losing $30,000 a month, and only had revenues of I think $400,000 or $500,000 in our first year they had enough confidence to make the investment. That wouldn't happen these days. It was [the year] 2000, it was a dot-com thing that was going on, and anything Internet-based was made of gold."

The $1 million was used up right away and the company continued to plod along, still struggling with cash flow. Although the company was profitable, there were always debts that the company was paying off, which continued to put a strain on cash flow, and the company constantly flirted with performing with a profit of only a few hundred thousand dollars each year.

Several offers to sell came along over the early years and some investors wanted to sell. Wayne wanted to hold on because the company's future looked bright, and if Wayne was right, his shares would be much more valuable at a later date. However, another partner became anxious because he did not want to deal with the uncertainty anymore, and wanted to sell his shares and walk away with a large cheque.

Wayne negotiated a deal with the ultimate buyer that would allow him and one other remaining shareholder to sell their shares at a multiple of profits. There would be uncertainty as to what the company would be worth four years down the road with a possibility that the company may collapse at some point. This sale was to be calculated on profits four years later. This created a real risk for Wayne, but knowing that the company was headed in the right direction, he was confident that this was the best way to maximize his return on a 10-year investment of time and effort.

Almost immediately after finalizing the agreement to sell the company and after a number of years of struggling, the company reached a tipping point where revenues and profits suddenly skyrocketed. Revenues jumped 40% annually and profits increased by a factor of 20 over the four years leading up to the sale.

Wayne attributes his ability to stay focused and continue despite all of the financial trials and tribulations because, as he says, he was "pig-committed".

"What pig-committed means is that if a chicken and a pig are thinking of throwing a breakfast for somebody, the chicken is involved because he has to deliver some eggs to the process, but he is still alive," he says. "The pig is committed because he is done."

As Wayne recounts, making an assumption that all would be fine during the analysis of the billing process almost resulted in a cash squeeze that would have put him and his team permanently out of business. If there are any doubts, then the team analyzing the process step must address these doubts, even if the process step needs to be revisited from start to finish. Doing this will ensure that all questions and concerns from all the stakeholders are addressed.

Although this may take more time, the alternative of not spending this kind of time will result in an inefficient number of steps, which, together, result in a much larger misstep in the process's outcome. The whole exercise may then have to be repeated, resulting in frustration and unhappy stakeholders. But the alternative is much better – just ask Wayne.

When implementing a process, some entrepreneurs focus on the outcome as a target rather than ensuring that there is efficiency built into each step of the process. By focusing on the actual process steps and making them as efficient as possible, the output would naturally be maximized. Focusing on a process's outcome had Vinay Sharma learning a lesson or two.

Never Focus on the Outcome

We excessively focused on the project outcomes instead of the process, and the results were disastrous, not once, but twice.

– Vinay Sharma, CEO – London Hydro

When companies begin to implement processes, a common mistake is to focus excessively on the outcome while paying little attention to the process itself. It is neither the end that justifies the means, nor the means that justifies the end; rather, a balanced approach where due consideration is given to both the process and the outcome is the key to success.

On a more broad level, entrepreneurs may do the same by looking at how much money the business can make, whereas the attention should be put into mapping out how the business could provide products and services to fulfill customers' needs on an ongoing basis.

Lack of due focus on the process or means could engender repetitive work, bottlenecks, or wasted time, rendering the processes inefficient. In some cases inefficiencies are masked, and although there could be some semblance of positive outcomes, over time inefficiencies could pile up, resulting in wasted efforts and wrong outcomes. Such was the case for Vinay Sharma, costing time, effort, and money.

Vinay Sharma is the CEO of London Hydro, a utility that provides electricity to the residents of London, Ontario. He originally joined London Hydro in 1998 and moved through various departments such as customer service, energy and conservation management, the Smart Meter initiative, retailer management, and business planning.

Bringing up the subject of business failures, Vinay immediately points to two distinct experiences in computer application project deployment. Both projects involved outside contractors, some offshore vendors and some North American vendors.

"The failure was quite simple in hindsight," he says. "The projects failed because we focused excessively on the results and, perhaps, not as much on the process." These challenges caused project cost overruns and delays in project timelines. Needless to say, a significant amount of money was spent to fix and redo the majority of the projects.

"One project, we did, we failed, we fixed it, and its life came to an end," Vinay says. "The second time, we did it again with almost similar technology, and we faced similar challenges again. The first one was $11.5 million and the second was $15 million. Significant!"

In both projects, management took all the steps to establish proper contracts and service level agreements and, perhaps mistakenly, assumed the contractor's adherence to the project requirements. Though there were a number of checkpoints and tests, just doing checkpoint testing is generally not sufficient; a contractor may be able to "show" a client confirmatory test results that adhere to contractual specifications with solutions that at times are cosmetic in nature; yet, the real problem persists.

"Often the right results were seen, but the underlying technological solution was questionable," he says. "I'll be in a meeting with the vendor representative alleging that 'My folks are saying this thing has failed, and the results are showing that this thing is not working.' And being an offshore vendor, he promises his folks will work overnight to fix it. So the fix comes, and the next morning the vendor says that all of the accounts that had failed are all fixed. Now this is a batch process, so when we do process another batch, which runs all night, the morning after we realized how the fix has failed and also caused many other failures. We did not realize until later what was happening; what was happening was that the offshore vendor was cycling the accounts manually by fixing it on an ad-hoc basis and not fixing the root cause. Either they did not know what the root cause was or they did not know how to fix it, or maybe the project manager was saying 'Don't spend money and time on this anymore.' I don't know what the reasons were, but this happened repeatedly, many, many, many times."

Vinay and his team again faced similar challenges, perhaps with a different shade, on a subsequent project.

"We had a contract with an offshore entity that began in 2007, to design billing for unmetered load such as streetlights," he recalls. "Today, we have 34,000 streetlights and a very special profile for billing purposes. The billing program got written by the offshore entity, and we have been exclusively using that program ever since. It got tested extensively, but, in hindsight, it seemed it was a partial solution as we did not know any better at the time. The test results came out and everything looked fine, and we go on. The contract ended early in 2009."

In January 2013, the streetlights bill for the electricity usage for December was sent to the customer, whose representative discovered a discrepancy upon examining the bill. The bill showed a smaller electricity demand calculation than the estimation. From 2009 to 2012, the number of streetlights had increased; naturally, this would have resulted in a higher electricity load. This discrepancy certainly prompted London Hydro to investigate.

"What was found was that the program that had been written [by the vendor] would give you the right results if nothing changed in the customer profiles," Vinay recounts. "But, over time, the number of streetlights goes up as subdivisions get built, and so on. Back in 2009, there were 24,000 streetlights, and we have added 10,000 streetlights since. Well firstly, the program was not accounting for the new streetlights and secondly, it was not applying the correct parameter, for example, new profiling parameter due to additional streetlights. We had to debug the program line by line to determine the root cause. If nothing changes, of course, the results would be perfect."

Only an inherent knowledge of the software's code would catch such a problem; a relatively heavy reliance on outside vendors together with relatively few qualified resources dedicated to the project magnified the potential for these slips.

"I guess we were good at managing projects in terms of budget and timeline, but we weren't really as good in understanding the designs behind-the-scenes," he says. "Our learning, perhaps my most important lesson, was to have an internal project manager that is not only an expert in the technology but also is 'all-knowing' of the business processes. Hindsight is reality, foresight is some planning whereas insight is intellect – we thought we had grown up in the first go-around, yet we had to learn it all over again."

At this point, Vinay decided it would be better to have resources in-house rather than relying on outside contractors. Increasing such resources would give him important internal capabilities to understand both the business processes and the technology supporting those business processes.

Vinay began adding resources to the IT department, going from using 70% contractors and 30% internal resources in 2001 to having 25% contractors and 75% internal resources today. These additional resources effectively doubled the IT department, going from 21 people, and heavily dependent on outside contractors, to 42 people who understood the projects being deployed. Vinay was quick to point out the advantages that this gave London Hydro.

"The first advantage was that major IT projects with the same scale and costs as those done previously, were successfully deployed with no failures whatsoever," he says. "The second advantage is that we have a deeper knowledge and understanding of all the IT projects. A third advantage was that, although adding resources may be seen as an overall cost increase, in fact, there was not only no increase as this money would have been spent on contractors at a higher rate, but we were also able to save money."

A result of this lesson is that London Hydro has demonstrated prudence in executing capital projects to its regulators. It has, through its efforts, earned a strong regulator reputation which has manifested into receiving nearly 95% – 99% success in regulatory approval of its cost.

"First, we never asked for more than we needed to," Vinay says. "Second, we had good plans to justify for what we are asking. To give you an example of our success, in 2000, London Hydro became a corporation and had a rate base of $172 million. Today, London Hydro has a *fully approved* rate base of $267 million, which represents significant shareholder growth. Now, I won't say that the customer rates were not affected, because they were. But the increase to our customer has been relatively lower than many of the other hydros. This can only be possible by running London Hydro as efficiently as possible."

Vinay believes in implementing technology to help increase efficiencies by allowing it to automate certain processes. For example, when the

Smart Meter initiative was being implemented, it was assumed that the number of calls coming into customer service would increase; however, London Hydro maintained its customer service staff levels in the call centre by automating much of the Smart Meter information management system.

"When the Smart Meter came in, we automated the majority of the business processes," he says. "For example, our online customer registration for Smart Meters is 40,000 out of 150,000. That is almost 1/3 of our customers! That is very high. And our paperless billing is running at a penetration of 11%, and we do direct billing ourselves. All of these have reduced the number of customer calls."

Vinay also led the development of technology to automate the tenancy change process. Many of the tenants in London are direct customers of London Hydro and at times the utility would be pulled into tenant/landlord disputes. To resolve these issues, London Hydro worked in conjunction with the local property management association to develop an online web portal for landlords/property managers to self-manage the hydro accounts on their properties; of course, without jeopardizing confidentiality and privacy of data.

"If there is any tenant that has given us a date to cancel the service, it shows up online in the property manager's web portal, and the property manager can seek to resolve the differences with tenants promptly," Vinay states. "With its implementation, calls from property managers have significantly reduced, and hence, there are efficiency gains. That is how we manage the technology investments versus using operational dollars to mitigate the impact on customer rates."

Because of Vinay's balanced focus on processes and results, he has been able to turn London Hydro into an industry leader. Among all the feathers in its cap, London Hydro has added one more for its strong delivery of energy conservation and demand management programs to its customers. London Hydro started these programs in 2005 when the government decided to bring about a culture of energy conservation in the province. Not only has London Hydro won many awards for these programs, but its customers have enjoyed relatively more benefits than others in the province of Ontario.

"Among 73 utilities in Ontario, London Hydro is the third-highest in achieving energy conservation success in the marketplace," says

Vinay. "So it has been good in that respect. The Ministry recognizes us for our ability to manage both technology deployment and energy management, and because of our regulator reputation, the Ministry requested us to provide leadership to two programs. The first was in asking London Hydro to lead the Smart Meter program on behalf of 67 smaller utilities. The Ministry also requested London Hydro, in addition to Hydro One, help design the Green Button initiative. This initiative is for customers to provide third-party access to their consumption data so that the service providers can devise programs and services for energy management."

The main reason for Vinay's success at implementing projects is his leadership style as an influencer, making it his priority to ensure that the employees are comfortable. Since joining London Hydro, he has successfully changed the internal culture to a collaborative culture. Surprisingly, this is a process unto itself.

Vinay makes it a priority to communicate with his employees. The company puts out a quarterly magazine which talks about many general things including employee stories, and Vinay sends a monthly note to the employees that have both a business and a personal message embedded in it.

"I find that people laugh at my stories sometimes, but it breaks that barrier and brings me closer to them," he says.

Vinay also engages with his employees by making worksite visits. He joins crews working in the field and spends quality time with them, taking the opportunity to meet as many employees as possible and at the same time, getting to see the quality of their work.

"I would spend an hour or two with them, whatever is required, and sometimes it will be in the dead middle of winter," he says. "They are certainly dressed for the cold and, generally, I'm not as warmly dressed. With frozen lips, my words don't come out right and they doubly laugh at me. They love me coming out; this increase in communication has really helped me a lot because I get to know them on a first-name basis. Secondly, they get to see me. And now, there is a connectedness, a little bit of a connection that I see, and they see it too."

Vinay also makes it a point to bring a group of staff members to the boardroom just to have a chat with them, but more importantly, to share information about the corporation's success.

"My message is always to teach them something about our company," he says. "Say financial issues such as credit rating, well, how do we get a credit rating? Sometimes, I'll talk to them about what capital structure is, what does equity mean, and so on. And we all learn."

When a business decides to take a balanced focus on both the process and the outcome, the process is well mapped out and inefficiencies are identified and mitigated. This tends to generate a realigned process that is much more efficient and well-resourced, much like what Vinay has done at London Hydro. This balanced focus on process and outcomes helps to save the company time, wasted efforts, and in most cases, results in a financial bump through either increased production or efficiency. Once the realignment is done, all the company needs to do is monitor the process to ensure that it continues to be efficient.

FAIL FAST ⬈ FAST ⬊ SUCCEED FASTER

PART 5

Can You Move
the Business Forward?

*Success has many fathers
but failure is an orphan.*

– John F. Kennedy

After running a successful business for a period of time, a discussion on how to move the business forward ensues. Moving the business forward could mean several things: expanding products and services, expanding into other territories or countries, or adapting to change.

Moving the business forward should involve a vigorous debate both internally with the company's resources and externally with advisors, board members, and mentors. Any expansion should make business sense, and the business should have the appropriate level of resources and capabilities to properly expand.

If the business expands without being fully ready, it may be taking on a level of risk that is harmful for the business. Of course, some risk is necessary to move the business forward, but there need to be supportive arguments that taking on such a level of risk will not put the business in harm's way.

The stories in this section look at some of the crucial considerations a business owner needs to examine when expanding. One can expand and have the financial statements show a nice temporary increase in top line revenues, but if done without proper preparation and advice, the expansion could jeopardize the entire business operation.

Most of the interviewees in this section were able to recover successfully with some bruising along the way and lessons learned, but not everyone was so lucky.

Establish a Local
Presence if Expanding

Because we did not have a local presence or controls put in place on the franchisees, we hurt the growth. We had to close the stores, and we had to walk away. I remember getting back on the plane and flying back to Vancouver, saying to my partner, George, we made a mistake. We should have opened an office there first.

– Jim Treliving, Chairman & Owner – Boston Pizza International Inc.

A common business mistake occurs when assuming that a particular business model could expand to other geographic locations through franchising without establishing a local presence. The problem stems from the different nuances in culture, behaviours, and habits of potential customers that are not taken into account. Without understanding those cultural elements, a business misses the opportunity to fully understand its customers.

The effect? A hit to profitability. When the business is looking to expand, it must establish a local presence. Of course, that is going to cost money, without immediate return on that investment. But for Jim Treliving, this is money well spent.

Jim Treliving is Chairman & Owner of Boston Pizza International Inc., Canada's number one casual dining brand. With Jim and his partner, George Melville, at the helm, Boston Pizza has been consistently recognized as one of Canada's "50 Best Managed Private Companies" and more recently as one of Canada's "Top Ten Most Admired Corporate Cultures".

Jim was a young RCMP officer in 1966 when he left to join "Boston Pizza and Spaghetti House" in Edmonton, opening his first Boston Pizza franchise in Penticton, British Columbia in 1968. From that small location, through hard work and dedication, Jim has expanded to over 350 franchise locations with almost $1 billion in annual sales today. Boston Pizza is now Canada's No. 1 casual dining brand with more than 325 restaurants from coast to coast.

The Boston Pizza franchise concept became successful in Western Canada, headquartered in Vancouver. To try to increase its brand presence, Boston Pizza became the official pizza supplier for Expo '86 in Vancouver. This turned out to be a winning move for the company. Following Expo '86, between the years of 1987 and 1990, Boston Pizza opened a number of franchise locations in Ontario, six locations in Taiwan, one in Japan, and one in Hong Kong, all at the same time.

Opening these franchise locations went well, but the expansion exposed some real problems as growth in the new areas flattened. The volumes in these franchise locations were doing well, but a lack of controls on the franchisees themselves proved to be an issue. When members of the head office were not present, the franchisees would act like franchisors.

Franchisees were making changes without approval from the head office – for example, one franchisee added fish and chips to the menu due to a customer suggestion. The customer suggested fish and chips because all the local restaurants used to have it on their menus. Not only was this undesirable for Jim and his management team, but the locals who ate at a Boston Pizza location expected Western food choices; local food was available everywhere else.

Without controls on the franchisees to prevent such situations, Jim and his management team would have trouble building a consistent concept for every franchise location, wherever they were in the world, as they desired.

"The challenge was that they didn't know the expectations we had as a North American company," says Jim. "We sold the franchise, but we did not have anybody on the ground to watch the business. The hardest part for us was sitting back and thinking about this after running the business for 10 years. Was it successful in terms of people coming? Yes. Was it successful in building the business? No. The reason being we did not put any people on the ground."

Having the head office in Vancouver, while operating franchises in different time zones, only compounded the problem. For example, if franchisees in Toronto had issues that the head office needed to answer, they were not always addressed right away. A problem that occurred at 9:00am in Toronto could not be resolved right away because it was 6:00am in Vancouver. This issue would be magnified for those franchisees overseas. This was not just a problem with Boston Pizza, but a general problem for any other company expanding franchise locations in different parts of the country and across time zones, or in different countries.

Additionally, certain parts of the day would inevitably be spent in airports and planes, time which could have been used to address franchisee issues.

"What would happen is that a franchise would be sold, the team would then fly out to the location, fly back to Toronto, sell another franchise, visit that location, fly back to Toronto, have the franchisee fly to Toronto to attend training, have the franchisee fly back out to the location, and so on," says Jim. "The problem with this was the time difference. Flying out to Vancouver in the morning and then back to Toronto would be full day. A 9:00am start in Toronto would result in a 5:00pm return."

The management team sat back and realized that what worked in Western Canada did not work for Eastern Canada due to differences in attitudes and lifestyle. For example, Western Canadians generally ate later.

"In Toronto, people generally work in shifts," Jim explains. "People start work at seven, finish at three, go home, pick up their kids at four and then go out to eat at five or six o'clock. In Vancouver, you don't go out to eat at six o'clock. You're getting home at six, and then you go out to eat at seven or eight o'clock. We got our butts kicked in Ontario and were told to go home because we weren't ready. We weren't ready for the volume, double the people than any of the other places in Western Canada. They eat at different times, they eat a lot, and they bring their families. So all of a sudden, we get hammered at five o'clock, and in Vancouver, there's nobody in our restaurants at five o'clock. We had deck ovens, so you're taking one thing out at a time or two at a time. We had to go to conveyor ovens to make it faster. People don't have two hours to sit there and wait. Some people got upset and would not return again. We slowly lowered the crowd to fit what we were doing."

The team agreed that, before opening up another franchise location, a template franchise structure staffed with the appropriate resources should be established locally before opening franchise locations in those geographic regions.

All of the franchisee locations outside of Eastern Canada were closed and over the next four or five years, a new expansion strategy was developed, with the inclusion of a local geographic presence in addition to the development of appropriate controls for franchisee owners.

After rolling out this new expansion strategy, Boston Pizza returned to Ontario in the late 1990s, with Jim actually moving back to Ontario to open the head office. In addition, regional offices in Québec and British Columbia were set up to be closer to the franchisees so they could be more in tune with local attitudes and integrate these into the restaurant operations to vastly improve the customer experience.

With the expansion model fixed, Jim moved down to Dallas to put the infrastructure in place for Boston Pizza to expand into the United States with as few hiccups as possible. Despite the US going through two wars, the attacks on September 11, 2001, and a major recession, Boston Pizza has been expanding in the US for close to 14 years. Jim has established 50 franchises in the United States, slowing down the expansion during the big recession, and ramping back up today to continue the growth. Jim quickly points out other well-known companies who have tried to expand into United States, treating it like another province, and failed because the systems and culture were so different.

"If I had not been there, we would have been forced to close down," he says. "Going to the US is going to another country with a different set of rules, regulations, the way they do business and the way they eat. Pricing is completely different, costs are completely different, and it's probably the toughest competition in the world. That's why it is number one in growth compared to everybody else."

The success of the expansion strategy also allowed Boston Pizza to tap into the Mexican market, establishing its first franchise location approximately nine years ago. There are currently five locations, with seven more to be added. Each location has the same look as the flagship store in Toronto, with no extra Mexican additions to the menu. Although the guacamole and salsa may taste better due to the franchise being located in Mexico, the pizza and pasta formulas remain unchanged. Surprisingly, all of these franchises are located outside the main tourist areas, and have long lineups to get into the restaurant.

Although some suggest that the menu be changed to adapt to the local culture, Jim's experience has been exactly the opposite. In fact, Boston Pizza re-opening the Taiwan location caused such a clamour for North American food that the wait time to be seated was upwards of three or four hours. Boston Pizza was not going to compete with the Chinese restaurants, nor was that the reason customers waited for so long. It was simple: They wanted North American food.

"What I've often said about people in those parts of the world, which is the same reason why people want to go franchise to places like India and all these other places," says Jim, "is that you've got to look at it and say, they've got all the choices in the world of their own food, but what they're looking at is saying I don't want to be American, I don't want to be Canadian. I want to be Chinese or I want to be Indian, but I want to have the choices of looking and seeing that I can dress and eat Western food."

Opening in these other countries requires respect for the appropriate local beliefs and customs. For example, when looking to expand to India, Boston Pizza will not have pork or beef on the menu, and will find appropriate substitutes. However, the overall menu will have relatively the same look and feel as any other franchise location in the world.

Being in these other countries also attracts the younger demographic, which is preferred. The older demographic may not want to experience Western food, and in some cases may not know how to eat it. For example, in China, the older demographic may not know how to eat pizza with chopsticks, and may not return to the restaurant because they would never eat food with their hands. On the other hand, the younger demographic would simply pick up the pizza and eat it with their hands. With the desire to have North American food, the younger demographic would then visit a franchise location on multiple occasions for at least another 25 years. This kind of popularity and patronage makes any other expansion franchise location successful as well.

Jim learned an important lesson when expanding. A classic expansion mistake is to generate the volume of sales first before spending the overhead costs required to open a regional head office. Jim moved from Vancouver to Toronto, spending the overhead costs before worrying about the volume, and putting in a full structure before he sold another franchise. Once this was fixed, Boston Pizza grew significantly.

Those considering expansion require a significant outlay of capital to expand. That capital needs to be in place for the expansion to be successful. Of course, there are always exceptions to the rule, but making a bet on being the exception may not be such a wise idea. Losing the bet could mean losing your business.

With the local presence established, expansion seems well on its way. If the company is expanding with the same products and services, then it is able to leverage the current knowledge base and can transfer the appropriate knowledge to the expanded entity. However, if a company is expanding into an area different from its core offerings, then it must be careful to ensure that it properly understands the operational and resource requirements to avoid taking attention and resources away from its core business, which will affect the company's profitability. In that case, expansion may not be a good idea, as was experienced by Larry Rosen.

Expanding Outside of
Your Core Competencies

When expanding to a new market, you need to properly assess the amount of time, focus, and management resources required. Otherwise, you will fail in that expansion and take valuable attention away from your core competence.

– Larry Rosen, Chairman & CEO – Harry Rosen

As a business grows and becomes accustomed to a steady stream of revenues, it is not uncommon for business owners to think about expanding. Expansion could come in many forms, including new products and services, increasing retail space, adding locations either across the country or internationally, or adding new businesses.

The caution when considering expansion is to maintain the core essence of what made the business successful, regardless of the form the expansion takes. For example, if the business is introducing a new product, customers should see how this product logically extends from the base of products the company already offers.

However, expansion can create a disconnection in the customer's mind between it and the original business, or shift attention and resources away from the core business. The core business then suffers, and the steady stream of revenues that were once enjoyed may start to slip – a similar situation to what Larry Rosen experienced.

Larry Rosen is Chairman & CEO of Harry Rosen, a successful Canadian chain of men's high-end fashion stores. Harry Rosen was first opened in 1954 by Larry's father, Harry, and his uncle, Lou. Harry and Lou personally dealt with the customers and kept records of their contact details and purchases, and called them back for sales and suggestions and hence earned their trust.

"Back then, client cards were used to track this information," says Larry. "Now, the stores are equipped with computers that capture customer information and provide staff with customer leads for those who would benefit from any special events."

Harry Rosen has leveraged this practice to reinforce its level of service, in-house expertise, and more importantly, trust from the customer to become a destination store for men's fashion.

"Harry Rosen is really an advisory service to men, assisting them to develop a confident personal image for any time, any place, and any occasion," Larry says. "One of the advantages of our brand is that it's about men. Men can be 18, or men can be 75. We are very cognizant of the demographics of the country, where the ages are going and the Baby Boomers retiring, and so on. We design stores, design offerings, and design advertising pieces to really speak to a lot of the demographic. When you go to our store, you can see that. You can see the areas where you'd probably say, this isn't for me or for younger people, but there are areas where you feel comfortable and say, yeah, they got it. I don't think the fact that we are experts at younger fashion and older fashion deters or detracts from one demographic. I think people understand that we are a men's store and we work very hard at that."

Larry inherited his biggest challenge in business when he took over as CEO in 2000. During the late '80s or early '90s, senior management thought Harry Rosen had to be bigger and needed to expand, so they decided to expand to the United States.

"It was thought that the Americans were very similar to Canadians in style and fashion, and with that assumption, Harry Rosen opened up a store in Buffalo, New York," Larry says. "It was quickly found out that the retail scene in the United States was much different."

The whole process of getting the store open and running meant dealing with different sourcing methods, different landlords, and different builders, just to name a few problems. This was not the case for the Canadian locations, where Harry Rosen's standards were executed consistently, no matter which part of the country a store was opened. Not only did this apply to the process of opening a store, but also to bringing Canadian culture to a different country.

"We have been very successful in rolling out our culture right across the country," Larry says. "We've never had any problems when we open up a Harry Rosen store. We bring our standards and our approach to doing business in a very consistent manner regardless of whether it's in Edmonton, Winnipeg, Toronto, Montréal, doesn't matter, French or English. We've been able to bring our standards and our vision and execute it very consistently across the country."

However, expansion into the United States exposed a number of obstacles to success, a big one being operational in nature.

"A big part of that challenge was in having a constant change in who ran the Buffalo, New York store and how [the franchise] was being bought," Larry says. "It was a very small part of the business and ended up being quite a distraction. To try and get the store to become more successful, more attention was given to this store than was needed."

In the late 1990s, Harry Rosen struck a venture with Hugo Boss to open up a number of boutique Hugo Boss stores in the US. Hugo Boss played a major part of Harry Rosen's collection in Canada, which meant that the product, the merchandise, and how to sell the brand were all well known. The first Hugo Boss store opened in Michigan in 1998, and the Buffalo store was then converted to a Hugo Boss boutique. Seven more stores were opened: one in Los Angeles, one in Boston, two in Chicago, one in Florida, one in Denver, and one outside New York City. The vision was to open up 150 Hugo Boss stores in the United States, so Harry Rosen invested greatly in these stores. Executives thought the expansion would be a slam-dunk, but it never was.

"One of the major issues was that these boutiques were 2,500 square-feet in size, whereas all of the other Canadian Harry Rosen stores were about 13,000 square-feet in size," Larry says. "There was a gap in the mentality of running a smaller store. These US locations were not being costed as boutique stores and thus they could not justify the expense, the training, and the service that a typical Harry Rosen store was used to. Despite a volume of $40 million being achieved through the nine stores, we were not making money."

Larry took over as CEO in 2000 and had to make a decision on this albatross hanging around his neck. In 2001, the recession hit, and Larry's key decision related to the US operations became urgent.

"Harry Rosen was making good money in Canada, but the US operation was absorbing a lot of key people, and their attention, in addition to losing money," he says. "There was a level of confidence that the operation could be turned around to profitability, but it would be at the expense of making very dramatic changes in the way the company approached the stores, with a lot of time that would need to be invested. I felt that the resources spent on the US stores were neglecting the Canadian operations. That same effort, time, and energy would result in much greater results for the Canadian operations much faster."

Larry decided to exit the US and sell the stores to Hugo Boss. He knew he had to take a write-down[38] on the US operations, but he had to be careful with the asking price because Hugo Boss was one of his largest suppliers in Canada. The deal had to be a win-win for both sides. Larry saw that Hugo Boss would be able to run those stores for a profit, although they were not ready to do so right away. However, Hugo Boss eventually bought the stores for an agreed discount.

"I have no doubt that this was the best decision at the time," Larry says. "We were able to refocus on Canada and within two to three years, we really recouped our losses and we had our Canadian operations running much, much better. And ever since then, it's been running better, and better, and better. From a business strategy point of view, it was cutting our losses."

There were a number of key lessons that Larry took from the US expansion experience.

"Firstly, before you jump into another venture, measure the potential impact it has on the existing venture. You don't want to kill the golden goose. You have a precious existing venture and you don't want to put too much risk on the mothership, and I believe we did," he says. "Number two is how much am I going to risk and how many resources does a new venture absorb? The biggest resource is not always capital. The biggest resource is people. You only have so many senior management people, people that can assume leadership roles vis-à-vis new ventures, and new ventures absorb much more senior management time

---

38 A write-down is performed due to the value of certain assets on a balance sheet (or book value) being lower than their market value (http://www.investopedia.com/terms/w/writedown.asp)

and effort, and organizational effort and time than existing ventures. You know, cookie-cutting out an existing business is a lot more effective than starting up something brand-new that isn't your core business. Even though we all aspire to break into the US market and be effective in the US market, the reality was that it was an extremely smart strategy to come back and focus on our core competency where we really had a competitive advantage, where we really were the best at what we were doing. The learning was really meaningful."

There were other key lessons that Larry shares.

"I learned the value of focus, and the value of how much management can take in terms of new challenges, and how to manage new challenges and make them fit within your organization," he says. "It was really from the failure of that business where I learned all those things. I also learned that because we're really good as Canadian retailers, it doesn't make us good US retailers. The US retailers that come up here are pretty poor Canadian retailers. Some do well, but most don't."

Larry applies the lessons from that incident to his business today and shares a few thoughts with business owners.

"A growing organization is important," he says. "If you're not growing, you are not giving new horizons and opportunities for your people. Your people are really what make you good. The way to retain people is to have a growing organization. I believe in a growing organization. Businesses are like sharks. If they aren't swimming, they die. Everybody talks about milking the cow. Well, yeah, you got to milk the cow, but you have to milk the cow and still move forward. There is nothing wrong with earning good money, but you constantly have to grow your business. If that means that you're in a segment where you are dominant and there's very little growth on the horizon, it means adding businesses. You know, we did not have a shoe business to speak of 10 years ago. Today we have a $25 million dollar shoe business. That's a new business."

To grow the business while maintaining its core essence, Larry has embraced social media as a tool to increase sales.

"We recognize that the social revolution and the virtual revolution where people are getting their information in different ways is changing the way that we communicate with people," he says. "It's very important that we hire people that are on top of that. Look, next door I have a photography lab for e-commerce. I never had that three years ago.

Now it's working 24/7 taking shots all the time. It's a reality. The reality is that I've had to expand my business in a lot of different areas. At the end of the day, the beauty of our business is that the core essence hasn't changed."

In particular, Larry leverages social media to fuel additional sales by using suggestive selling techniques.

"For a customer who is a regular purchaser, let's say you bought a Zegna shirt last year and you are enjoying it," he says. "Here's a couple of new Zegna shirts that just came in. Would these interest you? This would go with that navy blazer and we're sending you a picture, maybe even laying down the blazer. We're using the new technology to support the essence of our business."

Larry points out yet another example, this one involving e-commerce.

"Last week I asked our people for our top 25 e-commerce customers, because we've been at it for two years," he says. "And I sent each one a personal email saying, you know, here's where we're going, there are changes you're going to be seeing on the website in the next little while, I hope you've been happy with your purchases and let me know if you have any other ideas or suggestions in what we can do. I wanted to make it more personal. I didn't want these people thinking that they were just dealing with a computer, that there is an actual person behind the company. Half of them responded with some suggestions, ideas, and questions. I started a conversation with these people and let them know that our e-commerce is not just about clicking buttons. There's a real organization that offers advice. In each one of the emails, I said 'Sometimes there is stuff on the site that you need more information about, would you like me to get you an associate in a store might be able to converse with you on a regular basis?' A couple of them had asked for that as well. That's a different way of doing e-commerce. I don't think a lot of organizations would try to bring the personal touch to it."

Harry Rosen is not just a clothing store for men, but acts more as an advisory service to help men create and maintain a certain image. This is the core essence of its business, which has made it successful since inception.

"The beauty of our brand is that it's really an advisory position," Larry says. "We are really helping you develop a personal image. Our customers are the leaders of this country. If you care about how you present yourself, you are usually in a position of authority or leadership. Even if your concept is a jeans and a T-shirt, it's still an image, right? We're really here for people who want us to give them that confident, personal image. In our business, the brands we carry are very exclusive. Within those brands, we have a lot of exclusivity in product. Price is important to everybody. But for the kind of customer who is buying a consulting image, a leadership image, the price is less important than the advice on how it's put together and the fact that we stand behind our product and that we alter our products correctly and that we fit you correctly – that's really what we sell. And it's worked out well."

Although their expansion to the US also involved men's clothing, the key success factors for a typical Harry Rosen store required carrying a large variety of inventory with various brands in large stores located in major Canadian cities. Although there was profit made in the smaller US stores, the business model was not as attractive as those of the Canadian stores. In addition, the constant draw on the management team was a problem.

Business owners that expand into areas need to consider the similarities in operations between the main business and the expanded venture. If there are differences, bringing on resources familiar with the expansion model should help, but trying to do it with existing resources may not work. As seen in the case study above, a differing business model required more resource attention, energy and effort than expected.

Either get back to the basics, as Larry Rosen did, or allocate capital to assemble a team to understand the expansion venture, develop the business model and execute flawlessly, which Jim Treliving learned the hard way with Boston Pizza's expansion, illustrated earlier in this section.

When the business is moving forward, it may attempt to move into areas that are hoped will increase the overall profitability of the company. But what needs to be fully considered is that the profitability of the expanded venture is assessed. Without a thorough assessment, the new venture could result in financial losses, and one may need to hire a turnaround specialist, such as Pierre Blouin, to get the company back on track.

Know the Profitability of an Expansion

Knowing the profitability of a particular venture is paramount when comparing it to the other product or service offerings. If the profitability is weak, then you must regroup and even possibly shelve the venture and get back to what you were doing well, focus on perfect execution and make that better.

– Pierre Blouin, CEO – MTS Allstream

When trying to move a business forward, a company may look to other companies, industries, or geographic areas to see what business opportunities are successful and adopt them. If there is a low barrier to entry with little investment required to create a similar product or service, then replicating that opportunity is quite possible, assuming that the new opportunity fits with a company's current core competencies.

But there are cautions. If the other opportunities were developed with substantial time and effort, required a unique set of skills and abilities, was a result of a patented product or process, or served a particular customer base that is not reachable, this presents a high barrier to entry, and trying to replicate this opportunity would require a tremendous amount of time, effort, and money.

Some companies do try despite the high barrier to entry as they may have the financial wherewithal and the resources to do so, but if this strategy does not generate the expected results, the company must regroup and get "back to the basics" of what it was doing previously and try another expansion strategy.

For a wireless provider, doing this required the services of a turn-around expert, Pierre Blouin, who was tasked with getting the company "back to the drawing board". Through an innovative approach and trust in his team, he was able to turn the company around from a situation where it was losing share in its prime product line, resurrecting it back atop its perch as the Canadian market leader in cellular phones.

Pierre Blouin is CEO of Manitoba Telecom Services Inc. and MTS Allstream Holdings Inc. He previously held a number of senior executive and CEO positions in the Canadian telecom industry.

"For most of my career, I have played the role of a 'fireman' in the positions I have occupied," he says. "I have been tapped to fix groups, divisions, or companies that experienced operating or strategic challenges and helped them improve their performance. For example, a few years ago, MTS Allstream had gotten itself into a non-performing position in particular for its national division and I was hired to help turn it around."

Pierre had joined a wireless provider at a time when the Canadian cellular phone market was exploding, growing at a rate of about 15% per year. The industry was experiencing rapid technological evolution with cell phones moving away from being large and bulky, and in some cases being bolted to cars, to a smaller form. This made them easier to use in addition to having them include convenient features such as text messaging.

To buy a cellular handset, a typical cell phone customer would go to a retail dealer, select a handset from a limited choice of brands, and enter into a multi-year contract with a wireless service provider. The incentive for the customer to enter into a contract would typically be a substantially discounted cell phone price to eliminate, or significantly reduce, any upfront cost. That customer would then pay monthly for the use of the cell phone, as per the signed contract.

The pre-paid cellular phone market was popular in Europe, representing a large proportion of the cellular phone market. Customers paid for cell phones upfront and were not tied to any long-term contract. In the late 1990s, pre-paid cell phones were being introduced into the North American market. Canadian cellular carrier companies began to think about how they would incorporate this new market into their portfolio of offerings.

Based on the successes other companies had in Europe, the wireless provider that Pierre joined wanted to introduce pre-paid cell phones as another wireless choice for Canadian consumers and focused its major annual sales campaign in this area.

"This wireless provider did very well and achieved close to 50% market share in this emerging market in its territory," Pierre says. "Although this success was impressive, the strategy resulted in a business focus that took the company away from its most profitable product: cell phones that were under contract, called post-paid. Year-end results showed that they had lost share in the post-paid segment."

Profits took a hit because the revenue contribution from pre-paid cell phones at that time was about four times less than that of a post-paid cell phone user for most North American companies. With lower revenues, profitability was negatively affected, and Pierre was asked to quickly help get the company to a better level of performance.

"I faced two challenges," he says. "First, how do I turn around such a successful and focused strategy of gaining market share in the pre-paid market and bring the focus back to our base business, which was trying to acquire as many post-paid customers as possible. The second challenge was improving the performance of the new pre-paid business which, at that time, had very low monthly revenues of just over $10 per month for each customer."

The company had also fallen from being the clear Canadian market leader in cellular phones to the number two position, and it was in danger of falling to number three. With Pierre being the "new kid on the block" and leading a company with strong capabilities, he wanted to reinvent the company with a plan to get back to the number one position in the market by year-end.

First, Pierre tasked his direct reports to put forth their most innovative and non-conservative ideas that would result in the growth of the post-paid segment.

The team spent a few months evaluating data around these ideas and prepared innovative strategies and plans to put them in place.

One of the more innovative strategies put in place resulted in making the cellular purchase simple for consumers while also introducing more competitive pricing. This idea, termed "Wireless in a box", had consumers buy a cell phone, which was packaged in a tin can, directly off of a store shelf. The consumer would then take the unit home and activate it there.

In addition to generating sales, customer support was drastically increased by sending all available corporate employees to retail locations and stand-alone customer service centres during large sales campaigns.

"The main strategy was to substantially increase the number of post-paid customers by drastically increasing the number of customer activations," Pierre says. "This overall strategy was risky as more activations means even less profitability in the short term."

The risk in Pierre's strategy stemmed from the profitability the company would receive for a typical post-paid customer. Customers would often walk away with a "free" cell phone, and a commitment to pay the company on a monthly basis. But that cell phone was not "free". The company had to incur the upfront costs to subsidize the handset. In addition to this cost, the company also provided incentives to its retail partners for customers activated. Of course, these upfront costs would be recovered over time through the monthly revenues received from that customer, with the payback period at that time being around 10-12 months.

Pierre had to pitch this overall strategy to the board of directors to get approval before he could move ahead.

"I went in front of the board and explained why our wireless business was not performing to expectations and in line with peers, and took them through our aggressive and innovative customer acquisition strategy," he recalls. "They understood that it also meant that if successful, we were going to deliver, for a few months, even more negative financial results, at least in terms of profitability. We asked them to trust our team and the innovation that we would bring to the market, and committed to them that based on our forecasts, we would deliver growth again by early winter. The board approved the plan, and we moved forward knowing that we would not have a second chance."

The strategy worked. By year-end, the company passed the one million customer mark, and added another million customers in the following year, clearly establishing itself as the number one wireless provider in Canada, while also delivering the best customer satisfaction levels. The company had a double hit to the bottom line: an aggressive revenue increase and a large increase to its customer base.

"Those two years were the most successful in the history of the company," Pierre says.

There were several keys to the success of Pierre's strategy. His plan was clear, and based on the analysis his team undertook, he was convinced that it would work. He believed and trusted his team. He leveraged an innovative approach to lead the market. Pierre also articulated the plan and showed everybody how it would lead to success in the end. With a plan, a strategy, innovation, solid execution, and a focus toward a realistic and believable successful outcome, everyone bought in and focused on executing the strategy.

The company faced a business challenge when looking at different ways of bringing in additional customers. However, the company had previously failed to understand that the pre-paid cell phone user revenue model, while successful in Europe, had a different structure and market rules than the Canadian market. The company successfully attracted a large number of new customers, but the European companies had a different (lower) revenue and profitability model.

Lower revenue contributions from the pre-paid cell phone segment meant lower profitability when acquiring a typical customer. Success in the pre-paid segment would need to have both a lower cost of acquisition and further segment analysis of consumer spending patterns for the Canadian or North American markets, which would have given some more insights into the type of consumer that would buy a pre-paid phone.

Ultimately, innovation and a focused execution enabled a quick turnaround for the company, which created huge growth.

When a business looks to expand its products or services, it should examine customer behaviour in its markets and the overall profitability of that product or service and its fit with the current core business. The business also has to ensure that it does not confuse customers. If you are a high price-high margin-high value producer of products and services, be careful how you introduce products that could be construed in the customer's mind as low price-low margin-low value. Anything in between is also a recipe for disaster.

When expanding, it is also important that entrepreneurs take the time to examine how the expansion affects the current operations and whether expansion is consistent with a company's brand identity. For Andy and Carol Gates, suggestions are plenty, but they have a thick filter to ensure that the business opportunities they venture into have minimal impact on the business and are in line with the company's brand.

Be Consistent With Your Brand

*You have to be consistent with what your business is.
When looking at business ideas or options, don't just think
about the money. You need to think about how it impacts
operations and if it is in line with who you want as a customer.*

– Andy Gates, Co-owner – GT's Beach Bar and Grill

*Not doing this will get you into business areas that
are not consistent with who you are. And that is the
biggest mistake you can ever make.*

– Carol Gates, Co-owner – GT's Beach Bar and Grill

As a business becomes successful, entrepreneurs may begin to look for areas to move the business forward so that the business continually provides additional value to its customers. Certainly, many friends and colleagues seem to have ideas of how an entrepreneur can change or expand the business, often ensuing in an exciting discussion about how this would work, what the possible marketing avenues would be, how many people would come, and so on.

Of course, these sorts of discussions build excitement at the possibility of gaining additional customers; experiencing more revenues or shaving off some costs is always a good objective for a business. But actually implementing these ideas needs greater consideration because there are much deeper issues to think about before going ahead.

If these ideas seem to detract from the core business, or introduce significant operational inefficiencies, for example, then maybe implementing these ideas is not such a great idea.

What the entrepreneur needs to do is to take a step back and think about how the new business will be able to integrate into the existing operations. Sometimes, the headaches in integration and potential soft costs are too much to justify the potential monetary gains, something that Andy and Carol Gates always consider when entertaining suggestions on how their restaurant-style beach bar can provide more value to their customers.

Andy and Carol Gates, who own GT's, a restaurant-style beach bar located in Port Stanley, Ontario, are constantly looking to add value to their customers, and have gotten some great (and not-so-great) suggestions from friends and family of how to make the business better.

But they have always tested these ideas on whether they fit with their definition of the GT's brand, what impact the operational changes or additions have on their customers' experiences, and whether the incremental revenue comes out ahead of any hard and soft costs that are incurred.

They have a solid definition of the GT's brand, and every decision they make needs to be consistent with that definition. Their business decisions, from menu items, to the ordering of food, to expansion possibilities, must all be consistent with their identity as a business to their customers.

In the humblest way, Andy says that in spite of the challenges they have faced along the way, they have never really failed. Carol attributes their success at this business to learning from mistakes made in previous employment opportunities. By the time Andy and Carol took over the restaurant, they had over 40 years of combined experience that taught them how to run a restaurant and bar, and most importantly, what pitfalls to avoid.

Carol and Andy met many years ago, both working for a franchise-owned restaurant. After Carol left to work at GT's as a manager, Andy also left to work in another restaurant. Carol worked at GT's for 15 years before receiving an opportunity to buy it from the owner, and began running it, with Andy helping when he could as he worked full-time at another restaurant with varying shifts. Owning the business was never their dream, but given the opportunity, it made sense for them to do so, and so they went ahead.

Because the restaurant was seasonal, being shut in the winter meant that every spring, they would have to open the restaurant, and every winter, they would have to shut the whole operation down. To some this might seem an arduous annual task, but the Gates love the procedure because of their love for the business and their customers.

"In so many ways, I have opened up a brand-new restaurant 20 times in 20 years," says Carol. "You have to do a new menu, hire your staff, do a big training; you know, all the things you have to do to open up a brand-new restaurant we've done, or I've done, every single year. And it's big. The whole deck would be buried knee deep in sand. You have to dig it out, stain it, get everything turned back on and then at the end of the season we turn everything back off."

"At the end of the season, everything gets scrubbed," Andy adds. "We actually turn off all the fridges and freezers, and they get turned into storage areas. So everything that is not bolted down goes inside. I chain the tables up on the patio. But every chair, every light fixture, and every sign comes down and gets put away. Computer equipment and TVs come down, and even paint that you don't even use goes into a warm zone so it doesn't freeze in the winter. The snow fence goes up on the outside. The volleyball poles stay out there, but the nets, and the boxes that they go in, come inside. And then in the spring, you have to retrain everybody, reprint all the menus, and so on."

During the off-season, both Andy and Carol reflect on the year and spend their time researching new menu items and look at areas of the business to improve. Closer to spring, orders are put in with food vendors to begin stocking supplies, with Andy and Carol always looking for ways to maintain or even increase the food quality for their customers.

With no cash flow during this down time, both Andy and Carol need to make sure that they have enough cash to cover the expenses of opening of the restaurant, which includes training new staff, stocking the bar, the stock of food, and so on.

One of the first mistakes they talk about happened in their first year of operation. With a small family, their sons being six months and 18 months of age at the time, Carol would open the restaurant, and then race to her home in London, Ontario, about 45 minutes away, to relieve the nanny at 6:00pm. Because Andy worked nights at another restaurant, Carol relied on staff to close the restaurant. But this schedule affected the profitability.

As new owners, despite having incredible sales in the first full year of operation, the restaurant lost money. Carol could not rely on the managers to run the restaurant the way she and Andy preferred, and they had to come up with a solution, which began discussions on the possibility of Andy joining the business. This was risky because Andy and Carol had to trade off having an income from Andy's full-time employment with having no income in the winter because of the seasonality of GT's.

In the third year of their ownership, Andy made the leap and left his employment to concentrate on the restaurant. This had an immediate positive effect on the profitability and overall operations.

"In the long run, it wasn't much of a difference, and stress-wise, it made all the difference," Andy says. "It was a mistake to think that we can do that with children that age."

Carol relives that time. "Andy was working at his full-time job and then coming down to close on Friday and Saturday nights. It was a lot of stress. Buying a business and having two babies, I would not recommend. Don't do that!"

Learning from failures at previous restaurant jobs helped them through those first few years and kept further stressful situations from cropping up; one lesson in particular stands out for Carol.

"The previous owner was a big fan of buying equipment at auction and so he would buy this dirt cheap equipment, get it repaired and just thought it was the greatest thing you can do," she says. "Well, we've been dealing with that 'falling apart' equipment ever since. Now, we have the same philosophy as a car, which is buying it new, get the life of it, get the warranty and use it for the whole life of it."

From a business perspective, making the decision to save money is always a good idea. But, with the volume of customers in GT's, having a machine break down while serving customers during a peak period was not fun, and it took time and attention away from customers, not to mention the possible lost revenues from a slowing of turning tables around.

However, kitchen machinery breaking down is a secondary concern in the restaurant business; it does not matter if the stove works if customers do not order food, so Andy and Carol insisted on maintaining the quality of the food being offered. Andy and Carol feel GT's has two types of customers – casual diners, and food-savvy ones. They wanted their clientele to come to GT's both for the location and for the food. The previous owner had a menu consistent with a typical beach bar with items such as chicken fingers and fries. Certainly, GT's offers such standard fare, but having a different menu every year was important for them.

"That's a real niche. We are unique because nobody has what GT's has," Andy says. "Even the bars and restaurants in Grand Bend, nobody is truly on the beach as far as what we have. What I really like hearing is people saying that they were pleasantly surprised by what GT's offered. But it wasn't all deep-fried, but that you can get a fresh option, like perch or salads. The real advantage in being seasonal for us is that we spend the winter doing research. If you look at anything that has been on the menu for the last five years, I know where it has originated, and where the idea came from."

This has also changed the type of clientele for GT's. Given the strict laws against drinking on the beach and adhering to stringent noise bylaws, GT's has been able to operate successfully while remaining respectful of its corporate and residential neighbors. Andy and Carol could have had constant blasting music and live bands, but chose to forego the thousands of dollars of business they could have earned from operating in this way, in favour of being good neighbours. This attitude reflects the type of restaurant they wish to be: respectable clientele with excellent food.

"The neighbours are our customers, and they walk to GT's to enjoy the food," Andy adds. "The last thing I want to do is offend a hundred of them by having loud music."

Andy and Carol practice being good neighbours in other ways, such as being active in the community. Carol is involved with the local Business Association, something that the previous owner did not do. The town of Port Stanley has gone from having no festivals in 2012 to having three in 2013, and the spending of the contributions from local businesses now goes to smarter advertising driven by business goals and purposes.

Despite the success they've had with GT's, Andy and Carol are consistently offered ideas to expand or move the business forward. Opening up a winterized area to stay open all year has been one of the most popular suggestions, but this suggestion does not resonate with Andy and Carol's definition of the GT's brand.

"That is the biggest mistake we could ever make because you have to decide who you are, and what you are, and do that very well," says Carol. "We are a beach bar and we know we are weather dependent. It is important that we have a roofed area, but, as you can tell, it is the last place that people want to sit on a sunny day. They'll sit there if the rest the patio is full or if it's raining, using it as a last resort."

Another idea Andy and Carol commonly receive is opening for breakfast. However, given the cost of staff and other supporting costs, opening the restaurant earlier to accommodate this request does not seem feasible.

"We're already open 12 to 15 hours a day," Andy points out. "From what I can make off of breakfast, the tax on ourselves and staff to maybe clearing even $1,000 a week – if you take into account the X number of hours you add on, it doesn't make sense. Again, we're a beach bar."

The beach bar concept remains central to decision-making. As a weather dependent restaurant, they may face a rainy week with few customers, to having an incredible wave of excellent weather and being consistently full from open to close. Their process from the customer walking in the door to having that customer walk out must be as smooth and efficient as possible, regardless of the impact of weather. This makes staff scheduling and kitchen preparation a daily task.

Despite being seasonal and having a turnover of between 40% and 50% of serving staff, Andy and Carol's consistent style of running GT's has encouraged a number of managers to stay with them for close to eight years. In fact, the kitchen manager has been with the restaurant for over 20 years, since GT's opened.

Lack of consistency was one of the biggest mistakes Andy and Carol saw at the franchise restaurant they both had worked at, brought on by drastic cost-cutting. The franchisor brought in potential franchisees, sat them at the bar, poured a couple of cappuccinos and went on about how wonderful the restaurant was. The new franchisees had never owned a restaurant, and after two weeks of watching the operations from a couple of bar stools, they were given the keys to run the show, with a promise to send the head office a royalty cheque every month.

The previous owner stayed on for a month to transition the franchisee couple, but soon after that, the financial and operational realities of running a franchise restaurant hit them. After giving a royalty cheque to the franchisor, there was little money left for the franchisees, in addition to the operational disarray.

Under financial strain, the couple started cutting corners. Cheaper food products were sourced and the quality of the menu items declined. Faced with a substandard product, customers fled and Carol and Andy saw the operations go downhill.

"This definitely taught me what not to do in terms of inventory management," says Carol. "Every Sunday, we would have to ask the kitchen what we were out of because the order came out on Monday. They ran the inventory so lean that by Sunday, your table would sit down and you got to take the menu and say, just so you know folks, we are out of this, this, this, and this, this, this, and this. And we'd be borrowing from other stores. It was embarrassing. I can't stand running out of one item at GT's."

"Sometimes there wouldn't be enough cutlery to set all the tables," Carol adds. "Some people got their food, and there was literally no clean cutlery in the restaurant because they were too cheap to buy more, or they were mad because they lost cutlery through theft or by staff throwing it out by mistake. But that is the cost of doing business. But you can't run a restaurant without giving people forks."

Andy and Carol are not willing to cut corners with GT's.

"We are in it for the long haul," Andy says. "If I need to, I'll spend an extra $10,000 to start the year. But I don't waste time fixing equipment or chasing to save five dollars on a box of chicken because I know I have a good supplier with good food, who delivers up to me weekly, and he brings me the same product. It's not worth wasting my time saving five dollars on something like that. My time spent on maintaining the quality of products is more important, and people recognize that."

Andy and Carol know their customers realize when they are eating a sub-standard product. They will never compromise on the quality, despite the financial savings. In fact, they upgraded their chicken wings recently because they felt the wings they bought the previous season were poor quality, and they will buy better chicken wings for the next season.

What astounds Andy and Carol further is that when pricing a box of chicken, restaurant owners are more concerned about the price of the box, and not the actual per-piece price of the chicken. Not knowing this information would obscure the overall per-plate cost for each food item served, a number that Andy and Carol know intimately, and is essential financial information. According to a representative from one of the major food suppliers, only 4% to 6% of his overall customers know this information.

Andy and Carol advise those new to the restaurant industry that a love for golf or a love for eating does not mean that you can run a golf course or open a restaurant. It is not like hosting a party every night. Running a restaurant requires a lot of hard work and is all about the numbers.

Andy suggests, "If you dream of opening up a restaurant, work in one first, and start in the kitchen. Bartenders and servers do not receive exposure to information about the financials – that generally happens when watching the food preparation inventory in the kitchen. Also, see what a customer sees. Sit at a table and see if there is garbage on the floor that needs to be picked up, or a table that needs clearing."

In addition to being familiar with the different areas, Andy adds, "You also need to be a jack of all trades. If we are behind and I need someone in the kitchen, Carol can jump online and do fries, or do a line, or sometimes she serves, or sometimes she bartends. You should work every aspect. Conversely, even if you are a chef, you should have an idea of what it is like being in front of people and dealing with customers' complaints, and dealing with mistakes and to go up and apologize. How do you make someone happy without giving away the farm? Is it a small discount, is it simply talking to them, is it buying their meal?"

Andy and Carol's attention to quality, customer experience, and adherence to the GT's brand has brought them success. Many locals eat at the restaurant, and corporate clients look to GT's to host their events. In fact, GT's hosts corporate groups ranging in size between 20 and 200 guests every year, and 95% of their corporate clients return the following year because of the value, the quality, and the service they receive at GT's. Andy and Carol are justifiably proud of their restaurant.

Their attention to detail is always on display. Even on a patio devoid of customers, Carol points out to Andy that one table is too close to another. The chairs, when pushed back for diners to sit, would touch the chairs at another table, so Andy shifts the table about four inches away – just enough to make his customers comfortable when the patio does get busy. Carol and Andy refuse to accept even a minor discomfort for their patrons; no detail is too small, and no problem goes unattended.

GT's already has a bustling clientele that makes it a success every season, because Andy and Carol have established an identity for GT's. They know who they are and what they want to be, and everything else supports that. Businesses trying to add value need to make sure they stick with this identity. Not doing so may dilute the brand, confuse customers, and spread resources too thin in too many different areas. The last thing one wants is flat revenues as these can begin dipping quickly.

Customer tastes and preferences continually change as time passes, and entrepreneurs must adjust the business to ensure that its products and services still meet customers' expectations. This is an ongoing challenge, especially when the consumer has a tremendous number of choices as a substitute. If one fails to adapt to that change, customers simply go elsewhere, and that closes the curtain for the business. Not being able to adapt to change closed the curtain on Gloria Dona's business, taking her from $10 million in revenue to zero in one year.

Adapting to Change

We did not take into account the preferences of a shifting demographic in our clothing line. We missed the mark when ordering inventory and could not recover. That was the beginning of the end for my company.

– Gloria Dona, Former Founder & CEO – Optionelle

In the world we live in today, there is constant change. Technology evolves rapidly, the Internet has given consumers access to credible information to research products and services, and consumer tastes shift as companies introduce a plethora of products and services, supported by well-crafted marketing efforts, to get customers to buy their wares.

Ensuring that the company is in tune with this constant change, especially in its industry, management needs to continually research what products consumers tend to buy that are related to its products and services. A hint of a shift in consumers' tastes should signal management to take the appropriate steps to ensure that its products and services match those shifting tastes. However, if management is not able to do that, customers will likely move on. That is precisely the wrong time to begin thinking about making changes.

Not being prepared for this shift took Gloria Dona's company from $10 million in annual revenues in one year to the bank calling in the loan the next year, closing the company's doors and eventually auctioning off its assets.

Gloria Dona was Founder and CEO of Underlines Inc., which was rebranded as Optionelle.

A number of separate influences gave Gloria the impetus to start a business. Starting at 17 years of age, she took a fashion design course at a local college, was employed in direct sales as a part of the college program's co-op requirements, worked in a manufacturing facility after graduating, and wrote a business plan while working at the manufacturing facility.

Putting all these experiences together, at just 20 years old, Gloria opened the doors of Underlines Inc. in London, Ontario, a company that designed and manufactured an exclusive line of lingerie and women's lounge wear for the Canadian marketplace. Because her clothing line was exclusive, it was generally higher in price.

"I started in my parents' basement doing everything, and then grew it from me, to five people, to 10 people, and as sales grew over the next few years, we were able to move out of my parents' basement into a small industrial mall," she says.

She also used a unique direct sales model approach where independent sales persons would host parties at their homes and would showcase the clothing line, with compensation being a percentage of the overall sales. But using the direct sales approach to sell the clothing line proved difficult.

"These are independent sales reps. Think of them like volunteer sales reps because they don't owe you anything," she says. "[They hosted] home parties, like a Tupperware concept. It's a volunteer sales force in terms of getting them to do what you want. So, motivation is different than an employee sales force."

The business continued to grow year-in and year-out and the product lines were extended to meet the demands of the market, discovered through customer feedback.

"Obviously, it's really simple. This is what is selling, so you go in that direction," she says.

Based on the feedback, Gloria tweaked the clothing line here and there as she was manufacturing this herself, and it continued to sell well.

In the late '80s, the company was growing so fast that Gloria had to think about outsourcing manufacturing. In the early '90s, the apparel industry as a whole relied on taking their manufacturing offshore, and Gloria knew she had to make the same move as it was getting difficult to compete on price: the costs to manufacture overseas were considerably lower than doing the same in-house. But she had to make a trade-off in the flexibility of changing her designs because she needed to place orders well before the start of her selling season, which typically started in September and February of any given year.

Soon, her customers' buying behaviour changed, and Gloria decided to rebrand the company as Optionelle.

"Our product line had changed," she says. "We had to reinvent ourselves and came up with a new name because we weren't selling lingerie anymore. [The older clothing designs] started to wean out and customers began buying more of our sportswear. We migrated the brand, and started to put production in China."

Switching to the new line of clothing worked well and the company kept growing. Acquiring sales representatives from other direct selling companies that had closed helped Optionelle expand across Canada, collecting different information and ideas from each acquisition target.

"In my career, I had seen a lot of direct sales companies come and go because direct sales and apparel is not an easy game," she says. "When those companies closed, we usually acquired either a lot or parts of the network with a direct sales model."

By the early 2000s, 80% of the company's production had been overseas, typical of the industry at the time. By 2005, sales had peaked, and then started to flatten.

"We really had two customers," Gloria says. "Our sales force was one customer because they were the volunteers who were selling our clothing every season. We needed to inspire and motivate them to continue to sell and to buy into the company. And they had their network of customers. That demographic was aging. Our line had become very sophisticated, did well and was more expensive. But we were flat. How do we change this and how do we grow?"

Gloria decided to make a change in the clothing line to invigorate sales. Some aspects of the designs were tweaked, but revenues remained flat. She went back to the design team, tweaked the clothing line again to see what happened, but revenues were still flat.

"In business, I think in any industry, there is no such thing as zero growth," she says. "You're either on the point of a boat going down, right, or you're going up."

The constant tweaking of the clothing line continued, in addition to substantial internal discussions to try to figure out what needed to change.

"We knew we needed a younger demographic as one possibility," Gloria says. "We looked at the pricing of the collection, the product line. It's always a recipe. It's a formula. You can't just fix one thing. All the pieces have to work together. It's the sales force, the compensation plan, the product line, the pricing, how you bring it to market and how you sell it to the customers. We were looking at everything."

Because the company moved its production offshore, the supply chain became a challenge, which the company never recovered from.

"The biggest challenge was in forecasting and buying because of how we sell," she says. "We had a catalogue, and our sales reps went and sold the catalogue for the season. And because of the lead times, we would bring 'X' amount in, and what that 'X' was supposed to be was never right."

Gloria's company had to ensure that her sales estimates for that particular season were pinpoint accurate when ordering inventory for each of the different clothing lines. If not, she would either be left with too much inventory, which she was not able to return, or she would sell out, which resulted in unhappy customers and sales reps. Because of the restrictive lead times caused by the offshore manufacturing, the company simply had to get the numbers for each season right the first time.

"We were always playing with the supply chain, always working on that, and looking at actually trying to find collections that we could produce effectively, on time and profitably," Gloria says. "That was one of the core challenges. Because we went to offshore production the challenges were never really solved well, and in the end, it was part of the demise, really."

One of the signs that Gloria reflects on that signaled "the beginning of the end" was when a large national competitor with the same business model closed its doors in 2008. Having been in the business for 20 years, that company was the only other women's apparel company using the direct sales method in Canada, the US, and Europe. The reason for that company's demise was the same reason that resulted in Gloria's company losing revenue fast.

"So, really, our only competitor in Canada with direct sales of clothing went into receivership," she says. "Their challenges were the same challenge that we faced, which was an aging demographic. Their network, their sales network was getting older. We're selling clothing at home parties. When I'm a woman in her 30s and 40s, she needs more clothes. When she starts to get in her 50s, her lifestyle changes. Some of them are retiring and you don't need the business-wear, and maybe the disposable income is going to go to other things. They are more financially secure and don't need the extra money. They've already put their kids through school. A number of factors."

With this changing demographic, sales were directly affected as fewer customers purchased the company's clothing line. This directly affected the income of the sales reps that depended on the sales commissions from the home parties. The clothing line was also exclusive, carrying a higher price tag, which precluded the younger demographic from purchasing the clothing and buying into the business.

In 2008, Gloria approached a number of the sales reps from the competitor and convinced some to join her company, effectively doubling her sales force in Canada. Based on this additional sales force, Gloria adjusted her inventory forecasts, and with some lead time in hand, put in her order to the Asian manufacturer.

The competitor also had a warehouse in England and used sales reps in Europe to promote its clothing lines there. After closing shop, the sales reps approached Gloria and asked if she was interested in coming to Europe as they liked her clothing line, which was not available in Europe at that time.

"I said, sure. Let's do it. I thought, here's a trained sales force, and if you don't get them now, they're going to go somewhere else. Seize the moment. We had discussions and not everyone was in favour internally. With some of the key leaders from the sales force there supporting us, I made the decision to do this," she says.

The major naysayer was Gloria's CFO, who thought that this was a risky venture; the CFO was not convinced that there was enough time to turn the warehouse operations around to begin fully selling product at the beginning of the peak season. There were a large number of issues to attend to that needed to be resolved by September 1, THE key selling season for the company. This created a tremendous sense of urgency to resolve all of these issues as September was just around the corner.

"This was like July, and we were aiming for September. It's not just getting more product, but it's all the logistics," she says. "I said, 'Oh, but of course we can find solutions, we can do this, we can do anything.' So off we went. We secured the warehouse, secured office staff, recruiting people at the same time, and started working on getting a European company in place, logistics, customer service, getting our order processing system ready, paying for legal services and translation services because we had recruited people in Germany and Austria. It was a very painful and stressful season, and we weren't ready for September 1. We were barely ready for October 1. We had made commitments for the inventory, and we were behind in recruitment even though we had made our inventory commitments."

Whether it was due to timing or the economic turbulence in the fall of 2008, the sales in Europe did not materialize and only being ready for October 1 meant that the company missed all of September. The product started arriving late from China, and there were continuing issues with the order processing system. Further compounding the problem, the forecasts from the Canadian sales force were completely wrong.

"The product line was more sophisticated, and not all customers bought into it. Some of the people who had joined [from the competitor] had already left, and then jumped on and then jumped off. By the end of that fall season, we had really bought twice as much inventory as we needed. Between the cost of expanding to Europe, all the legal costs, the travel, and then the amount of leftover inventory we had, we went from cash flow positive and a good balance sheet to like this," she says, gesturing downward with her arm. "We just never really recovered from that."

In 2009, the bank started taking a look at the company's financial records and soon called in the loan. A forbearance agreement[39] was negotiated and Gloria ran the company for the last six months with a hope to turn it around and buy it back from the bank. While working under the bank, delayed product, back orders, and the challenges of a

---

39 An agreement to delay, reduce or suspend payments due on a loan for a limited period of time.

new enterprise resource planning system proved to be too many hurdles to overcome, and in late spring, Gloria announced that Optionelle was closing. The bank took over and began to auction off all the assets.

"The challenges that the company faced were really much earlier than at the end," Gloria says. "The way I look at it, it was a quick and painful ending, but I think we were facing a slow death. Well, that's the $1 million question – were we able to find a solution to the model? But that's a moot point, it doesn't matter. The question is could we have reinvented ourselves, as we have done in the past, very successfully, or was it the end of the lifecycle? We hit maturity. I felt that because we were successful, and reinvented ourselves in the past, we should be able to do it. Or, was it a business that had come and just reached the end of its time?"

She also points out that although there could be a sense that companies reach the end of their time because of external factors, the responsibility of seeing these factors and adjusting to them still lies with the person running the organization.

"You can blame the external environment, you can blame this, and you can blame that. In the end, they were my decisions and my risks," she says. "I failed to plan and react to the aging demographic, I failed to properly tweak my designs to adjust, and I made a knee-jerk reaction to take over that warehouse in England despite others saying it wasn't a good idea. I have to take full responsibility."

Because of the shift in demographics, factors such as the high price point for clothing, the problems with the supply chain, and the constant tweaking of the apparel design never seemed to satisfy the new demographic that replaced the old one. In hindsight, Gloria may have been able to begin looking at the younger demographic much earlier to blend the two sets of clothing collections together. That way, as the older demographic started to reduce their purchasing habits, Gloria could have increased inventory with the new collection and attract sales from the younger demographic replacing the old demographic.

The key lesson is that management must always be on the lookout for these shifts in consumer tastes and market trends to ensure that the company's products and services are still in demand. Companies such as Blockbuster and Kodak are prime examples of what can happen when management delivers products that are no longer in vogue. Making changes at the last minute only serves to drain the bank account much faster.

Elaine Paquin's company produced a product that had to be in fashion, and so she had to know what trends were happening. She experienced a classic mistake of working IN the business and not ON the business. She missed the trend. She missed the boat. And she narrowly missed closing down.

Keeping Up With the Trend

Our failure was that we spent too much time concentrating on the business, and not enough time watching the market. Because of that, we almost went out of business.

– Elaine Paquin, President – Quinco & Cie Inc.

With the incredible choices consumers have, it becomes difficult to predict with certainty what consumers will want and what trends will be established. There is a lot of market research performed that will help spot trends, and entrepreneurs may want to perform their own market analysis as well to ensure that the products and services being offered match the consumer's trendy choices.

Some trends last longer than others. Certain trends such as consuming organic foods are slow to change once started, and hence, those looking into providing organic products will have a good chance of making healthy profits from quite some time if the business is run efficiently.

Other trends, such as clothing styles, may change rapidly from one season to another. To ensure profitability in this industry, the entrepreneur needs to gather the right information quickly before the selling season to ensure that the business has the right styles in the proper colour schemes to match consumer demand, a problem that Gloria Dona faced in the previous chapter.

If an entrepreneur predicts the trend incorrectly in a quick-changing industry, or simply does not see the trend happen, then the business continues making products that are out of date. The business will be saddled with excess inventory that can only be sold at a discount, resulting in lost revenues and lost opportunity.

In this type of industry, the entrepreneur needs to have his or her head up to watch the trends and adjust the manufacturing process accordingly. If the entrepreneur's head is down, as was the case for Elaine Paquin, the trend can easily be missed, and the result may be too taxing for the business to continue.

In 1999, Elaine Paquin and a partner started a company called Quinco & Cie Inc., based out of Quebec. Their company manufactures a peel and stick tile, a product that did not exist in the market at the time. The idea came to Elaine while she was trying to choose ceramic tiles to use for the backsplash in her kitchen. If she picked any ceramic tile, because of its permanency, she knew it would be difficult to change, yet she also knew that she would likely tire of the same look after a couple of years. The idea involved a less permanent product that would be easy to install.

Identifying a solution to Elaine's problem, the company started with a product that would be easy to apply and easy to take off, with the target market being the home décor industry. Because Elaine had been stung investing in a previous business, she began to put more of her time in the company rather than making a huge investment in manufacturing and selling the tile. She contacted other manufacturers and subcontracted the making of the tile to them.

After a couple of years, the market for this product became much more attractive, and the company decided to manufacture the product itself. Quinco & Cie took on some fixed costs such as rented space, employees, and manufacturing equipment, and began to manufacture and sell the product, reaching close to $800,000 in sales. Due to the nature of the home décor market with shifting consumer tastes, Elaine and her partner needed to have a pulse on that change. A shift in the home décor trend did happen; once-popular colours and patterns changed, and the company was caught flat-footed, not prepared for the shift.

"After three or four years, the product was doing well," Elaine says, "but we were so caught up in doing everything that we really did not see the shift in the home décor trend. And that was our big mistake.

We were in over our heads with everything else – learning the manufacturing, learning about having employees and dealing with them... We did not see the shift coming. So, we started to go down because everything we were designing, at that point, was not what people were asking for."

In 2006, revenues fell drastically and the company hovered on the edge of closing for the next three years. To stay afloat, Elaine acquired a licensing deal with a major North American company the year prior to put characters on tiles. That deal brought enough cash to survive, but did not result in many sales, and the deal was shut down five years later.

Within those three years, on two occasions, the accountant asked Elaine to think about closing the business. At the same time, Elaine engaged in discussions with a major national home décor retailer to carry her product, but the actual order kept getting pushed back.

Going through those difficult three years had Elaine asking, "Even though we realize sales are coming down, okay then, what else can we come up with? You know, you have to be constantly reinventing yourself. So it's not just saying, okay, this is no longer working, but what else we can do? We had to come up with a second generation product."

Eventually, Elaine and her team designed a glass tile imitation product, which they introduced to the market in 2009. This product was a hit and pulled Elaine's company out of trouble.

The experience taught Elaine that her industry was particularly sensitive to change. Consumers' tastes changed on a regular basis, so Elaine's product needed to change to match the tastes at the time. To that end, Elaine hired people to take care of sales and operations so that she could focus solely on new product innovation. "That is really what is going to keep us alive in the future," she says. Today, Quinco & Cie enjoys sales of over $6 million a year.

Having a pulse on changes in consumers' tastes requires attention be paid in that area. Those who solely own their businesses need to find a balance between looking internally to ensure that the actual business runs smoothly, and looking externally to work on the strategy. This becomes more important when selling a product that changes rapidly in design and function, such as technology, as compared to an industry such as furniture, where the trends change more slowly. After suffering a "near business death experience", Elaine dedicates her time to paying attention to market trends and trusts her employees to take care of the business.

In conversations with entrepreneurs, many will share their experiences of making a decision that helped the company move forward, but disclose that their decision was based solely on intuition, or a gut feeling. It is hard to explain as it sometimes defies the underlying logic, but nevertheless, the intuitive decision is made and the business thrives.

In the previous section, we were able to see how Kelsey Ramsden was better at tapping into her intuition, somehow resulting in the right decision being made at the right time, whereas Christine Siegel ignored her intuition, which resulted in continued troubling events.

Stephen Brooks successfully tapped into his intuition to realize that he needed to expand the demographic that would come and watch the Toronto Blue Jays baseball club. The business challenge he faced was in generating successful marketing programs that resonated not only with the younger demographic, but also with the existing stable of season ticket holders and sponsors, in an uncertain environment where a string of player injuries or team losses could result in more empty seats at games, a crucial hit to revenues.

Tapping Into Intuition

In baseball, business decisions are based on what happens on the baseball field. With always changing factors on the field, such as injuries or player slumps, you need to trust your gut and move forward with a marketing plan despite the challenges of continuing to increase revenues from gate receipts.

– Stephen Brooks, Senior Vice-President of Business Operations – Toronto Blue Jays Baseball Club

Entrepreneurs may not have the luxury of having 100% of the information all the time. Yet, the business must go forward and decisions must be made. Tapping into mentors, advisors, or resources within the company should help make effective decisions based on past experience. In some cases, that may not be enough, or the entrepreneur has an inkling that there is a better way to go. That inkling is an intuition, or gut feeling, that the entrepreneur taps into that somehow results in the right business decision made at the right time. For Stephen Brooks, tapping into his intuition resulted in a wider and younger demographic coming to baseball games and sponsors throwing their support behind the team while hoping that the baseball players remain healthy and continue to win baseball games.

Stephen Brooks is Senior Vice-President of Business Operations for the Toronto Blue Jays baseball club. One of the unique challenges that Stephen faces is that in the sports business, the product changes almost every day. From a business perspective, the product on the field tries to encourage those with disposable income looking for an entertainment outlet to attend baseball games in addition to season-ticket sales and corporate sponsors.

In trying to put an excellent team on the field that is going to win, under performance and injuries make it hard to market the team. Because of the unique nature of the business he is in, Stephen needs to make calculated business decisions, often going with his intuition.

One of the gut feelings that Stephen has sensed is that, despite relying on ticket sales from corporate sponsors and season-ticket holders, there needs to be a push to involve the younger demographic. At some point, the younger demographic will be looking for an entertainment outlet. One challenge that Stephen faces is to balance his marketing programs to not only cater to the existing fan base, but also implement marketing and communication tools that are familiar with the younger demographic.

"In the past year, the marketing efforts for the Toronto Blue Jays have been geared towards engaging the 18 to 34 year demographic, complemented by the nature of the ads, the players being social media savvy, and the music being geared towards this demographic," says Stephen. "In addition, changing uniforms back to the older colours based on the history of the club and cross-Canada events with the players resonated with the broader demographic. This complemented the positive and well-received moves and direction from the baseball perspective."

An additional challenge that Stephen faced, although he was not with the team at the time, was in dealing with a disconnection with baseball fans in general after the 1994-1995 lockout, the Montréal Expos baseball team relocating to Washington, DC, and the Toronto Blue Jays not making the playoffs. Although several years had passed since those events, this trifecta created a long-term disengagement with baseball. To meet this challenge, instead of bringing fans to the Toronto Blue Jays, he brought the Toronto Blue Jays to the fans.

The Blue Jays instituted a number of baseball camps across the country, holding 14 camps in 10 provinces with 25 to 30 one-day camps across the province of Ontario, having 18 alumni players come to help, and having the current players go on a winter tour, all in an effort to get the baseball players and the brand back out across the country.

"It is important for us to demonstrate that commitment and for us to re-engage the fans with the Blue Jays brand and the game of baseball," Stephen says. "Those things together, I think, are starting to now pay dividends, particularly for that 18 to 34 demographic on which we have focused. As an organization, I think we have done an admirable job of re-engaging the brand. You learn from your mistakes and can always do more. But I know that when I look around the stands during our games and I see so many 20-somethings coming to the games, and that to me is a good sign, a healthy sign. Most importantly, it starts with an on-field product that is engaging with the promise of success. The marketing efforts then have to complement the on-field product. We have tried to re-engage the younger demographic through a series of instructional camps across the country with our alumni players, the Winter Tour with our players, our partnerships with Baseball Canada and Little League Canada as well as our sponsorships of various amateur baseball programs across the country. This has been coupled with various in-game elements over the last couple of years to appeal to that younger demographic. I believe that there is evidence that this is showing results – our research indicates that the 18-34 demographic has grown, particularly our female demographic; our Junior Jays programs have grown exponentially, and I think that we have done some good in keeping the profile of the game of baseball at the forefront."

Stephen's marketing decisions and efforts need to work hand-in-hand with the delicate balance between the business side and the product on the field. The baseball side is the biggest driver of revenues that attracts people to come to the baseball games. From the business side, the marketing programs rely on this revenue base to generate marketing campaigns that will try to increase ticket sales. This presents an interesting chicken and egg scenario, but Stephen needs to use his past experience and success to make a decision and take a plunge with a particular marketing program to move things forward.

"You can put a good team on the field, a team that you think is going to win, and like last year, with injuries and team under performance relative to expectations, winning becomes elusive," he says. "It becomes challenging to market because in sports, what matters is winning. On the other hand, a winning team markets itself where you then try to do things from a marketing perspective that complement or follow from that on-field success. In our business, you can turn things around by winning games. At the end of the day, fans expect to win and rightly so – that is what it is all about."

If the business side of that delicate balance becomes out of sync with an excellent product on the field, the overall organization suffers.

"You can have a tremendous team on the field, but if the fundamentals of the business are not sound, such as the right ticket price, lack of interest from the corporate community or a lacklustre brand that does not resonate with people, you miss an opportunity to maximize the return from the team on the field," Stephen says. "One needs to be careful as a winning team can mask weaknesses in business fundamentals, and you then forfeit the ability to maximize your return on the product."

The overall organization also suffers when the tables are turned in that delicate balance if the business side does well, but the product on the field has problems.

"The reverse is problematic as well," Stephen explains. "If the business side gets ahead of the baseball team, then people will only buy hope for so long. They expect to see tangible results otherwise they will be looking elsewhere for entertainment. I know I'm being repetitive but at the end of the day, the driver of this business is not slick advertisements or promotions, it is about on-field performance. It is about winning. On the baseball side, there were a number of key injuries, and our manager left the organization. These are the things that make the sports business so interesting. Specifically, the business side has to adapt to changes like these; changes that every sports team faces."

To compound this problem, Stephen has to deal with the sheer magnitude of dollars involved in putting a team together. Other sports have salary caps for the athletes but in baseball there is no such cap. This provides a unique entrepreneurial spirit for the business of baseball as one essentially needs to get the business headed in the right direction, spend money if possible or desired, and be accountable for those decisions. This leads to an interesting risk/reward ratio which is much higher for baseball than other sports.

Stephen's ability to channel his intuition into a successful business decision has resulted in the support of fans and success in bringing sponsors on board. Because Toronto has the only Canadian baseball team, he has the luxury of promoting the team, and the sport, across Canada with the only competition being teams in other sports. This allows him to take a unique approach when dealing with corporate sponsors. Rather than just having a corporate sign on a rig board or on an outfield wall, Stephen has looked at increasing the spirit of partnership with sponsors by focusing more on how to get the collective brands into the marketplace. This has worked extremely well.

"In the summer of 2012, Budweiser added the Toronto Blue Jays logo to all their beer cans in Ontario," Stephen says. "Tim Horton's Cold Stone Creamery ice cream was engaged in getting the Blue Jays brand into their stores. And WestJet has become a new partner whose first foray into the sports sponsorship world started with the Toronto Blue Jays. Getting them active in promoting our brand and us in promoting their brand, that is how corporate partners in the sports world should work. Not just a sign on a wall. We have worked hard to elevate the Blue Jays brand again with our partners. The enthusiasm of our partners in wanting to activate our brands nationally has been tremendous. There are always challenges and we need to continue to grow nationally, but this is how partnerships need to work."

At the end of the day, the Toronto Blue Jays are in the entertainment business. When a game is going on or events are planned before and after the game, it is much like a theatre or musical production. Stephen and his team need to react to unexpected events, just like any other business in the same industry. He may not have all the information, and because of this, he needs to tap into his experience and effective intuition to bring an exciting product to Canadian baseball fans.

"You need to adapt your marketing and overcome, because the show must go on," he says.

There is no rule book to follow when it comes to tapping into intuition. Over time, an ability to make the right decision at the right time can consistently be made when there is a synergy between creative solutions and logical thought. Once the entrepreneur is able to successfully tap into this intuition, the business can only benefit. In Stephen's case, he understood that he needed to bring in a different demographic to baseball games while coping with the balance between the business and product.

A business's expansion plans may include the acquisition of another entity. To ensure that the marriage of the two entities goes smoothly, both sets of management members must work together to integrate the culture and business processes for a certain period of time. However, at some point, some of the management members should be asked to leave as the combined company does not need two sets of management. The timing of when this should happen is crucial; extending the stay of the temporary management members does more harm than good, as Patrick Lauzon experienced.

Keep Only Essential Resources

When integrating or acquiring companies, you have to find that point where you need to let the leadership of these companies go. Holding onto them longer only produces diminishing returns.

– Patrick Lauzon, Former President – Mediative Inc.,
SVP Interactive Marketing Platforms - TC Media

When companies integrate or acquire, it is important that proper benchmarks are established to determine which processes will be used, what resources will stay, and which corporate culture will be adopted, and the sooner that this is done, the smoother the transition. For the leadership transitioning in, there comes a point where keeping them on becomes ineffective, unless they are a key part of the integration. Keeping leadership longer than necessary was a problem for Patrick Lauzon, former President of Mediative Inc.

Patrick has always been an influencer of change in the companies that he has worked with. He started at a large telecommunications firm in the dot-com era and quickly gained a reputation for being the go-to person when it came to anything in the digital space.

After exiting a couple of partnership opportunities, Patrick joined one of Canada's largest media companies and was tasked with moving this firm forward in the digital media area. The main challenge was that for a number of years this company's structure consisted of many fiefdoms with hierarchical decision-making. Each fiefdom, numbering over 300 employees within the firm, would have its own individual decision-maker. Trying to orchestrate changes for the betterment of the overall company was a nightmare.

"Trying to convince 300 people that we need to go in one direction is impossible," Patrick says. "Everybody having an opinion is a good way of getting nowhere fast. It was extremely difficult to influence change to convince people that we needed to change, and that we needed to change fast. A lot of the individuals still to this day believe that, you know, the Internet is a fad. Some people don't see it, and they don't believe that business needs to change. They say the old ways need to stay."

Although Patrick had the authority to move the company forward, he constantly faced pushback. There were some wins with some lessons learned, but clearly this company was not ready to adopt anything digital that would help them become more competitive.

Patrick moved on and joined another firm in the media industry. This company had large national clients looking for help in the digital media area. To help with this, Patrick was tasked with building a digital media strategy nationally for this company, with the goal of becoming a leader in its space.

Patrick was much more comfortable moving forward at this company because the decision-making structure was centralized. This meant that, compared to the previous firm, where he had to convince 300 individual people to go a certain direction, Patrick would only have to convince a core senior management team that had the decision-making power for the whole firm nationally.

Patrick proposed that a separate company be formed, located in a different city so it could be perceived as a separate brand. This would not only allow the separate company to work on the national accounts, but it could also operate autonomously and become a national leader in its own right. Patrick would also be free to create a digital media culture that might not be possible if this separate company was somehow physically attached to the parent company.

In 2010, Patrick was given the go-ahead, and became president of Mediative Incorporated as a separate entity from the parent company. Mediative was put together through an integration of business units from the parent company as well as acquiring four other separate companies while at the same time bringing on fresh new resources.

Patrick also established a strong digital media culture which continues today.

With the integration of the companies, Patrick kept the senior management of those companies to smooth out the transition from the parent company and into Mediative. Yet Patrick still had to wrestle with the decision of when to part ways with the leaders from these other companies.

This was tricky because Patrick needed them for the transition; however, keeping those senior managers on too long stunted the efficiency of the transition. After a clear point in time, keeping the senior managers on had diminishing returns. Unfortunately, Patrick kept them past this point. The momentum of the business vision slowed and the employees were being affected as they were pulled in two different directions. This, obviously, affected the culture and the work environment.

"I kept the old leadership team a little too long," he says. "I kept them for two to two-and-a-half years, and they were important and essential for the transition, but I would've cut them sooner. I would have given the second line – not the head of those organizations, but the body of those organizations – an opportunity to grow faster. They were to help in the integration, but I don't think they helped because it became very personal for them; they liked their old brand and fought back with the integration more than anyone else. On the other hand, they were very good ambassadors. They are leaders and a lot of people know them. Integrating eight companies into one single company took a lot of time with little bumps in the road. It was crucial that these other leaders were on board to help in the transition."

Patrick learned that by keeping these leaders on board for longer than necessary, they ended up not adding value to the transition, and being a distraction. This not only affected the forward movement of the business vision Patrick had, but it also affected the culture he was trying to build. Eventually they were let go, and Patrick was able to concentrate on moving the business forward.

Ultimately, moving the business forward requires that it provide additional value to its customers. If the business decides to stay put, then competitors will overtake its market share. If the business fails to provide customers with additional value that is in sync with its current offerings, customers may move on. Kevin O'Brien, Pierre Morrissette and Kevin Higgins share how they are able to provide additional value to their customers.

Providing Additional Value
to Your Customers

Given the competitive landscape, the business challenge for Aeroplan is in continually providing additional value to its members. We're getting very good at doing that, but we consistently need to keep at it.

– Kevin O'Brien, Chief Commercial Officer – Aeroplan

Despite being a market leader, it is still necessary to be innovative and nimble to survive because of an ever-changing industry. We invest in technology even before there is any business case to support it. Risky? Yes. Necessary? Absolutely! That is why we are a consistent market leader.

– Pierre Morrissette, Executive Chairman – Pelmorex Media Inc. and Chairman, President & CEO – Pelmorex Investments Inc.

Trying to find growth opportunities given a very slow economy is very difficult and provides a major business challenge for a company. With innovative thinking, we are able to meet that challenge.

– Kevin Higgins, Vice-President, Industrial Business Group – 3M Canada

With a state of constant change in consumer tastes and preferences, companies need to continually innovate and adapt their products and services to appease their customers. The challenge when making these changes is to ensure that the new products and services are viewed as logical extensions of a company's core set of offerings and still provide value in the customer's eyes. If the company is wrong, customers simply keep their money in their pockets or go elsewhere. If the company is right, then not only do existing customers stay happy, but there is a strong possibility that new customers will also come on board. A company needs to keep asking itself how it can keep adding value – a question that Kevin O'Brien faces today.

Kevin O'Brien is Chief Commercial Officer (CCO) for Aeroplan. In this role, Kevin has accountability for leading and growing the Aeroplan business and direct responsibility for all commercial elements. Since joining Aeroplan in 2009, Kevin has contributed to the development and execution of the company's strategic direction.

Kevin came to Aeroplan after an illustrious management consulting career, helping large multinational firms with their strategic issues. The opportunity at Aeroplan hit all the right markers for him. The position had to have a strong Toronto presence, international exposure without a lot of travel, an analytical component to the job, and a great culture. Upon joining Aeroplan, he started in a strategic role and, within two years, moved into a commercial role as CCO.

One challenge Kevin faces is trying to provide enhanced value for existing and potential customers, prompted by the uptick of competitors offering travel in exchange for loyalty points.

"Historically, before I came on, Aeroplan's point of differentiation was having amazing value but with uncertainty," he says. "When looking at the whole travel process for typical Aeroplan members, they can book hotels and rent cars for a time period of their choosing, but the flight may not be available, which adds friction to the process. Members had to generally be flexible to unlock the value that they see from earning miles, trade-offs members were willing to make."

The Canadian banks realized they had an opportunity to capture customers by not only providing a credit card with travel points, but giving the customer complete autonomy in the booking experience.

"Canadian banks spent a significant amount of money offering credit cards that allowed individuals to collect points and redeem them for flights any time, any place and anywhere," says Kevin. "Although the value from a dollar spent per mile for these destinations was often not as good as that offered by Aeroplan, the marketing message shifted a customer away from thinking about the value in redeeming points for a flight to ensuring certainty in getting on that flight. Segments of customers heard the message, liked what they heard, and as long as the competitors were able to keep to their promises, people used their services."

To an Aeroplan member, this meant he or she would book a flight using Aeroplan first, and if a particular flight was not available, he or she might pick up the phone and book the flight with a competitor, if they had more than one credit card in their wallet, even though it may cost more.

"The value for the traveler is that there is certainty from start to finish in the travel process," says Kevin. "It is clear that Aeroplan needs to address the certainty as it has increased in importance, even for free travel."

Despite the fact that Aeroplan issues more than 1.5 million reward flights annually and that recent analysis has confirmed that Aeroplan's "Classic" tickets remain value leaders – especially in business class, a key strength of the program – Aeroplan needs to do a better job of delivering on members' expectations by making more effective use of the fact that they have access to all seats on every Air Canada flight – not just those offered as a Classic seat. Getting to the issue of certainty and increasing inventory at acceptable reward prices comes at a cost, and Aeroplan needs to find out how to defray those costs.

Another avenue Kevin sees to provide enhanced value to the customer would be to provide additional redemption opportunities by adding more partners.

"Most Aeroplan members join because they want to fly for free," he says. "That puts all of the pressure to deliver member satisfaction on the redemption experience: getting the flight. Aeroplan needs to make the rest of the relationship – the period and interactions between redemptions – a key part of member engagement. This will be done by having the right accumulation partners and focusing on the experience throughout a member's life."

Kevin sees an opportunity in emphasizing and extending Aeroplan's premium position. At one time, Aeroplan was focused on becoming more "mass". The assumption was that retailers would want the program to apply to most of their customers. In practice, however, Aeroplan has found value in focusing on the "right" part of the market. Aeroplan is a strong brand with premium Canadian consumers and these Canadians spend more and buy higher margin products.

"From a retailer's point of view, this is a very attractive group," Kevin says. "Because Aeroplan captures a significant portion of that premium segment, its partners can target their marketing efforts to that segment. As an example, a typical Aeroplan member may not purchase a high-end refrigerator every year. However, if one of the Aeroplan partners was a high-end refrigerator manufacturer or retailer, it can market directly to that member at a much lower marketing spend than using other marketing methods as a non-partner. The other advantage is that Aeroplan could put together data that might suggest that a particular member is doing a renovation, which may include the purchase of a refrigerator. Just knowing this provides tremendous value to the refrigerator manufacturer as a partner as it has now found the ideal customer to market to."

With a changing competitive landscape, Kevin had to find better ways to provide additional value to Aeroplan members. More important, he recognizes that providing additional value must be a continuous function; not doing so would result in the real potential to lose members to the competition.

Providing continuous additional value is a business challenge in and of itself as a company must keep thinking about new opportunities. But this may mean that one has to be innovative and nimble, such as Pierre Morrissette, where he aggressively adopts new technologies, being first to market despite not having a supporting business case.

Pierre Morrissette founded Pelmorex Media Inc. in 1989, and purchased The Weather Network and MeteoMedia in 1993. Pierre began his career in the banking industry, but by 1977, had become heavily involved in communications. From 1977 to 1979, he was Vice-President of Finance with Telemedia Communications Inc., and Senior Vice-President & Chief Financial Officer of the company from 1979 to 1982. He also served as President of Telemedia Ventures (1983) and Canadian Satellite Communications (1983-1989), which used satellite to distribute media to various locations.

Under Pierre's direction, the company has taken the broadcasting of weather information into a national business enterprise that uses the resources of almost every technology available to deliver highly accurate and often specialized weather information.

Pierre faced the challenge of trying to be successful despite a consolidation in the media industry which resulted in all of the independent media companies joining other companies, leaving Pierre's company as the only independent media company left.

"Today, we're the last one," he says. "Last man standing. We're the biggest independent now. When you're surrounded by three, four, or five major media players who are all competing for eyeballs and ad dollars, and when you are dependent on distribution, and now four or five distributors represent 95% of Canadian households, that level of concentration is tough for an independent. When you combine the very large media players vertically integrating with the very large distributors, it makes it even tougher. To survive in that kind of world, you have to have a really good niche that you are a market leader in."

Pierre insists that you have to be innovative and nimble to tackle the fast-paced change and disruptiveness of technology, especially in his industry.

"There is disruptive technology happening all over in media," he says. "Look what's happened with newspapers, magazines, and regular television. All of them are going like that [shows a declining slope]. But, the new segments are the ones that are taking share away and growing. I decided a long time ago, in the '90s, that you need to understand your customers and meet their needs better than anybody else, giving them the best value proposition of anybody. And you'll win a good chunk of that market share."

When considering his competition, Pierre uses market information to "know them better than they know themselves". He then applies that to his strategy to win customers. A unique process that Pierre uses is assuming the position of a competitor.

"We've had, for a long time, a process where we ask ourselves, 'If you are a competitor how do you beat us?' And I want to know the answers to that question, because, if there's a gap or an opportunity in the marketplace that could take share away from us somewhere down the road, we want to be there, and we want to cannibalize ourselves," he says.

Where other companies shy away from cannibalization, Pierre encourages it.

"I have been a fan of cannibalization forever," he says. "I remember when we launched our first website, people asked why would we invest money in that? It's going to take share away from TV. I said, yes, because if we don't, someone else will. We've been very early adopters of web desktop applications, mobile applications and new screen tablets. And we invest a lot of money in those new things before there's even a business case to support it. Someday, there will be a business case, and we will figure it out. In the meantime we have to occupy that territory, be there first and gain market share. A lot of what we do is free. We rely on gaining a very good share: a lot of reach[40], a lot of frequency[41] and then we'll convert that to advertising."

Pierre describes how important it is to be on top of your game, especially in areas not well known yet.

"You have to be an expert in that new field that nobody knows anything," he says. "You've got to learn. You've got to develop the business case yourself. So, it's being innovative, it's being early in the market, it's creating your own competition."

Although to some this may seem risky, it is exactly what is needed to become a leader in the industry. The results speak for themselves.

"We are in our 24th year now," Pierre says. "We are in every home and TV, the most frequently consulted television network, Canada's number one Canadian website, number one app of all apps on tablets, number three of all apps, including the US, on smart phones, and number one in desktop apps."

Despite these accolades, Pierre keeps innovating and competing against himself. One such example is a project called "The Traveler's Network", which was at the beta testing stage at the time of writing.

---

40 Reach – number of individuals (or homes) you want to expose your product to through specific media scheduled over a given period of time (http://www.entrepreneur.com/encyclopedia/media-planning)

41 Frequency – Using specific media, how many times, on average, should the individuals in your target audience be exposed to your advertising message? (http://www.entrepreneur.com/encyclopedia/media-planning)

"The most popular category on our website after local weather was road conditions, traffic conditions, and traffic cameras," Pierre says. "I said, 'Someday, somebody is going to focus on that category and make it a business because it meets market needs, it's a big market, and nobody does a really good job of it.' So, we spent two years, spending $2 million in developing the science, the capabilities, and platforms to operate in a traveler network space. What is that? It's from getting A to B, whether it's around the corner or around the globe through any mode of transportation. We'll tell you what the current conditions are, the future schedules of public transit, air, rail, bus, if there are delays, alternate routes or alternate flights or alternate departures and other peripheral information because that meets the needs of everybody."

This ability to be nimble, innovative, and forward-thinking brings Pierre and The Weather Network continued success today.

Given the economic challenges and a highly competitive environment, companies must always be on the hunt for new opportunities and products, and need to change the ways of doing business from before. Those who decide to stick with the old ways may eventually see revenues flatten. In addition, when trying to increase shareholder value, one cannot assume that "just being here" matters.

For Kevin Higgins, moving forward is of utmost importance and makes it a priority to continually look at identifying other growth areas in Canada, such as healthcare.

Kevin Higgins holds the position of Vice-President of the Industrial Business Group for 3M Canada. He joined 3M in 1980 as Marketing Manager and National Sales Manager for the Copying Products Division. Since then, he has held marketing, sales leadership, and business management positions in a number of 3M business units ranging from Engineering Systems Division to Medical and Health Care products.

One of the challenges Kevin faces is continually trying to find new opportunities for the products for which he is responsible.

"Companies nowadays must be able to adapt and change. If not, there is a risk of being stuck in an old business model," he says.

By continually looking for growth opportunities, Kevin has been successful at growing the areas he oversees, and in most cases they have grown faster than the overall company. The crux of Kevin's challenge is that the Canadian manufacturing economy is expected to be stagnant over the next three to four years, and trying to find opportunities in a "slow-to-no-growth" environment is extremely difficult.

"In the past four years, when I had taken over the industrial division, I tasked my team to focus on areas of Canada where the industrial products would have a winning opportunity," Kevin says.

He had his team look at the Canadian marketplace differently than it had in the past by looking at markets and opportunities that would "stay at home".

For example, four years earlier, Kevin needed to decide where to market a protection film for cars.

"This film is designed to protect cars from stone chips and cracks," he says. "The product could be sold to the OEMs[42] and hence, locate the production facilities and associated brand relatively close to them."

However, he and his team wondered if that was a smart move as the number of auto assembly plants would likely decline in Canada.

"The smarter choice was to focus marketing and sales efforts at where people bought their cars, as close to two million cars would be sold in Canada on an annual basis," he says. "It was thought the focus could be put on the car dealers to get the buyers to purchase the film for their asset, giving 3M greater longevity in the film protection business. Sure enough, this proved to be a very fruitful decision."

Given the ongoing changes in the economy, and industry, technology and consumer tastes, companies must be able to continually move forward with new products, new services, and even new ways of running a business to support those products and services. The companies that will win at making this transition will be those continuing to

---

42 OEM, also known as the Original Equipment Manufacturer, is a company that buys a product and incorporates or re-brands it into a new product under its own name. (http://www.investopedia.com/terms/o/oem.asp)

provide innovative products and services that resonate with changing customer values.

Despite facing competitive pressures for Aeroplan, an ever-changing industry for The Weather Network or a slowing economy for 3M, the fact remains that a business needs to change to remain competitive, and that change needs to connect with both existing customers and new ones. Making those changes will ultimately result in a successful transition, as can be seen in these three cases, whereas sticking with the old way of doing things will most probably result in a consistently dwindling market share.

Conclusions

As you can see, there is a tremendous complexity to running a business, starting with one's skills and abilities all the way to thinking about how to move a business forward. The hope, as mentioned before, is that one appreciates the enormous variety of issues that need to be considered.

If one is thinking of starting a business or is in the process of putting one together, then this book will provide tremendous value to you, getting you to really take a step back to reflect on the path that may lie ahead for you and the business. The book is not meant to discourage you from going ahead, it merely gives you a chance to ask the right questions and think about business hurdles that you may encounter, and how you will prepare for them when met.

For those who are already in business and are facing some of these business challenges, of course, the book is equally valuable, providing a window into future business challenges, and an opportunity to reminisce about the business hurdles that you have overcome.

In both cases, it is essential that you find a qualified mentor to help you address the business hurdles you will encounter, someone you feel comfortable working with, and who has the appropriate level of experience to guide you. This is an excellent investment to make early, with an incredible return on the investment when you think about those individuals who lost their savings or those businesses that lost revenues, market share, or collapsed.

If you are struggling to make your business a success, and are potentially overwhelmed after reading this book, then you may want to pause, take a step back and really ask whether it is worth moving ahead.

Certainly, there is no shame in cutting your losses early and saving you from further financial repercussions. That, to me, is also success.

In the end, a business must be able to make money to be successful, with success being in the eye of the beholder, so to speak. This book will provide you with a number of lessons to help you be better prepared for the business challenges that may lie ahead.

If you are better prepared, then the business challenges will be handled with much more efficiency, saving you time, money, and resources in the process, ensuring that you fail fast, and succeed faster.

If you enjoyed reading my book, I ask you to spread the word to your family, friends, and colleagues to encourage them to purchase a copy for their personal library so that they can also enjoy reading about the business challenges and failures of the interviewees who have contributed to the book.

Be sure to visit my website, www.failfastsucceedfaster.com to read blogs, listen to audio podcasts, or watch videos as others continually share their stories of business challenges and failures.

Also take the time to visit www.radicalsolutionsgroup.com to find out how you can get more information on seminars, webcasts, conferences, or courseware on how to be prepared for the business challenges that may lie ahead. If you are looking to find a qualified mentor, call us to have a conversation with one of my team members on how my organization can help you fail fast and succeed faster.

Thank you.

Sunil Godse